David Henry Montgomery

**The Two Great Retreats of History**

1. The retreat of the ten thousand. 2. Napoleon's retreat from Moscow

David Henry Montgomery

**The Two Great Retreats of History**

*1. The retreat of the ten thousand. 2. Napoleon's retreat from Moscow*

ISBN/EAN: 9783337197193

Printed in Europe, USA, Canada, Australia, Japan

Cover: Foto ©ninafisch / pixelio.de

More available books at **www.hansebooks.com**

THE

# Two Great Retreats of History.

I. THE RETREAT OF THE TEN THOUSAND.
II. NAPOLEON'S RETREAT FROM MOSCOW.

*WITH INTRODUCTIONS AND NOTES*

BY

D. H. M.

BOSTON, U.S.A.:
PUBLISHED BY GINN & COMPANY.
1889.

TYPOGRAPHY BY J. S. CUSHING & CO., BOSTON, U.S.A.
PRESSWORK BY GINN & CO., BOSTON, U.S.A.

## PREFATORY NOTE.

THE two following selections contain, first, Grote's account of the Retreat of the Ten Thousand Greeks, taken from his "History of Greece," and, secondly, an abridgment of Count Ségur's narrative of Napoleon's retreat from Russia.

Grote's History, based on Xenophon's, is given entire, with the exception that, in a very few instances, some slight verbal change has been made in order to better adapt the work to school use.

Two maps are furnished, an introduction is prefixed to each selection, and all needed notes subjoined.

D. H. M.

# TABLE OF CONTENTS.

## I. Retreat of the Ten Thousand.

|  | PAGE |
|---|---|
| Sketch of Cyrus the Younger (Introductory to the Retreat of the Ten Thousand) | v |
| § 1. Effect of the death of Cyrus on the Greeks; they resolve to retreat | 1 |
| § 2. Commencement of the retreat | 6 |
| § 3. Negotiations with Tissaphernês | 10 |
| § 4. Treachery of Tissaphernês | 19 |
| § 5. Xenophon's dream and its results | 29 |
| § 6. The Greeks cross the Zab | 42 |
| § 7. The Greeks fight their way across the Karduchian Mountains | 50 |
| § 8. March through Armenia; great suffering from cold and hunger | 60 |
| § 9. The Greeks come in sight of the Black Sea | 70 |
| § 10. The Greek cities on the Black Sea; their feelings toward the Ten Thousand | 75 |
| § 11. Plans of the army for the future | 79 |
| § 12. The Ten Thousand begin their march westward | 82 |
| § 13. Plan of Xenophon for founding a city on the Black Sea | 88 |
| § 14. Xenophon defends himself against false accusations | 95 |
| § 15. The army passes by sea to Sinôpê | 104 |
| § 16. The army crosses the Bosphorus to Byzantium; false promises of Anaxibius and their results | 116 |
| § 17. Mutiny of the army in leaving Byzantium | 120 |
| § 18. Xenophon's speech to the soldiers | 123 |
| § 19. The army finally leaves Byzantium; Seuthês offers to hire them | 128 |
| § 20. The army enters the service of Seuthês | 135 |
| § 21. Xenophon crosses over with the army to Asia | 138 |
| § 22. Xenophon takes leave of the army. Conclusion | 143 |

## II. Napoleon's Retreat from Moscow.

|  | PAGE |
|---|---|
| Sketch of Napoleon (Introductory to the Retreat from Moscow) | 152 |
| § 1. Description of Moscow; arrival of the Czar | 157 |
| § 2. Alarm in Moscow at the advance of the French army; preparations for the destruction of the city | 162 |
| § 3. Departure of the Russian governor from Moscow | 168 |
| § 4. Napoleon's first view of Moscow; the French enter the city | 175 |
| § 5. Napoleon takes up his quarters in the Kremlin; the city discovered to be on fire | 182 |
| § 6. The fire compels Napoleon to leave the city | 190 |
| § 7. Napoleon returns to the Kremlin; plunder of the city | 195 |
| § 8. Rostopchin sets fire to his country-seat; anxiety of Napoleon at not hearing from the Czar | 201 |
| § 9. Napoleon determines to leave Moscow | 215 |
| § 10. Departure from Moscow; the first battle | 224 |
| § 11. Napoleon holds a council of war, and decides to retreat northward | 233 |
| § 12. Napoleon's attempt to destroy the Kremlin; view of the battle-field of Borodino | 238 |
| § 13. Napoleon reaches Viazma; battle near that place | 243 |
| § 14. Dreadful snow-storm on the 6th of November; its effect upon the troops | 247 |
| § 15. Defeat and entire dissolution of Prince Eugene's corps at the passage of the Wop | 253 |
| § 16. The Grand Army reaches Smolensk | 257 |
| § 17. Napoleon leaves Smolensk; battle of Krasnoë | 263 |
| § 18. Napoleon reaches Dombrowna and Orcha; he holds a council | 267 |
| § 19. Arrival of Marshal Ney | 272 |
| § 20. Capture of Minsk by the Russians | 277 |
| § 21. March through the forest of Minsk; passage of the Berezina | 280 |
| § 22. Napoleon abandons the Grand Army, and sets out for Paris | 291 |
| § 23. Sufferings of the Grand Army after Napoleon's departure; arrival at Wilna | 298 |
| § 24. Conclusion | 308 |
| Index to notes and list of proper names with their pronunciation | 316 |

# MAPS.

|   |   | PAGE |
|---|---|---|
| 1. | The advance and the retreat of the Ten Thousand, facing . . | 1 |
| 2. | The advance and the retreat of Napoleon in his Russian campaign, facing . . . . . . . . . . . . | 1 |

# SKETCH OF CYRUS THE YOUNGER.

(INTRODUCTORY TO THE RETREAT OF THE TEN THOUSAND GREEKS.)

IN the year 423 B.C. Darius Nothus ascended the throne of Persia. That country was then the greatest empire in the world, and had an area nearly equal to that of the United States. The capital of this seemingly powerful realm was the ancient city of Babylon on the lower Euphrates. Here the Great King, as he was styled, had his principal palace, from which he issued orders to his twenty or more satraps or governors whose provinces extended in name at least from the shores of the Mediterranean to the banks of the Indus, and from the Persian Gulf to the Black Sea.

Darius had married his half-sister Parysatis, a high-spirited but unscrupulous woman, by whom he had two sons, destined to be known in history. The eldest was Artaxerxês, a youth of but little character; and the second, Cyrus, who inherited the decided qualities of his mother. In order to distinguish him from Cyrus the Great, the founder of the Persian Empire, who died more than a hundred years earlier, he is commonly called Cyrus the Younger.

He was his mother's favorite, and as he was born after Darius assumed the crown, while Artaxerxês was born before that date, Parysatis seems to have encouraged Cyrus to consider himself the true heir to the throne, since he was in fact the *king's* eldest son. Through her influence he was appointed satrap of Lydia and the adjacent provinces of western Asia Minor when he was but sixteen. This position, since it made him the military ruler of that populous and wealthy section of country, was one of great importance, and doubtless had no small influence in shaping the young man's future career.

In 404 Cyrus was summoned from Sardis, the capital of Lydia, to Babylon, and shortly after, his father died, leaving his crown to Artaxerxês, who, from his remarkable memory which appears to have been his chief characteristic, got the title of Artaxerxês Mnemon. But Cyrus certainly was not deficient in this mental quality, for he seems to have remembered his mother's suggestions about his being the rightful heir to the throne so well, that at the coronation of Artaxerxês he plotted his assassination; or at least, Tissaphernês, a neighboring satrap,[1] accused him of it. Cyrus, who appears to have had no adequate defence to make, was forthwith arrested and would probably have been summarily put to death — for in Persia the law's delays were unknown — had not Parysatis interfered. Realizing her son's imminent peril, she rushed forward and, clasping him in her arms, wound her long flowing hair about him, and pressed his neck to hers in such a way that the executioner must have beheaded her with the same stroke with which he decapitated Cyrus.

The prayers and entreaties of Parysatis saved the young man's life, and he was even permitted to return to Sardis and resume his power. He went; but with no intention of remaining in that subordinate position. Not only was he resolved to be revenged on Tissaphernês, but he was equally determined to overthrow the mild Artaxerxês and convince him of the mistake of yielding to a woman's tears.

Cyrus had learned from his residence on the Mediterranean coast, how far superior Greek soldiers were to the troops of Persia. The former would not only fight from patriotic motives, but what was more, they would readily fight outside of Greece, if they were paid well for it; the latter would only fight when they were flogged to it, and officers had to carry whips to drive them into battle by the sting of the lash.

Under the pretext that he was about to engage in a local

---

[1] Tissaphernês was a satrap of Caria, a province of Asia Minor south of Lydia.

and private war with his enemy Tissaphernês, Cyrus managed to gradually collect an army of about ten thousand Greeks whom Klearchus, an ex-governor of Byzantium, hired for him. These ten thousand were the real core of the expedition, though in addition a hundred thousand Asiatics were to form the bulk of it. With this force the young satrap believed that he could take Babylon, and with it that title of Great King which he coveted. It was true that Artaxerxês would meet him with an army of ten men to his one; but, as Cyrus said, mere "numbers and noise" did not tell on the battle-field, and "numbers and noise" were all that the Persian sovereign had to rely on.

When all was ready, Cyrus set out from Sardis on his memorable march in the spring of 401. Among the Greeks was a volunteer named Xenophon, who had been persuaded to go by his friend Proxenus, a general in the army of Cyrus. Xenophon, as we shall see, eventually saved his countrymen from destruction, and became not only the leader, but the historian of the expedition.

With the exception of Klearchus, none of the army seem to have known the real object of the campaign, but supposed that Cyrus was going to attack the Pisidians, robber tribes that inhabited the mountainous country southeast of Sardis. Artaxerxês appears to have been equally in the dark, and though he knew Cyrus was advancing in the direction of Babylon, he thought that his ultimate purpose was to make war on Tissaphernês, and so gave himself no more trouble about the matter.

All went well with Cyrus and his Greek mercenaries until they reached that city of Tarsus in Cilicia, which was later to become famous as the birthplace of the apostle Paul. When they reached that place, Xenophon's countrymen saw that they had been deceived, and that Cyrus evidently had some greater foe in view than the rough banditti of the Pisidian highlands. At first they were on the point of mutinying, and of stoning Klearchus to give proper emphasis to their feelings; but sober second thought showed them that it was doubtful whether they would gain anything by such a course. Klearchus, who was quite equal to the emergency, bade them reflect that they were now a long distance from home, and that Cyrus had it in his power to make it difficult for them to get back without his permission. Next, they were promised a decided increase of pay if they would keep on. These considerations so influenced the Greeks that they finally resolved to continue their march and take the chances of war. Cyrus still refused to divulge his real purpose; and though there cannot be much doubt that the Ten Thousand felt pretty reasonably certain what it was, yet they probably believed he had chances enough of success to make it worth their while to run the risk with him.

Accordingly the army resumed their forward movement, following the trend of the coast round the Gulf of Issus, and then striking southeasterly again, until some time in the summer they reached and crossed the Euphrates at Thapsacus. From that point they marched down the left bank of the river, through the hilly desert of Arabia, toward the great city of Babylon. Early in September they reached a point on the Tigris, nearly opposite Bagdad, and about two days' march from Kunaxa, a place not very far northwest of the Persian capital.

Up to this time Cyrus had met with no opposition, though he was daily expecting to see the advance-guard of his brother's army. Before going further he thought it prudent to hold a grand review of his troops, which he did at midnight, as it was now reported that Artaxerxês, with an army of over a million, was coming to give him battle.

But the million did not make their appearance, and so Cyrus decided to keep on until he should encounter them. The next day the invading army reached a trench which had evidently been recently dug to obstruct their advance. It stretched across the plain between the Euphrates and the Tigris, in connection with the ruins of the old Median Wall, built probably in the days of Nebuchadnezzar as one of the defences of Babylon. This trench was eighteen feet deep, thirty feet wide, and upwards of forty miles in length; it stopped short of the Euphrates by only twenty feet. Over that narrow strip of ground, which the Persian king might easily have held with a small number of resolute men, the Cyreian forces passed, with no one to hinder them. The great trench, on which so much labor had been expended, was, therefore, not only useless as a defence to Artaxerxês, but it was a positive encouragement to Cyrus and his men, for it revealed the inefficiency and the cowardice of the Persians. The whole army now moved rapidly forward, confident of an easy victory, many even supposing that Artaxerxês would make no stand at all, but abandon his capital to them. The Great King, however, was not so hopelessly pusillanimous as that; for, when Cyrus reached Kunaxa, scouts brought word that the enemy's hosts were not far behind. This time the intelligence was correct. That very afternoon a great cloud of white dust rolled up from the plain, and as it kept advancing the invaders caught sight of the flash of brazen armor and a forest of spears.

When all was ready for the battle to begin, the Greeks, not waiting to be attacked, charged on the run against the Persian left wing. The Persians, who seem to have thought that on such an occasion absence of body was a good deal better than presence of mind, waited just long enough to hear the Greeks give a fierce shout to Mars, accompanied by a significant clatter of spears and shields. That satisfied them, and, turning like a flock of frightened sheep, they ran for their lives.

Cyrus, who had refused to put on a helmet, now dashed into the fight with uncovered head, making straight for King Artaxerxês, who occupied the centre of his army. "I see the man!" he cried, and, hurling his lance, he struck and slightly wounded the Great King; but that fratricidal blow was the last, for just then a javelin pierced Cyrus under the eye, and he fell from his horse and was slain. His head and right hand were then cut off to serve as a warning to traitors. The native or Asiatic troops, seeing the disaster, fled, and did not stop till they had reached a former camp eight miles away.

Meanwhile the victorious Ten Thousand, knowing nothing of what had happened to Cyrus, pursued the Persians as long as light lasted; then when the sun had set they returned to find that their camp had been plundered by the enemy, and that they must go to bed supperless. It was not until sunrise of the next day that they learned that Cyrus was dead; that their companions in arms had fled; and that they were left a mere handful of men without a leader, and without provisions, in the heart of the enemy's country.

How to retreat from such a position was the supreme question. They could not return the way they came, for that road led them through the desert, where it would be impossible to get food. If they were to get back alive they must take the northern route to the shores of the Black Sea. This would lead them through a fertile but rough country, in which they would have to find their way as best they could across rivers and over mountains, harassed by the Persians in the rear, and encountering savage tribes who would dispute their progress. At the shortest such a march would be about six hundred miles even in an air line, with prospect of something like six hundred more before they reached the Mediterranean.

After many delays, this latter course was the one they finally resolved to take, and owing to Xenophon's courage and resolution it turned out successfully.

After eight months of wandering, hardships, and peril, they all came in sight of the Euxine, and perhaps no shipwrecked sailors clinging to a raft ever cried "Land!" "Land!" with more joy than those Greeks who had climbed a hill-top shouted "The Sea!" "The Sea!"

Thanks to their own bravery, to their able leader, and finally to Persian vacillation and cowardice, this little army had now reached a place of safety. It was long, however, before they got back to their native country, and when they did, they were not to arrive at its shores asleep, on shipboard, as the much wandering and storm-tossed Ulysses came to his beloved Ithaca.

It is doubtful, indeed, how many of them ever got back to their Spartan or Athenian homes, for we know that most of them could not make up their minds to live quiet lives of peace again; but preferred fighting in behalf of the independence of the Ionian cities which Greece had planted on the coast of Asia Minor.

Such was the Retreat of the Ten Thousand. If we may accept the judgment of Rollin, a once noted historian, it has never had a parallel in history. If we consider its results, it certainly merits all that Rollin claims for it, for it convinced the Greek people that the apparent power of the Persian empire was utterly unreal. They saw that, as Cyrus had said, its only strength was in " numbers and noise." This conviction grew, and two generations after Xenophon's return, it led to that grand invasion of Persia by Alexander the Great which was to revolutionize the ancient world.

What, then, had the retreat of the Greeks accomplished? First, it proved that ten thousand men not afraid to die are worth more than a million who lack that courage; and next, though it was a retreat, yet it suggested that advance which eventually spread the Greek language, Greek culture and Greek civilization in countries where they were before unknown.

D. H. M.

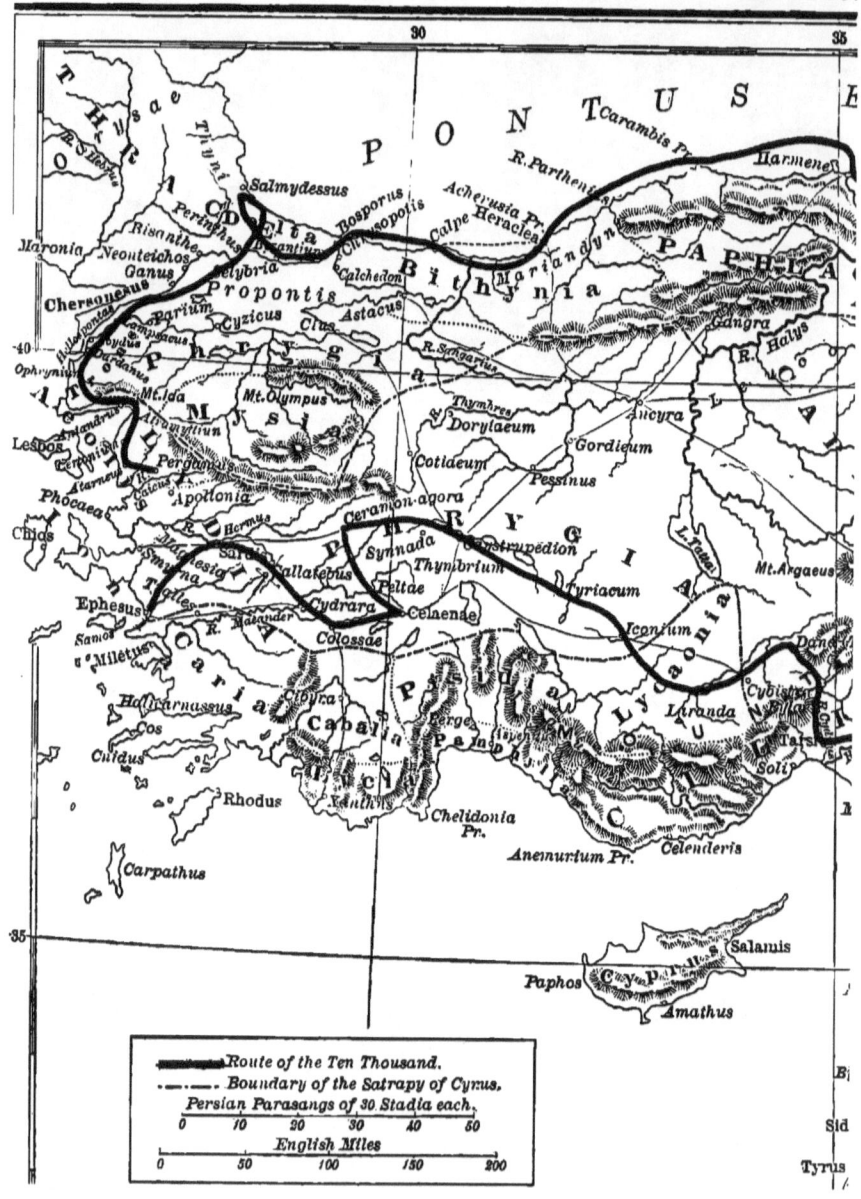

# HOUSAND GREEKS.
## ANABASIS.

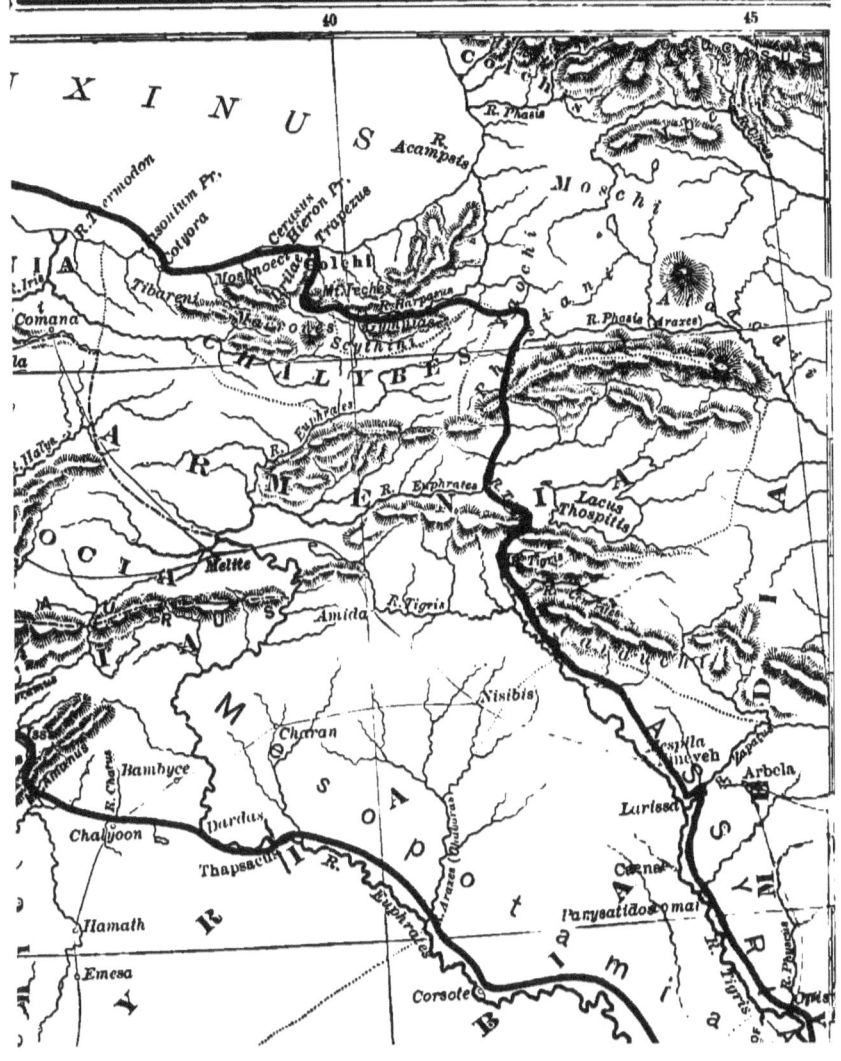

SKETCH MAP OF EUROPE
SHOWING
PRINCIPAL BATTLES OF NAPOLEON.

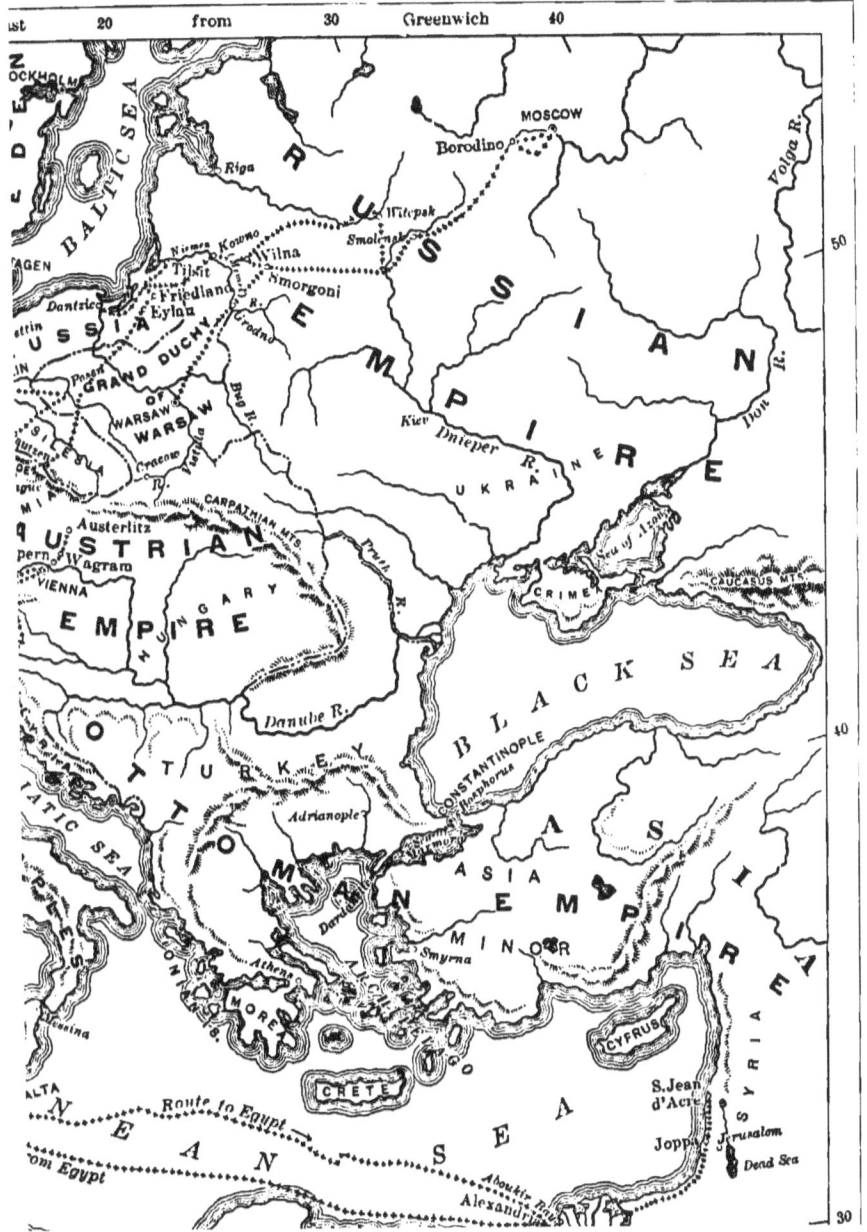

# RETREAT OF THE TEN THOUSAND GREEKS.

## § 1. Effect of the death of Cyrus on the Greeks; they resolve to retreat.

THE first triumphant feeling of the Greek troops at Kunaxa[1] was exchanged, as soon as they learnt the death of Cyrus, for dismay and sorrow; accompanied by unavailing repentance for the venture into which he and Klearchus had seduced them. Probably Klearchus himself too repented, and with good reason, of having displayed, in his manner of fighting the battle, so little foresight, and so little regard either to the injunctions or to the safety of Cyrus. Nevertheless he still maintained the tone of a victor in the field, and after expressions of grief for the fate of the young prince, desired Proklês and Glûs to return to Ariæus, with the reply, that the Greeks on their side were conquerors without any enemy remaining; that they were about to march onward against Artaxerxês; and that if Ariæus would join them, they would place him on the throne which had been intended for Cyrus. While this reply was conveyed to Ariæus by his particular friend Menon along with the messengers, the Greeks procured a meal as well as they could, having no bread, by killing some of the baggage animals; and by kindling fire to cook their meat, from the arrows, the wooden Egyptian shields which had been thrown away on the field, and the baggage carts.

[1] **Kunaxa**: see Introduction.

Before any answer could be received fromAriæus, heralds[1] appeared coming from Artaxerxês; among them being Phalînus, a Greek from Zakynthus, and the Greek surgeon Ktesias of Knidus, who was in the service of the Persian king. Phalînus, an officer of some military experience and in the confidence of Tissaphernês, addressed himself to the Greek commanders; requiring them on the part of the King, since he was now victor and had slain Cyrus, to surrender their arms and appeal to his mercy. To this summons, painful in the extreme to a Grecian ear, Klearchus replied that it was not the practice for victorious men to lay down their arms. Being then called away to examine the sacrifice[2] which was going on, he left the interview to the other officers, who met the summons of Phalînus by an emphatic negative. "If the King thinks himself strong enough to ask for our arms unconditionally, let him come and try to seize them."—"The King (rejoined Phalînus) thinks that you are in his power, being in the midst of his territory, hemmed in by impassable rivers, and encompassed by his innumerable subjects." — "Our arms and our valor are all that remain to us (replied a young Athenian); we shall not be fools enough to hand over to you our only remaining treasures, but shall employ them still to have a fight for *your* treasure." But though several spoke in this resolute tone, there were not wanting others

[1] **Heralds**: officers who proclaimed war or peace, challenged to battle, and were bearers of messages from the commander-in-chief or king; here, messengers.

[2] **Sacrifice**: it was the custom of the Greeks to examine the entrails of the animals they sacrificed, in order that from their appearance they might learn the will of the gods; and next, that they might gain a knowledge of coming events.

In all important undertakings these signs were carefully consulted before any decisive action was taken.

disposed to encourage a negotiation; saying that they had been faithful to Cyrus as long as he lived, and would now be faithful to Artaxerxês, if he wanted their services in Egypt or anywhere else. In the midst of this parley Klearchus returned, and was requested by Phalînus to return a final answer on behalf of all. He at first asked the advice of Phalînus himself; appealing to the common feeling of Hellenic[1] patriotism, and anticipating, with very little judgment, that the latter would encourage the Greeks in holding out. "If (replied Phalînus) I saw one chance out of ten thousand in your favor, in the event of a contest with the King, I should advise you to refuse the surrender of your arms. But as there is no chance of safety for you against the King's consent, I recommend you to look out for safety in the only quarter where it presents itself." Sensible of the mistake which he had made in asking the question, Klearchus rejoined—"That is *your* opinion: now report our answer. We think we shall be better friends to the King, if we are to be his friends, — or more effective enemies, if we are to be his enemies, — with our arms, than without them." Phalînus, in retiring, said that the King proclaimed a truce so long as they remained in their present position — but war, if they moved, either onward or backward. And to this Klearchus acceded, without declaring which he intended to do.

Shortly after the departure of Phalînus, the envoys despatched to Ariæus returned; communicating his reply that the Persian grandees would never tolerate any pretensions on his part to the crown, and that he intended to depart early the next morning on his return; if the Greeks wished to accompany him, they must join him during the

[1] **Hellenic:** pertaining to the Hellenes, or Greeks; Grecian.

night. In the evening, Klearchus, convening the generals and the captains, acquainted them that the morning sacrifice had been of a nature to forbid their marching against the King — a prohibition, of which he now understood the reason, from having since learnt that the King was on the other side of the Tigris, and therefore out of their reach — but that it was favorable for rejoining Ariæus. He gave directions accordingly for a night-march back along the Euphratês, to the station where they had passed the last night but one prior to the battle. The other Grecian generals, without any formal choice of Klearchus as chief, tacitly acquiesced in his orders, from a sense of his superior decision and experience, in an emergency when no one knew what to propose. The night-march was successfully accomplished, so that they joined Ariæus at the preceding station about midnight; not without the alarming symptom, however, that Miltokythês the Thracian deserted to the King at the head of 340 of his countrymen, partly horse, partly foot.

The first proceeding of the Grecian generals was to exchange solemn oaths of reciprocal fidelity and fraternity with Ariæus. According to an ancient and impressive practice, a bull, a wolf, a boar, and a ram, were all slain, and their blood allowed to run into the hollow of a shield; in which the Greek generals dipped a sword, and Ariæus, with his chief companions, a spear. The latter, besides the promise of alliance, engaged also to guide the Greeks in good faith down to the Asiatic coast. Klearchus immediately began to ask what route he proposed to take; whether to return by that along which they had come up, or by any other. To this Ariæus replied, that the road along which they had marched was impracticable for retreat, from the utter want of provisions through seventeen days of desert; but that he intended to choose another road, which, though longer, would be sufficiently productive to furnish them with provisions. There was, however, a necessity (he added), that the first two or three days' marches should be of extreme length, in order that they might get out of the reach of the king's forces, who would hardly be able to overtake them afterwards with any considerable numbers.

They had now come 93 days' march from Ephesus, or 90 from Sardis. The distance from Sardis to Kunaxa is 1464 miles. There had been at least 96 days of rest, enjoyed at various places, so that the total of time elapsed must have at least been 189 days, or a little more than half a year: but it was probably greater, since some intervals of rest are not specified in number of days.

How to retrace their steps was now the problem, apparently insoluble. As to the military force of Persia in the field, indeed, not merely the easy victory at Kunaxa, but still more the undisputed march throughout so long a space, left them no serious apprehension. In spite of this great extent, population, and riches, they had been allowed to pass through the most difficult and defensible country, and to ford the broad Euphratês, without a blow: nay, the King had shrunk from defending the long trench which he had specially caused to be dug for the protection of Babylonia. But the difficulties which stood between them and their homes were of a very different character. How were they to find their way back, or obtain provisions, in defiance of a numerous hostile cavalry, which, not without efficiency even in a pitched battle, would be most formidable in opposing their retreat? The line of their upward march had all been planned, with supplies furnished, by Cyrus: — yet even under such advantages, supplies had been on the point of failing, in one part of the march. They were now, for the first time, called upon to think and provide for themselves; without knowledge of either roads or distances — without trustworthy guides — without any one to furnish or even to indicate supplies — and with a territory all hostile, traversed by rivers which they had no means of crossing. Klearchus himself knew nothing of the country, nor of any other river except the Euphratês; nor does he indeed in his heart seem to have conceived retreat as practicable without the consent of the King. The reader who casts his eye on a map of Asia, and imagines the situation of this Greek division on the left bank of the Euphratês, near the parallel of latitude 33° 30' — will hardly be surprised at any measure of despair, on the part either of general or soldiers. And we may add that Klearchus had not even the advantage of such a map, or probably of any map at all, to enable him to shape his course.

In this dilemma, the first and most natural impulse was to consult Ariæus; who (as has been already stated) pronounced, with good reason, that return by the same road was impracticable; and promised to conduct them home by another road — longer indeed, yet better supplied.

### § 2. Commencement of the Retreat.

At daybreak on the ensuing morning, they began their march in an easterly direction, anticipating that before night they should reach some villages of the Babylonian territory, as in fact they did; yet not before they had been alarmed in the afternoon by the supposed approach of some of the enemy's horse, and by evidences that the enemy were not far off, which induced them to slacken their march for the purpose of more cautious array.[1] Hence they did not reach the first villages before dark ; these too had been pillaged by the enemy while retreating before them, so that only the first-comers under Klearchus could obtain accommodation, while the succeeding troops, coming up in the dark, pitched as they could without any order. The whole camp was a scene of clamor, dispute, and even alarm, throughout the night. No provisions could be obtained. Early the next morning Klearchus ordered them under arms ; and desiring to expose the groundless nature of the alarm, caused the herald[2] to proclaim, that whoever would denounce the person who had let the ass[3] into the camp on the preceding night, should be rewarded with a talent[4] of silver.

What was the project of route entertained byAriæus, we cannot ascertain ; since it was not farther pursued. For the effect of the unexpected arrival of the Greeks as if to attack the enemy — and even the clamor and shouting of the camp during the night — so intimidated the Persian commanders, that they sent heralds the next morning to treat about a truce. The contrast between this message, and the haughty summons of the preceding day to lay down their arms, was sensibly felt by the Grecian officers, and taught them that the proper way of dealing with the

---

[1] **Array**: disposition of forces with reference to defence or attack.

[2] **Herald**: here used apparently in the sense of a public crier.

[3] This seems to have been a standing military jest, to make the soldiers laugh at their past panic.

[4] **Talent**: about 57 pounds avoirdupois; or, taking silver at its present value, about $1250.

Persians was by a bold and aggressive demeanor. When Klearchus was apprised of the arrival of the heralds, he desired them at first to wait at the outposts until he was at leisure: then, having put his troops into the best possible order, with a phalanx[1] compact on every side to the eye, and the unarmed persons out of sight, he desired the heralds to be admitted. He marched out to meet them with the most showy and best-armed soldiers immediately around him, and when they informed him that they had come from the King with instructions to propose a truce, and to report on what conditions the Greeks would agree to it, Klearchus replied abruptly — "Well then — go and tell the King, that our first business must be to fight; for we have nothing to eat, nor will any man presume to talk to Greeks about a truce, without first providing dinner for them." With this reply the heralds rode off, but returned very speedily; thus making it plain that the King, or the commanding officer, was near at hand. They brought word that the King thought their answer reasonable, and had sent guides to conduct them to a place where they would obtain provisions, if the truce should be concluded.

After an affected delay and hesitation, in order to impose upon the Persians, Klearchus concluded the truce, and desired that the guides should conduct the army to those quarters where provisions could be had. He was most circumspect in maintaining exact order during the march, himself taking charge of the rear guard. The guides led them over many ditches and channels, full of water, and cut

---

[1] **Phalanx**: a body of troops in compact array, with their shields joined and their pikes or spears crossing each other, so as to present a firm, unbroken front to the foe.

for the purpose of irrigation[1]; some so broad and deep that they could not be crossed without bridges. The army had to put together bridges for the occasion, from palm-trees either already fallen, or expressly cut down. This was a troublesome business, which Klearchus himself superintended with peculiar strictness. He carried his spear in the left hand, his stick in the right; employing the latter to chastise any soldier who seemed remiss — and even plunging into the mud and lending his own hands in aid wherever it was necessary. As it was not the usual season of irrigation for crops he suspected that the canals had been filled on this occasion expressly to intimidate the Greeks, by impressing them with the difficulties of their prospective march; and he was anxious to demonstrate to the Persians that these difficulties were no more than Grecian energy could easily surmount.

At length they reached certain villages indicated by their guides for quarters and provisions; and here for the first time they had a sample of that unparalleled abundance of the Babylonian territory, which Herodotus is afraid to describe with numerical precision. Large quantities of corn,[2] — dates not only in great numbers, but of such beauty, freshness, size, and flavor, as no Greek had ever seen or tasted, insomuch that fruit like what was imported into Greece, was disregarded and left for the slaves — wine

[1] **Irrigation**: during the long dry summer the crops in this region would have perished from drought if the fields had not been watered. This was done by a system of canals, in which the supply of water, drawn from the overflow of the Tigris and Euphrates during the spring floods, was stored up to be used when needed. So abundant was the growth of grain on this rich soil that Herodotus did not dare state the amount for fear that he would be thought guilty of exaggeration.

[2] **Corn**: any kind of grain used for food.

and vinegar, both also made from the date-palm; these are the luxuries which Xenophon is eloquent in describing, after his recent period of scanty fare and anxious apprehension; not without also noticing the headaches which such new and luscious food, in unlimited quantity, brought upon himself and others.

### § 3. Negotiations with Tissaphernês.

After three days passed in these restorative quarters, they were visited by Tissaphernês, accompanied by four Persian grandees and a suite of slaves. The satrap[1] began to open a negotiation with Klearchus and the other generals. Speaking through an interpreter, he stated to them that the vicinity of his province to Greece impressed him with a strong interest in favor of the Cyreian Greeks,[2] and made him anxious to rescue them out of their present desperate situation; that he had solicited the King's permission to save them, as a personal recompense to himself for having been the first to forewarn him of the schemes of Cyrus, and for having been the only Persian who had not fled before the Greeks at Kunaxa; that the King had promised to consider this point, and had sent him in the mean time to ask the Greeks what their purpose was in coming up to attack him; and that he trusted the Greeks would give him a conciliatory answer to carry back, in order that he might have less difficulty in realizing what he desired for their benefit. To this Klearchus, after first deliberating apart with the other officers, replied, that the army had come together, and had even commenced their

---

[1] **Satrap**: the governor of a Persian province.
[2] **Cyreian Greeks**: those Greeks who had engaged in the expedition or Cyrus in his attempt to seize the throne of Persia. See Introduction.

march, without any purpose of hostility to the King; that Cyrus had brought them up the country under false pretences, but that they had been ashamed to desert him in the midst of danger, since he had always treated them generously; that since Cyrus was now dead, they had no purpose of hostility against the King, but were only anxious to return home; that they were prepared to repel hostility from all quarters, but would be not less prompt in requiting favor or assistance. With this answer Tissaphernês departed, and returned on the next day but one, informing them that he had obtained the King's permission to save the Grecian army — though not without great opposition, since many Persian counsellors contended that it was unworthy of the King's dignity to suffer those who had assailed him to escape. "I am now ready (said he) to conclude a covenant [1] and exchange oaths with you; engaging to conduct you safely back into Greece, with the country friendly, and with a regular market for you to purchase provisions. You must stipulate on your part always to pay for your provisions, and to do no damage to the country: if I do not furnish you with provisions to buy, you are then at liberty to take them where you can find them." Well were the Greeks content to enter into such a covenant, which was sworn, with hands given upon it, by Klearchus, the other generals, and the captains on their side — and by Tissaphernês with the King's brother-in-law on the other. Tissaphernês then left them, saying that he would go back to the King, make preparations, and return to reconduct the Greeks home; going himself to his own province.

[1] **Covenant:** a solemn agreement or treaty which both parties bound themselves to keep by oath, calling on their respective gods to punish them if they violated the compact.

The statements of Ktesias, though known to us only indirectly, and not to be received without caution, afford ground for believing that Queen Parysatis decidedly wished success to her son Cyrus in his contest for the throne — that the first report conveyed to her of the battle of Kunaxa, announcing the victory of Cyrus, filled her with joy, which was exchanged for bitter sorrow when she was informed of his death, — that she caused to be slain with horrible tortures all those, who, though acting in the Persian army and for the defence of Artaxerxês, had any participation in the death of Cyrus — and that she showed favorable dispositions towards the Cyreian Greeks. It may seem probable, farther, that her influence may have been exerted to procure for them an unimpeded retreat, without anticipating the use afterwards made by Tissaphernês (as will soon appear) of the present convention.[1] And in one point of view the Persian king had an interest in facilitating their retreat. For the very circumstance which rendered retreat difficult, also rendered the Greeks dangerous to him in their actual position. They were in the heart of the Persian Empire, within seventy miles of Babylon; in a country not only teeming with fertility, but also extremely defensible; especially against cavalry, from the multiplicity of canals, as Herodotus observed respecting Lower Egypt. And Klearchus might say to his Grecian soldiers — what Xenophon was afterwards preparing to say to them at Kalpê on the Euxine Sea, and what Nikias also affirmed to the unhappy Athenian army whom he afterwards conducted away from Syracuse[2] — that wherever they sat down, they were sufficiently numerous

---

[1] Convention: treaty or agreement.
[2] See note on p. 38.

and well-organized to become at once a city. A body of such troops might effectually assist, and would perhaps encourage, the Babylonian population to throw off the Persian yoke, and to relieve themselves from the prodigious tribute [1] which they now paid to the satrap. For these reasons, the advisers of Artaxerxês thought it advantageous to convey the Greeks across the Tigris out of Babylonia, beyond all possibility of returning thither. This was at any rate the primary object of the convention. And it was the more necessary to conciliate the goodwill of the Greeks, because there seems to have been but one bridge over the Tigris; which bridge could only be reached by inviting them to advance considerably farther into the interior of Babylonia.

Such was the state of fears and hopes on both sides, at the time when Tissaphernês left the Greeks, after concluding his convention. For twenty days did they await his return, without receiving from him any communication; the Cyreian Persians [2] under Ariæus being encamped near them. Such prolonged and unexplained delay became, after a few days, the source of much uneasiness to the Greeks; the more so, as Ariæus received during this interval several visits from his Persian kinsmen, and friendly messages from the King, promising amnesty [3] for his recent services under Cyrus. Of these messages the effects were painfully felt, in manifest coldness of demeanor on the part of his Persian troops towards the Greeks.

[1] **Tribute:** this was an annual tax so heavy and so cruelly extorted that it kept the great body of the people in a state little better than that of slavery.

[2] **Cyreian Persians:** those Persians who had espoused the cause of Cyrus in his attempt to seize the throne.

[3] **Amnesty:** pardon.

Impatient and suspicious, the Greek soldiers impressed upon Klearchus their fears, that the King had concluded the recent convention only to arrest their movements, until he should have assembled a larger army and blocked up more effectually the roads against their return. To this Klearchus replied — "I am aware of all that you say. Yet if we now strike our tents,[1] it will be a breach of the convention, and a declaration of war. No one will furnish us with provisions: we shall have no guides:Ariæus will desert us forthwith, so that we shall have his troops as enemies instead of friends. Whether there be any other river for us to cross, I know not; but we know that the Euphratês itself can never be crossed, if there be an enemy to resist us. Nor have we any cavalry, — while cavalry is the best and most numerous force of our enemies. If the King, having all these advantages, really wishes to destroy us, I do not know why he should falsely exchange all these oaths and solemnities, and thus make his own word worthless in the eyes both of Greeks and barbarians."[2]

Such words from Klearchus are remarkable, as they testify his own complete despair of the situation — certainly a very natural despair — except by amicable dealing with the Persians; and also his ignorance of geography and the country to be traversed. This feeling helps to explain his imprudent confidence afterwards in Tissaphernês.

That satrap, however, after twenty days, at last came

[1] **Strike our tents:** take down our tents.
[2] **Barbarians:** the Greeks called all foreigners "barbarians." This word, however, did not generally express contempt, or necessarily imply lack of civilization, but was used to designate those who spoke another language than Greek.

back, with his army prepared to return to Ionia[1] — with
the King's daughter, whom he had just received in marriage — and with another grandee named Orontas. Tissaphernês took the conduct of the march, providing supplies
for the Greek troops to purchase; while Ariæus and his
division now separated themselves altogether from the
Greeks, and became intermingled with the other Persians.
Klearchus and the Greeks followed them, at the distance
of about three miles in the rear, with a separate guide for
themselves; not without jealousy and mistrust, sometimes
shown in individual conflicts, while collecting wood or
forage, between them and the Persians of Ariæus. After
three days' march (that is, apparently, three days, calculated from the moment when they began their retreat with
Ariæus) they came to the Wall of Media,[2] and passed
through it, prosecuting their march onward through the
country on its other or interior side. It was of bricks
cemented with bitumen,[3] 100 feet high, and 20 feet broad;
it was said to extend a length of about 70 miles, and to
be not far distant from Babylon. Two days of farther
march, computed at 28 miles, brought them to the Tigris.
During these two days they crossed two great ship-canals,
one of them over a permanent bridge, the other over a
temporary bridge laid on seven boats. Canals of such
magnitude must probably have been two among the four
stated by Xenophon to be drawn from the river Tigris,
each of them about three miles and a half distant from
the other. They were 100 feet broad, and deep enough

[1] Ionia: see note on p. 21.
[2] **Wall of Media**: a wall supposed to have extended from the Euphrates
to the Tigris. It cannot now be traced with certainty.
[3] **Bitumen**: mineral pitch or asphalt. It is now much used for cement,
for making pavements, and for covering flat roofs.

even for heavy vessels; they were distributed by means of numerous smaller channels and ditches for the irrigation of the soil; and they were said to fall into the Euphratês; or rather perhaps they terminated in one main larger canal cut directly from the Euphratês to the Tigris, each of them joining this larger canal at a different point of its course. Within less than two miles of the Tigris was a large and populous city named Sittakê, near which the Greeks pitched their camp, on the verge of a beautiful park or thick grove full of all kinds of trees; while the Persians all crossed the Tigris, at the neighboring bridge.

As Proxenus and Xenophon were here walking in front of the camp after supper, a man was brought up who had asked for the former at the advanced posts. This man said that he came with instructions from Ariæus. He advised the Greeks to be on their guard, as there were troops concealed in the adjoining grove, for the purpose of attacking them during the night — and also to send and occupy the bridge over the Tigris, since Tissaphernês intended to break it down, in order that the Greeks might be caught without possibility of escape between the river and the canal. On discussing this information with Klearchus, who was much alarmed by it, a young Greek present remarked that the two matters stated by the informant contradicted each other; for that if Tissaphernês intended to attack the Greeks during the night, he would not break down the bridge, so as both to prevent his own troops on the other side from crossing to aid, and to deprive those on this side of all retreat if they were beaten, — while, if the Greeks were beaten, there was no escape open to them, whether the bridge continued or not. This remark induced Klearchus to ask the messenger, what was the extent of ground between the Tigris and the canal. The messenger replied that it was a great extent of country, comprising many large cities and villages. Reflecting on this communication, the Greek officers came to the conclusion that the message was a stratagem on the part of Tissaphernês to frighten them and hasten their passage across the Tigris; under the apprehension that they might conceive the plan of seizing or breaking the bridge and occupying a permanent position in the spot where they were; which was an island, fortified on one side by the Tigris,—on the other sides, by intersecting canals between the Euphratês and the Tigris. Such an island was a defensible position, having a most productive territory with numerous cultivators, so as to furnish shelter and means of hostility for all the King's enemies: Tissaphernês calculated that the message now delivered would induce the Greeks to become alarmed with their actual position, and to cross the Tigris with as little delay as possible. At least this was the interpretation which the Greek officers put upon his proceeding; an interpretation highly plausible, since, in order to reach the bridge over the Tigris, he had been obliged to conduct the Greek troops into a position sufficiently tempting for them to hold—and since he knew that his own purposes were purely treacherous. But the Greeks, officers as well as soldiers, were animated only by the wish of reaching home. They trusted, though not without misgivings, in the promise of Tissaphernês to conduct them; and never for a moment thought of taking permanent post in this fertile island. They did not however neglect the precaution of sending a guard during the night to the bridge over the Tigris, which no enemy came to assail. On the next morning they passed over it in a body, in cautious and mistrustful array, and found themselves on the eastern bank of the Tigris, — not only without attack, but even without sight of a single Persian, except Glûs the interpreter and a few others watching their motions.

After having crossed by a bridge laid upon thirty-seven pontoons,[1] the Greeks continued their march to the northward upon the eastern side of the Tigris, for four days to the river Physkus; said to be seventy miles. The Physkus was 100 feet wide, with a bridge, and the large city of Opis near it. Here, at the frontier of Assyria and Media, the road from the eastern regions to Babylon joined the road northerly on which the Greeks were marching. An illegitimate brother of Artaxerxês was seen at the head of a numerous force, which he was conducting from Susa and Ekbatana as a reinforcement to the royal army. This great host halted to see the Greeks pass by; and Klearchus ordered the march in column of two abreast, employing himself actively to maintain an excellent array, and halting more than once. The army thus occupied so long a time in passing by the Persian host that their numbers appeared greater than the reality, even to themselves; while the effect upon the Persian spectators was very imposing. Here Assyria ended and Media began. They marched, still in a northerly direction, for six days through a portion of Media almost unpeopled, until they came to some flourishing villages which formed a portion of the domain of Queen Parysatis; probably these villages, forming so marked an exception to the desert character of the remaining march, were situated on the Lesser Zab, which flows

---

[1] **Pontoons**: light framework or floats on which a platform or roadway is laid for a temporary bridge. Boats or canoes, placed side by side, and covered with planks, are not infrequently so used.

into the Tigris, and which Xenophon must have crossed, though he makes no mention of it. According to the order of march stipulated between the Greeks and Tissaphernês, the latter only provided a supply of provisions for the former to purchase; but on the present halt, he allowed the Greeks to plunder the villages, which were rich and full of all sorts of subsistence — yet without carrying off the slaves. The wish of the satrap to put an insult on Cyrus, as his personal enemy, through Parysatis, thus proved a sentence of ruin to these unhappy villagers. Five more days' march, called seventy miles, brought them to the banks of the river Zabatus, or the Greater Zab, which flows into the Tigris near a town now called Senn. During the first of these five days, they saw on the opposite side of the Tigris a large town called Kænæ, from whence they received supplies of provisions, brought across by the inhabitants upon rafts supported by inflated skins.[1]

### § 4. Treachery of Tissaphernês.

On the banks of the Great Zab they halted three days — days of serious and tragical moment. Having been under feelings of mistrust, ever since the convention with Tissaphernês, they had followed throughout the whole march, with separate guides of their own, in the rear of his army, always maintaining their encampment apart. During their halt on the Zab, so many various manifestations occurred to aggravate the mistrust, that hostilities seemed on the point of breaking out between the two camps. To obviate this danger Klearchus demanded an

[1] **Inflated skins:** bags or vessels made of the skins of sheep and other animals. They are quite commonly used in the East for carrying wine and other liquids. When inflated they are also employed as above mentioned.

interview with Tissaphernês, represented to him the threatening attitude of affairs, and insisted on the necessity of coming to a clear understanding. He impressed upon the satrap that, over and above the solemn oaths which had been interchanged, the Greeks on their side could have no conceivable motive to quarrel with him; that they had everything to hope from his friendship, and everything to fear, even to the loss of all chance of safe return, from his hostility; that Tissaphernês also could gain nothing by destroying them, but would find them, if he chose, the best and most faithful instruments for his own aggrandizement and for conquering the Mysians and Pisidians [1] — as Cyrus had experienced while he was alive. Klearchus concluded his protest by requesting to be informed, what malicious reporter had been filling the mind of Tissaphernês with causeless suspicions against the Greeks.

"Klearchus (replied the satrap), I rejoice to hear such excellent sense from your lips. You remark truly, that if you were to meditate evil against me, it would recoil upon yourselves. I shall prove to you, in my turn, that you have no cause to mistrust either the King or me. If we had wished to destroy you, nothing would be easier. We have superabundant forces for the purpose: there are wide plains in which you would be starved — besides mountains and rivers which you would be unable to pass, without our help. Having thus the means of destroying you in our hands, and having nevertheless bound ourselves by solemn oaths to save you, we shall not be fools and knaves enough to attempt it now, when we should draw upon ourselves the just indignation of the gods. It is my peculiar affection for my neighbors the Greeks — and my wish to

[1] **Mysians and Pisidians:** see note on p. 35.

attach to my own person, by ties of gratitude, the Greek soldiers of Cyrus — which have made me eager to conduct you to Ionia[1] in safety. For I know that when you are in my service, though the King is the only man who can wear his tiara[2] erect *upon his head*, I shall be able to wear mine erect upon *my heart*, in full pride and confidence."

So powerful was the impression made upon Klearchus by these assurances, that he exclaimed — "Surely those informers deserve the severest punishment, who try to put us at enmity, when we are such good friends to each other, and have so much reason to be so." "Yes (replied Tissaphernês), they deserve nothing less: and if you, with the other generals and captains, will come into my tent tomorrow, I will tell you who the calumniators are." "To-be-sure I will (rejoined Klearchus), and bring the other generals with me. I shall tell you at the same time who are the parties that seek to prejudice us against you." The conversation then ended, the satrap detaining Klearchus to dinner, and treating him in the most hospitable and confidential manner.

[1] **Ionia**: the central part of the western coast of Asia Minor. Here, at a very early period, flourishing Greek colonies were planted, and Ionia became celebrated for its art, its literature, and its cities, such as Ephesus and Miletus. But the country could not maintain its independence against the Eastern kings, and was at this period tributary to Persia. If the Ten Thousand could reach Ionia they would be among fellow-countrymen and friends, and within easy sail of all parts of Greece.

[2] **Tiara**: a flexible cap worn by the Persians. The king alone had the right to wear it erect and high, as a badge of royal authority. Some suppose that when Tissaphernês says that though he cannot openly place the high tiara on his head, but shall wear it on his heart (feeling like a king if not looking like one), that he purposely uses the language "the better to blind Klearchus," and make him think that if the Greeks will aid him with their arms, he will revolt and aspire to become king in fact.

On the next morning, Klearchus communicated what had passed to the Greeks, insisting on the necessity that all the generals should go to Tissaphernês pursuant to his invitation; in order to re-establish that confidence which unworthy calumniators had shaken, and to punish such of the calumniators as might be Greeks. So emphatically did he pledge himself for the good faith and philhellenic [1] dispositions of the satrap, that he overruled the opposition of many among the soldiers; who, still continuing to entertain their former suspicions, remonstrated especially against the extreme imprudence of putting all the generals at once into the power of Tissaphernês. The urgency of Klearchus prevailed. Himself with four other generals — Proxenus, Menon, Agias, and Sokratês — and twenty captains — went to visit the satrap in his tent; about 200 of the soldiers going along with them, to make purchases for their own account in the Persian camp-market.

On reaching the quarters of Tissaphernês — distant nearly three miles from the Persian camp according to habit — the five generals were admitted into the interior, while the captains remained at the entrance. A purple flag, hoisted from the top of the tent, betrayed too late the purpose for which they had been invited to come. The captains, with the Grecian soldiers who had accompanied them, were surprised and cut down, while the generals in the interior were detained, put in chains, and carried up as prisoners to the Persian court. Here Klearchus, Proxenus, Agias, and Sokratês, were beheaded, after a short imprisonment. Queen Parysatis, indeed, from affection to Cyrus, not only furnished many comforts to Klearchus in the prison (by the hands of her surgeon Ktesias), but used

[1] **Philhellenic:** Greek-loving.

all her influence with her son Artaxerxês to save his life; though her efforts were counteracted, on this occasion, by the superior influence of Queen Stateira, his wife. The rivalry between these two royal women, doubtless arising out of many other circumstances besides the death of Klearchus, became soon afterwards so furious, that Parysatis caused Stateira to be poisoned.

Menon was not put to death along with the other generals. He appears to have taken credit at the Persian court for the treason of entrapping his colleagues into the hands of Tissaphernês. But his life was only prolonged to perish a year afterwards in disgrace and torture — probably by the requisition of Parysatis, who thus avenged the death of Klearchus. The queen-mother had always power enough to perpetrate cruelties, though not always to avert them. She had already brought to a miserable end every one, even faithful defenders of Artaxerxês, concerned in the death of her son Cyrus.

Though Menon thought it convenient, when brought up to Babylon, to boast of having been the instrument through whom the generals were entrapped into the fatal tent, this boast is not to be treated as matter of fact. For not only does Xenophon explain the catastrophe differently, but in the delineation which he gives of Menon, dark and odious as it is in the extreme, he does not advance any such imputation; indirectly, indeed, he sets it aside.

Unfortunately for the reputation of Klearchus, no such reasonable excuse can be offered for his credulity, which brought himself as well as his colleagues to so melancholy an end, and his whole army to the brink of ruin. It appears that the general sentiment of the Grecian army, taking just measure of the character of Tissaphernês, was disposed to greater circumspection in dealing with him. Upon that system Klearchus himself had hitherto acted; and the necessity of it might have been especially present to *his* mind, since he had served with the Lacedæmonian fleet at Miletus[1] in 411 B.C., and had therefore had fuller experience than other men in the army, of the satrap's real character. On a sudden he now turns round, and on the faith of a few verbal declarations, puts all the military chiefs into the most defenceless posture and the most obvious peril, such as hardly the strongest grounds for confidence could have justified. Though the remark of Machiavel is justified by large experience — that from the short-sightedness of men and their obedience to present impulse, the most notorious deceiver will always find new persons to trust him — still such misjudgment on the part of an officer of age and experience is difficult to explain. Polyænus intimates that beautiful women, exhibited by the satrap at his first banquet to Klearchus alone, served as a lure to attract him with all his colleagues to the second; while Xenophon imputes the error to continuance of a jealous rivalry with Menon. The latter, it appears, having always been intimate withAriæus, had been thus brought into previous communication with Tissaphernês, by whom he had been well received, and by whom he was also encouraged to lay plans for detaching the whole Grecian army from Klearchus so as to bring it all under his (Menon's)

---

[1] **Miletus:** a city of Ionia, subject in a measure to Athens, revolted in 412 B.C. The next year the Lacedæmonians, or Spartans, who were the enemies of Athens, sent over a fleet to aid the people of Miletus. Tissaphernês, the Persian satrap, desiring to see the power of Athens completely overthrown, promised to pay the Spartan soldiers (of whom Klearchus was one), but afterwards made up his mind not to do so, and left them to fight at their own expense.

command into the services of the satrap. Such at least was the suspicion of Klearchus; who, jealous in the extreme of his own military authority, tried to defeat the scheme by bidding still higher himself for the favor of Tissaphernês. Imagining that Menon was the unknown calumniator who prejudiced the satrap against him, he hoped to prevail on the satrap to disclose his name and dismiss him. Such jealousy seems to have robbed Klearchus of his customary prudence. We must also allow for another impression deeply fixed in his mind; that the salvation of the army was hopeless without the consent of Tissaphernês, and therefore, since the latter had conducted them thus far in safety, when he might have destroyed them before, that his designs at the bottom could not be hostile.

Notwithstanding these two great mistakes — one on the present occasion, one previously, at the battle of Kunaxa, in keeping the Greeks on the right contrary to the order of Cyrus — both committed by Klearchus, the loss of that officer was doubtless a great misfortune to the army; while, on the contrary, the removal of Menon was a signal benefit — perhaps a condition of ultimate safety. A man so treacherous and unprincipled as Xenophon depicts Menon, would probably have ended by really committing towards the army that treason, for which he falsely took credit at the Persian court in reference to the seizure of the generals.

The impression entertained by Klearchus, respecting the hopeless position of the Greeks in the heart of the Persian territory after the death of Cyrus was perfectly natural in a military man who could appreciate all the means of attack and obstruction which the enemy had it in their power to employ. Nothing is so unaccountable in this expedition as the manner in which such means were thrown away — the spectacle of Persian impotence. First, the whole line of upward march, including the passage of the Euphratês, left undefended; next, the long trench dug across the frontier of Babylonia, with only a passage of twenty feet wide left near the Euphratês, abandoned without a guard; lastly, the line of the Wall of Media and the canals which offered such favorable positions for keeping the Greeks out of the cultivated territory of Babylonia, neglected in like manner, and a convention concluded whereby the Persians engaged to escort the invaders safe to the Ionian coast, beginning by conducting them through the heart of Babylonia, amidst canals affording inexpugnable defences if the Greeks had chosen to take up a position among them. The plan of Tissaphernês, as far as we can understand it, seems to have been, to draw the Greeks to some considerable distance from the heart of the Persian empire, and then to open his schemes of treasonable hostility, which the imprudence of Klearchus enabled him to do, on the banks of the Great Zab, with chances of success such as he could hardly have contemplated. We have here a fresh example of the wonderful impotence of the Persians. We should have expected that, after having committed so flagrant an act of perfidy, Tissaphernês would at least have tried to turn it to account; that he would have poured with all his forces and all his vigor on the Grecian camp, at the moment when it was unprepared, disorganized, and without commanders. Instead of which, when the generals (with those who accompanied them to the Persian camp) had been seized or slain, no attack whatever was made except by small detachments of Persian cavalry upon individual Greek stragglers in the plain. One of the companions of the generals, an Arcadian,[1] named Nikarchus, ran wounded into the Grecian camp, where the soldiers were looking from afar at the horsemen scouring the plain without knowing what they were about, — exclaiming that the Persians were massacring all the Greeks, officers as well as soldiers. Immediately the Greek soldiers hastened to put themselves in defence, expecting a general attack to be made upon their camp; but no more Persians came near than a body of about 300 horse, under Ariæus and Mithridatês (the confidential companions of the deceased Cyrus), accompanied by the brother of Tissaphernês. These men, approaching the Greek lines as friends, called for the Greek officers to come forth, as they had a message to deliver from the King. Accordingly, Kleanor and Sophænetus with an adequate guard, came to the front, accompanied by Xenophon, who was anxious to hear news about Proxenus. Ariæus then acquainted them that Klearchus, having been detected in a breach of the convention to which he had sworn, had been put to death; that Proxenus and Menon, who had divulged his treason, were in high honor at the Persian quarters. He concluded by saying — "The King calls upon you to surrender your arms, which now (he says) belong to him, since they formerly belonged to his slave Cyrus."

The step here taken seems to testify a belief on the part of these Persians, that the generals being now in their power the Grecian soldiers had become defenceless, and might be required to surrender their arms, even to men who had just been guilty of the most deadly fraud and

[1] **Arcadian**: an inhabitant of Arcadia, a district of the Peloponnesian peninsula, Greece.

injury towards them. IfAriæus entertained such an expectation, he was at once undeceived by the language of Kleanor and Xenophon, which breathed nothing but indignant reproach; so that he soon retired and left the Greeks to their own reflections.

While their camp yet remained unmolested, every man within it was a prey to the most agonizing apprehensions. Ruin appeared impending and inevitable, though no one could tell in what precise form it would come. The Greeks were in the midst of a hostile country, nearly 1200 miles from home, surrounded by enemies, blocked up by impassable mountains and rivers, without guides, without provisions, without cavalry to aid their retreat, without generals to give orders. A stupor of sorrow and conscious helplessness seized upon all. Few came to the evening muster; few lighted fires to cook their suppers; every man lay down to rest where he was; yet no man could sleep, for fear, anguish, and yearning after relatives whom he was never again to behold.

Amidst the many causes of despondency which weighed down this forlorn army, there was none more serious than the fact, that not a single man among them had now either authority to command, or obligation to take the initiative. Nor was any ambitious candidate likely to volunteer his pretensions, at a moment when the post promised nothing but the maximum of difficulty as well as of hazard. A new, self-kindled light — and self-originated stimulus — was required, to vivify the embers of suspended hope and action, in a mass paralyzed for the moment, but every way capable of effort. And the inspiration now fell, happily for the army, upon one in whom a full measure of soldierly strength and courage was combined with the education of an Athenian, a democrat, and a philosopher.[1]

### § 5. Xenophon's Dream and its Results.

It is in true Homeric vein, and in something like Homeric language, that Xenophon (to whom we owe the whole narrative of the expedition) describes his dream, or the intervention of Oneirus,[2] sent by Zeus,[3] from which this renovating impulse took its rise. Lying mournful and restless like his comrades, he caught a short repose; when he dreamt that he heard thunder, and saw the burning thunderbolt fall upon his paternal house, which became forthwith encircled by flames. Awaking, full of terror, he instantly sprang up; upon which the dream began to fit on and blend itself with his waking thoughts, and with the cruel realities of his position. His pious and excited fancy generated a series of shadowy analogies. The dream was sent by Zeus the King, since it was from him that thunder and lightning proceeded. In one respect, the sign was auspicious — that a great light had appeared to him from Zeus in the midst of peril and suffering. But on the other hand, it was alarming, that the house had appeared to be completely encircled by flames, preventing all egress,

---

[1] **Democrat and philosopher**: Xenophon (431?-355 B.C.) belonged to that party in Athens that maintained the principle of government "of the people, by the people, and for the people," in opposition to the party that, like the Spartans, believed that all political power should be monopolized by a favored few. Xenophon was also the disciple and friend of Socrates the philosopher, of whom some account will be given later on.

[2] **Oneirus**: the god of dreams and messenger of Zeus (Jupiter), father of gods and men, sometimes called Zeus the Preserver, Saviour, or Deliverer.

[3] **Zeus**: see note above on Oneirus.

because this seemed to indicate that he would remain confined where he was in the Persian dominions, without being able to overcome the difficulties which hedged him in. Yet doubtful as the promise was, it was still the message of Zeus addressed to himself, serving as a stimulus to him to break through the common stupor and take the initiative movement. "Why am I lying here? Night is advancing; at daybreak the enemy will be on us, and we shall be put to death with tortures. Not a man is stirring to take measures of defence. Why do I wait for any man older than myself, or for any man of a different city, to begin?"

With these reflections, interesting in themselves, and given with Homeric vivacity, he instantly went to convene the captains who had served under his late friend Proxenus. He impressed upon them emphatically the necessity of standing forward to put the army in a posture of defence. "I cannot sleep, fellow-soldiers; neither, I presume, can you, under our present perils. The enemy will be upon us at daybreak — prepared to kill us all with tortures, as his worst enemies. For my part, I rejoice that his villanous perjury has put an end to a truce by which we were the great losers; a truce, under which we, mindful of our oaths, have passed through all the rich possessions of the King, without touching anything except what we could purchase with our own scanty means. Now, we have our hands free: all these rich spoils stand between us and him, as prizes for the better man. The gods, who preside over the match, will assuredly be on the side of us, who have kept our oaths in spite of strong temptations, against these perjurers. Moreover, our bodies are more enduring, and our spirit more gallant, than theirs. They are easier to wound, and easier to kill, than we are, under the same favor of the gods as we experienced at Kunaxa.

"Probably others also are feeling just as we feel. But let us not wait for any one else to come as monitors to us: let us take the lead, and communicate the stimulus of honor to others. Do you show yourselves now the best among the captains — more worthy of being generals than the generals themselves. Begin at once, and I desire only to follow you. But if you order me into the front rank, I shall obey without pleading my youth as an excuse — accounting myself to be of complete maturity, when the purpose is to save myself from ruin."

All the captains who heard Xenophon cordially concurred in his suggestion, and desired him to take the lead in executing it. One captain alone — Apollonidês, speaking in the Bœotian dialect [1] — protested against it as insane; enlarging upon their desperate position, and insisting upon submission to the King as the only chance of safety. "How? (replied Xenophon). Have you forgotten the courteous treatment which we received from the Persians in Babylonia when we replied to their demand for the surrender of our arms by showing a bold front? Do not you see the miserable fate which has befallen Klearchus, when he trusted himself unarmed in their hands, in reliance on their oaths? And yet you scout our exhortations to resistance, again advising us to go and plead for indulgence! My friends, such a Greek as this man, disgraces not only his own city, but all Greece besides. Let us banish him from our councils, cashier[2] him, and make

---

[1] **Bœotian dialect:** the inhabitants of the Greek province of Bœotia were considered by the Athenians to be a dull and unprogressive people. They spoke a broad, coarse dialect.

[2] **Cashier:** to dismiss from service.

a slave of him to carry baggage." "Nay (observed Agasias of Stymphalus), the man has nothing to do with Greece: I myself have seen his ears bored, like a true Lydian."[1] Apollonidês was degraded accordingly.

Xenophon with the rest then distributed themselves in order to bring together the chief remaining officers in the army, who were presently convened, to the number of about one hundred. The senior captain of the earlier body next desired Xenophon to repeat to this larger body the topics upon which he had just before been insisting. Xenophon obeyed, enlarging yet more emphatically on the situation, perilous, yet not without hope — on the proper measures to be taken — and especially on the necessity that they, the chief officers remaining, should put themselves forward prominently, first fix upon effective commanders, then afterwards submit the names to be confirmed by the army, accompanied with suitable exhortations and encouragement. His speech was applauded and welcomed, especially by the Lacedæmonian general Cheirisophus, who had joined Cyrus with a body of 700 heavy-armed foot-soldiers at Issus in Kilikia.[2] Cheirisophus urged the captains to retire forthwith, and agree upon their commanders instead of the five who had been seized; after which the herald must be summoned, and the entire body of soldiers convened without delay. Accordingly Timasion of Dardanus was chosen instead of Klearchus; Xanthiklês in place of Sokratês; Kleanor in place of Agias; Philesius

[1] **Ears bored**: this was an Eastern (Lydian) custom, which the Greeks despised as only befitting slaves, since with them it was a mark of servitude. Agasias intimates that Apollonidês either had been a slave or at least ought to be one.

[2] **Kilikia** (also spelled Cilicia): Asia Minor.

in place of Menon; and Xenophon instead of Proxenus. The captains, who had served under each of the departed generals, separately chose a successor to the captain thus promoted. It is to be recollected that the five now chosen were not the only generals in the camp; thus for example, Cheirisophus had the command of his own separate division, and there may have been one or two others similarly placed. But it was now necessary for all the generals to form a Board and act in concert.

At daybreak the newly-constituted Board of generals placed proper outposts in advance, and then convened the army in general assembly, in order that the new appointments might be submitted and confirmed. As soon as this had been done, probably on the proposition of Cheirisophus (who had been in command before), that general addressed a few words of exhortation and encouragement to the soldiers. He was followed by Kleanor, who delivered, with the like brevity, an earnest protest against the perfidy of Tissaphernês and Ariæus. Both of them left to Xenophon the task, alike important and arduous at this moment of despondency, of setting forth the case at length,— working up the feelings of the soldiers to that pitch of resolution which the emergency required,—and above all extinguishing all those inclinations to acquiesce in new treacherous proposals from the enemy, which the perils of the situation would be likely to suggest.

Xenophon had equipped himself in his finest military costume at this his first official appearance before the army, when the scales seemed to tremble between life and death. Taking up the protest of Kleanor against the treachery of the Persians, he insisted that any attempt to enter into convention or trust with such liars, would be utter ruin — but that if energetic resolution were taken to deal with them only at the point of the sword, and punish their misdeeds, there was good hope of the favor of the gods and of ultimate preservation. As he pronounced this last word, one of the soldiers near him happened to sneeze.[1] Immediately the whole army around shouted with one accord the accustomed invocation to Zeus the Preserver; and Xenophon, taking up the accident, continued — " Since, fellow-soldiers, this omen from Zeus the Preserver has appeared at the instant when we were talking about preservation, let us here vow to offer the preserving sacrifice to that god, and at the same time to sacrifice to the remaining gods as well as we can, in the first friendly country which we may reach. Let every man who agrees with me hold up his hand." All held up their hands: all then joined in the vow, and shouted the pæan.[2]

This accident, so dexterously turned to profit by the rhetorical skill of Xenophon, was eminently beneficial in raising the army out of the depression which weighed them down, and in disposing them to listen to his animating appeal. Repeating his assurances that the gods were on their side, and hostile to their perjured enemy, he recalled to their memory the great invasions of Greece by Darius and Xerxes, — how the vast hosts of Persia had been disgracefully repelled. The army had shown themselves on the field of Kunaxa worthy of such forefathers; and they

[1] **Sneeze:** any sudden, involuntary outburst, like sneezing, was considered a sign of the divine will for good or evil. As it occurred here just as Xenophon pronounced the auspicious word "preservation," it was regarded as a favorable omen sent by Zeus himself. The accustomed invocation was like the old English custom of crying "God bless you" when one sneezed.

[2] **Pæan:** war-song, song of triumph; originally addressed to the god Apollo.

would for the future be yet bolder, knowing by that battle of what stuff the Persians were made. As for Ariæus and his troops, alike traitors and cowards, their desertion was rather a gain than a loss. The enemy were superior in horsemen: but men on horseback were after all only men, half occupied in the fear of losing their seats — incapable of prevailing against infantry firm on the ground, — and only better able to run away. Now that the satrap refused to furnish them with provisions to buy, they on their side were released from their covenant, and would take provisions without buying. Then as to the rivers; those were indeed difficult to be crossed, in the middle of their course; but the army would march up to their sources, and could then pass them without wetting the knee. Or indeed, the Greeks might renounce the idea of retreat, and establish themselves permanently in the King's own country, defying all his force, like the Mysians and Pisidians.[1] "If (said Xenophon) we plant ourselves here at our ease in a rich country, with these tall, stately and beautiful Median and Persian women for our companions — we shall be only too ready, like the Lotos-eaters,[2] to forget our way home. We ought first to go back to Greece, and tell our countrymen that if they remain poor, it is their own fault, when there are rich settlements in this country awaiting all who choose to come, and who have courage to seize them. Let us

---

[1] **Mysians and Pisidians**: rude tribes inhabiting mountainous districts of Asia Minor, and maintaining their independence in spite of the efforts of the Persian kings to subjugate them.

[2] **Lotos-eaters**: the lotos is a date-like fruit, fabled by Homer in the "Odyssey" to be so delicious and possessed of such marvellous properties that those who once tasted it forgot home and friends and wished only to remain where they might continue to eat it forever. See "Odyssey," Book IX., and compare Tennyson's poem of the "Lotos-Eaters."

burn our baggage wagons and tents, and carry with us nothing but what is of the strictest necessity. Above all things, let us maintain order, discipline, and obedience to the commanders, upon which our entire hope of safety depends. Let every man promise to lend his hand to the commanders in punishing any disobedient individuals; and let us thus show the enemy that we have ten thousand persons like Klearchus, instead of that one whom they have so perfidiously seized. Now is the time for action. If any man, however obscure, has anything better to suggest, let him come forward and state it; for we have all but one object — the common safety."

It appears that no one else desired to say a word, and that the speech of Xenophon gave unqualified satisfaction; for when Cheirisophus put the question, that the meeting should sanction his recommendations, and finally elect the new generals proposed — every man held up his hand. Xenophon then moved that the army should break up immediately, and march to some well-stored villages, rather more than two miles distant; that the march should be in a hollow square, with the baggage in the centre; that Cheirisophus, as a Lacedæmonian, should lead the van; while Kleanor, and the other senior officers, would command on each flank, — and himself with Timasion, as the two youngest of the generals, would lead the rear guard.

This proposition was at once adopted, and the assembly broke up; proceeding forthwith to destroy, or distribute among one another, every man's superfluous baggage — and then to take their morning meal previous to the march.

The scene just described is interesting and illustrative in more than one point of view. It exhibits that susceptibility to the influence of persuasive discourse which formed so marked a feature in the Grecian character — a resurrection of the collective body out of the depth of despair, under the exhortation of one who had no established ascendency, nor anything to recommend him, except his intelligence, his oratorical power, and his community of interest with themselves. Next, it manifests, still more strikingly, the superiority of Athenian training as compared with that of other parts of Greece. Cheirisophus had not only been before in office as one of the generals, but was also a native of Sparta, whose supremacy and name was at that moment all-powerful; Kleanor had been before, not indeed a general, but a captain, or one in the second rank of officers: — he was an elderly man — and he was an Arcadian, while more than the numerical half of the army consisted of Arcadians and Achæans.[1] Either of these two therefore, and various others besides, enjoyed a sort of prerogative, or established starting-point, for taking the initiative in reference to the dispirited army. But Xenophon was comparatively a young man, with little military experience: — he was not an officer at all, either in the first or second grade, but simply a volunteer, companion of Proxenus: — he was moreover a native of Athens, a city at that time unpopular among the great body of Greeks, and especially of Peloponnesians,[2] with whom her recent long war had been carried on. Not only therefore he had no advantages compared with others, but he was

---

[1] **Achæans**: inhabitants of Achaia, in the Peloponnesian peninsula.

[2] **Peloponnesians**: inhabitants of the Greek peninsula of the Peloponnesus (or so-called Island of Pelops), now known as the Morea. They were considered the best soldiers in Greece. Sparta, the rival and enemy of Athens, was the ruling city of this district.

under positive disadvantages. He had nothing to start with except his personal qualities and previous training; in spite of which we find him not merely the prime mover, but also the superior person for whom the others make way. In him are exemplified those peculiarities of Athens, attested not less by the denunciation of her enemies than by the panegyric of her own citizens, — spontaneous and forward impulse, as well in conception as in execution — confidence under circumstances which made others despair — persuasive discourse and publicity of discussion, made subservient to practical business, so as at once to appeal to the intelligence, and stimulate the active zeal, of the multitude. Such peculiarities stood out more remarkably from being contrasted with the opposite qualities in Spartans — mistrust in conception, slackness in execution, secrecy in counsel, silent and passive obedience. Though Spartans and Athenians formed the two extremities of the scale, other Greeks stood nearer on this point to the former than to the latter.

If, even in that encouraging autumn which followed immediately upon the great Athenian catastrophe[1] before Syracuse, the inertia of Sparta could not be stirred into vigorous action without the vehemence of the Athenian Alkibiadês — much more was it necessary, under the depressing circumstances which now overclouded the unofficered Grecian army, that an Athenian bosom should be

---

[1] **Athenian catastrophe:** in 415 B.C. the Athenians sent out a powerful expedition to conquer Syracuse in Sicily. They met with a disastrous defeat, both by land and sea, many thousands being taken captive and sold as slaves. Alkibiadês, an Athenian who had taken refuge in Sparta, now urged the Spartans to attack Athens, their old rival and enemy. His vehement eloquence was eventually successful.

found as the source of new life and impulse. Nor would any one, probably, except an Athenian, either have felt or obeyed the promptings to stand forward as a volunteer at that moment, when there was every motive to decline responsibility, and no special duty to impel him. But if by chance a Spartan or an Arcadian had been found thus forward, he would have been destitute of such talents as would enable him to work on the minds of others — of that flexibility, resource, familiarity with the temper and movements of an assembled crowd, power of enforcing the essential views and touching the opportune chords, which Athenian democratical training imparted. Even Brasidas and Gylippus, individual Spartans of splendid merit, and equal or superior to Xenophon in military resource, would not have combined with it that political and rhetorical accomplishment which the position of the latter demanded. Obvious as the wisdom of his propositions appears, each of them is left to him not only to initiate, but to enforce: Cheirisophus and Kleanor, after a few words of introduction, consign to him the duty of working up the minds of the army to the proper pitch.

How well he performed this, may be seen by his speech to the army, which bears in its general tenor a remarkable resemblance to that of Periklês[1] addressed to the Athenian public in the second year of the war,[2] at the moment when

[1] **Periklês:** leader of the party of the people in Athens, and for a long time governor of the city; he was perhaps the greatest statesman that Greece produced.

[2] **The war:** the Peloponnesian War, 431-404 B.C. This was a desperate struggle for supremacy between the two chief powers of Greece, Sparta and Athens. The Spartans were a rough, military people, despising all intellectual culture and maintaining a narrow and tyrannical form of government from which the body of the people was wholly excluded. The Athenians, on the

the miseries of the epidemic, combined with those of invasion, had driven them almost to despair. It breathes a strain of exaggerated confidence, and an undervaluing of real dangers, highly suitable for the occasion, but which neither Periklês nor Xenophon would have employed at any other moment. Throughout the whole of his speech, and especially in regard to the accidental sneeze near at hand which interrupted the beginning of it, Xenophon displayed that skill and practice in dealing with a numerous audience, and a given situation, which characterized more or less every educated Athenian. Other Greeks, Lacedæmonians or Arcadians, could act, with bravery and in concert; but the Athenian Xenophon was among the few who could think, speak, and act, with equal efficiency. It was this threefold accomplishment which an aspiring youth was compelled to set before himself as an aim, in the democracy of Athens; and which the Sophists[1] as well as the democratical institutions — both of them so hardly depreciated by most critics — helped and encouraged him to acquire. It was this threefold accomplishment, the exclusive possession of which, in spite of constant jealousy on the part of Bœotian officers and comrades of Proxenus, elevated Xenophon into the most ascendent person of the Cyreian army,

contrary, wished to maintain a republic in which all citizens should take part; they represented the highest civilization of Greece, and were in one sense the schoolmasters of the world.

[1] **Sophists**: a class of philosophers or teachers who gave instruction in rhetoric and the art of disputation. They went about from city to city, and, contrary to the general custom of Greek philosophers, took fees from their pupils. "What the Sophists, among other things conducive to success in life, really taught the people, was the art of conducting their own cases before the great citizen-juries, where every man was forced to be his own advocate." [See Myers's "Outlines of Ancient History."]

from the present moment until the time when it broke up, — as will be seen in the subsequent history.

I think it the more necessary to notice this fact, — that the accomplishments whereby Xenophon leaped on a sudden into such extraordinary ascendency, and rendered such eminent service to his army, were accomplishments belonging in an especial manner to the Athenian democracy and education — because Xenophon himself has throughout his writings treated Athens not merely without the attachment of a citizen, but with feelings more like the positive antipathy of an exile. His sympathies are all in favor of the perpetual drill, the mechanical obedience, the secret government proceedings, the narrow and prescribed range of ideas, the silent and deferential demeanor, the methodical, though tardy, action — of Sparta. Whatever may be the justice of his preference, certain it is, that the qualities whereby he was himself enabled to contribute so much both to the rescue of the Cyreian army, and to his own reputation — were Athenian far more than Spartan.

While the Grecian army, after sanctioning the propositions of Xenophon, were taking their morning meal before they commenced their march, Mithridatês, one of the Persians previously attached to Cyrus, appeared with a few horsemen on a mission of pretended friendship. But it was soon found out that his purposes were treacherous, and that he came merely to seduce individual soldiers to desertion — with a few of whom he succeeded. Accordingly, the resolution was taken to admit no more heralds or envoys.

## § 6. The Greeks cross the Zab.

Disembarrassed of superfluous baggage, and refreshed, the army now crossed the Great Zab River, and pursued their march on the other side, having their baggage and attendants in the centre, and Cheirisophus leading the van, with a select body of 300 heavy-armed foot-soldiers. As no mention is made of a bridge, we are to presume that they forded the river, — which furnishes a ford still commonly used, at a place between thirty and forty miles from its junction with the Tigris. When they had got a little way forward, Mithridatês again appeared with a few hundred cavalry and bowmen. He approached them like a friend; but as soon as he was near enough, suddenly began to harass the rear with a shower of missiles. What surprises us most, is, that the Persians, with their very numerous force, made no attempt to hinder them from crossing so very considerable a river; for Xenophon estimates the Zab at 400 feet broad, — and this seems below the statement of modern travellers, who inform us that it contains not much less water than the Tigris; and though usually deeper and narrower, cannot be much narrower at any fordable place. It is to be recollected that the Persians, habitually marching in advance of the Greeks, must have reached the river first, and were therefore in possession of the crossing, whether bridge or ford. Though on the watch for every opportunity of perfidy, Tissaphernês did not dare to resist the Greeks, even in the most advantageous position, and ventured only upon sending Mithridatês to harass the rear; which he executed with considerable effect. The bowmen and darters of the Greeks, few in number, were at the same time inferior to those of the Persians; and when Xenophon employed his rearguard, heavy-armed foot-soldiers and light-armed foot-soldiers, to charge and repel them, he not only could never overtake any one, but suffered much in getting back to rejoin his own main body. Even when retiring, the Persian horseman could discharge his arrow or cast his javelin[1] behind him with effect; a dexterity which the Parthians exhibited afterwards still more signally, and which the Persian horsemen of the present day parallel with their carbines.[2] This was the first experience which the Greeks had of marching under the harassing attack of cavalry. Even the small detachment of Mithridatês greatly delayed their progress; so that they accomplished little more than two miles, reaching the villages in the evening, with many wounded, and much discouragement.

"Thank Heaven" (said Xenophon in the evening, when Cheirisophus reproached him for imprudence in quitting the main body to charge cavalry, whom yet he could not reach), "Thank Heaven, that our enemies attacked us with a small detachment only, and not with their great numbers. They have given us a valuable lesson, without doing us any serious harm." Profiting by the lesson, the Greek leaders organized during the night and during the halt of the next day, a small body of fifty cavalry; with 200 Rhodian[3] slingers, whose slings, furnished with leaden bullets, both carried farther and struck harder than those of the Persians hurling large stones. On the ensuing morning, they started before daybreak, since there lay in

[1] **Javelin**: a light spear.
[2] **Carbines**: short muskets, or rifles.
[3] **Rhodian**: pertaining to the island of Rhodes, off the southwest coast of Asia Minor.

their way a ravine difficult to pass. They found the ravine undefended (according to the usual stupidity of Persian proceedings), but when they had got nearly a mile beyond it, Mithridatês reappeared in pursuit with a body of 4000 horsemen and darters. Confident from his achievement of the preceding day, he had promised, with a body of that force, to deliver the Greeks into the hands of the satrap. But the latter were now better prepared. As soon as he began to attack them, the trumpet sounded,—and forthwith the horsemen, slingers, and darters, issued forth to charge the Persians, sustained by the heavy-armed foot-soldiers in the rear. So effective was the charge, that the Persians fled in dismay, notwithstanding their superiority in number; while the ravine so impeded their flight that many of them were slain, and eighteen prisoners made. The Greek soldiers of their own accord mutilated the dead bodies, in order to strike terror into the enemy. At the end of the day's march, they reached the Tigris, near the deserted city of Larissa, the vast, massive, and lofty brick walls of which (25 feet in thickness, 100 feet high, seven miles in circumference) attested its former grandeur. Near this place was a stone pyramid, 100 feet in breadth, and 200 feet high; the summit of which was crowded with fugitives out of the neighboring villages. Another day's march up the course of the Tigris brought the army to a second deserted city called Mespila, nearly opposite to the modern city of Mosul. Although these two cities, which seem to have formed the continuation of (or the substitute for) the once colossal Nineveh [1] or Ninus, were completely

---

[1] Nineveh: "an exceeding great city" (Jonah iii. 3), larger, says Strabo, than Babylon, having walls with 1500 towers 200 feet high. (Diodorus.)

deserted, — yet the country around them was so well furnished with villages and population, that the Greeks not only obtained provisions, but also strings for the making of new bows, and lead for bullets to be used by the slingers.

During the next day's march, in a course generally parallel with the Tigris, and ascending the stream, Tissaphernês, coming up along with some other grandees, and with a numerous army, enveloped the Greeks both in flanks and rear. In spite of his advantage of numbers, he did not venture upon any actual charge, but kept up a fire of arrows, darts, and stones. He was however so well answered by the newly-trained archers and slingers of the Greeks, that on the whole they had the advantage, in spite of the superior size of the Persian bows, many of which were taken and effectively employed on the Grecian side. Having passed the night in a well-stocked village, they halted there the next day in order to stock themselves with provisions, and then pursued their march for four successive days along a level country, until on the fifth day they reached hilly ground with the prospect of still higher hills beyond. All this march was made under unremitting annoyance from the enemy, insomuch that though the order of the Greeks was never broken, a considerable number of their men were wounded. Experience taught them, that it was inconvenient for the whole army to march in one inflexible, undivided, hollow square; and they accordingly constituted six regiments of 100 men each, subdivided into companies of 50, and smaller companies of 25, each with a special officer (conformably to the Spartan practice) to move separately on each flank, and either to fall back, or fall in, as might suit the fluctuations of the central mass, arising from impediments in the road or menaces of the enemy. On reaching the hills, in sight of an elevated citadel or palace, with several villages around it, the Greeks anticipated some remission of the Persian attack. But after having passed over one hill, they were proceeding to ascend the second, when they found themselves assailed with unwonted vigor by the Persian cavalry from the summit of it, whose leaders were seen flogging on the men to the attack. This charge was so efficacious, that the Greek light troops were driven in with loss, and forced to take shelter within the ranks of the heavy-armed foot-soldiers. After a march both slow and full of suffering, they could only reach their night-quarters by sending a detachment to get possession of some ground above the Persians, who thus became afraid of a double attack.

The villages which they now reached were unusually rich in provisions; magazines of flour, barley, and wine, having been collected there for the Persian satrap. They reposed here three days, chiefly in order to tend the numerous wounded, for whose necessities, eight of the most competent persons were singled out to act as surgeons. On the fourth day they resumed their march, descending into the plain. But experience had now satisfied them that it was imprudent to continue in march under the attack of cavalry, so that when Tissaphernês appeared and began to harass them, they halted at the first village, and when thus in station, easily repelled him. As the afternoon advanced, the Persian assailants began to retire; for they were always in the habit of taking up their night-post at a distance of near seven miles from the Grecian position; being very apprehensive of nocturnal attack in their camp, when their horses were tied by the leg and without either saddle or bridle. As soon as they had departed, the Greeks resumed their march, and made so much advance during the night, that the Persians did not overtake them either on the next day or the day after.

On the ensuing day, however, the Persians, having made a forced march by night, were seen not only in advance of the Greeks, but in occupation of a spur of high and precipitous ground overhanging immediately the road whereby the Greeks were to descend into the plain. When Cheirisophus approached, he at once saw that descent was impracticable in the face of an enemy thus posted. He therefore halted, sent for Xenophon from the rear, and desired him to bring forward the light-armed foot-soldiers to the van. But Xenophon, though he obeyed the summons in person and galloped his horse to the front, did not think it prudent to move the light-armed foot-soldiers from the rear, because he saw Tissaphernês, with another portion of the army, just coming up; so that the Grecian army was at once impeded in front, and threatened by the enemy closing upon them behind. The Persians on the high ground in front could not be directly assailed. But Xenophon observed, that on the right of the Grecian army, there was an accessible mountain summit yet higher, from whence a descent might be made for a flank attack upon the Persian position. Pointing out this summit to Cheirisophus, as affording the only means of dislodging the troops in front, he urged that one of them should immediately hasten with a detachment to take possession of it and offered to Cheirisophus the choice either of going, or staying with the army. "Choose for yourself," said Cheirisophus. "Well then (said Xenophon), I will go; since I am the younger of the two." Accordingly, at the head of a select detachment from the van and centre of the army, he immediately commenced his flank march up the steep ascent to this highest summit. So soon as the enemy saw their purpose, they also detached troops on their side, hoping to get to the summit first; and the two detachments were seen mounting at the same time, each struggling with the utmost efforts to get before the other, — each being encouraged by shouts and clamor from the two armies respectively.

As Xenophon was riding by the side of his soldiers, cheering them on and reminding them that their chance of seeing their country and their families all depended upon success in the effort before them, a Sikyonian heavy-armed foot-soldier in the ranks, named Sotêridas, said to him — "You and I are not on an equal footing, Xenophon. You are on horseback : — I am painfully struggling upon foot, with my shield to carry." Stung with this taunt, Xenophon sprang from his horse, pushed Sotêridas out of his place in the ranks, took his shield as well as his place, and began to march forward afoot along with the rest. Though thus weighed down at once by the shield belonging to a heavy-armed foot-soldier, and by the heavy cuirass[1] of a horseman (who carried no shield), he nevertheless put forth all his strength to advance under such double incumbrance, and to continue his incitement to the rest. But the soldiers around him were so indignant at the proceeding of Sotêridas, that they reproached and even struck him, until they compelled him to resume his shield as well as his place in the ranks. Xenophon then remounted and ascended the hill on horseback as far as the ground per-

[1] **Cuirass**: defensive armor, covering the body from the neck to the girdle.

mitted; but was obliged again to dismount presently, in consequence of the steepness of the uppermost portion. Such energetic efforts enabled him and his detachment to reach the summit first. As soon as the enemy saw this, they desisted from their ascent, and dispersed in all directions; leaving the forward march open to the main Grecian army, which Cheirisophus accordingly conducted safely down into the plain. Here he was rejoined by Xenophon on descending from the summit. All found themselves in comfortable quarters, amidst several well-stocked villages on the banks of the Tigris. They acquired moreover an additional booty of large droves of cattle, intercepted when on the point of being transported across the river; where a considerable body of horse was seen assembled on the opposite bank.

Though here disturbed only by some desultory attacks on the part of the Persians, who burnt several of the villages which lay in their forward line of march, the Greeks became seriously embarrassed whither to direct their steps; for on their left flank was the Tigris, so deep that their spears found no bottom, — and on their right, mountains of exceeding height. As the generals and the captains were taking counsel, a Rhodian soldier came to them with a proposition for transporting the whole army across to the other bank of the river by means of inflated skins, which could be furnished in abundance by the animals in their possession. But this ingenious scheme, in itself feasible, was put out of the question by the view of the Persian cavalry on the opposite bank; and as the villages in their front had been burnt, the army had no choice except to return back one day's march to those in which they had before halted. Here the generals again deliberated, questioning all their prisoners as to the different bearings of the country. The road from the south was that in which they had already marched from Babylon and Media; that to the westward, going to Lydia and Ionia, was barred to them by the interposing Tigris; eastward (they were informed) was the way to Ekbatana and Susa; northward, lay the rugged and inhospitable mountains of the Karduchians, — fierce freemen who despised the Great King, and defied all his efforts to conquer them; having once destroyed a Persian invading army of 120,000 men. On the other side of Karduchia, however, lay the rich Persian satrapy of Armenia, wherein both the Euphratês and the Tigris could be crossed near their sources, and from whence they could choose their farther course easily towards Greece. Like Mysia, Pisidia, and other mountainous regions, Karduchia was a free territory surrounded on all sides by the dominions of the Great King, who reigned only in the cities and on the plains.

### § 7. The Greeks fight their way across the Karduchian mountains.

Determining to fight their way across these difficult mountains into Armenia, but refraining from any public announcement, for fear that the passes should be occupied beforehand — the generals sacrificed[1] forthwith, in order that they might be ready for breaking up at a moment's notice. They then began their march a little after midnight, so that soon after daybreak they reached the first of the Karduchian mountain-passes, which they found unde-

---

[1] **Sacrificed**: not only to propitiate the gods, but to obtain omens or signs for their future guidance.

fended. Cheirisophus, with his front division and all the light troops, made haste to ascend the pass, and having got over the first mountain, descended on the other side to some villages in the valley or nooks beneath; while Xenophon, with the heavy-armed and the baggage, followed at a slower pace,— not reaching the villages until dark, as the road was both steep and narrow. The Karduchians, taken completely by surprise, abandoned the villages as the Greeks approached, and took refuge on the mountains; leaving to the intruders plenty of provisions, comfortable houses, and especially, abundance of copper vessels. At first the Greeks were careful to do no damage, trying to invite the natives to amicable colloquy. But none of the latter would come near, and at length necessity drove the Greeks to take what was necessary for refreshment. It was just when Xenophon and the rear-guard were coming in at night, that some few Karduchians first set upon them; by surprise and with considerable success — so that if their numbers had been greater, serious mischief might have ensued.

Many fires were discovered burning on the mountains, an indication of resistance during the next day; which satisfied the Greek generals that they must lighten the army, in order to ensure greater expedition as well as a fuller complement of available hands during the coming march. They therefore gave orders to burn all the baggage except what was indispensable, and to dismiss all the prisoners; planting themselves in a narrow strait, through which the army had to pass, in order to see that their directions were executed. The women, however, of whom there were many with the army, could not be abandoned; and it seems farther that a considerable stock of baggage was still retained : nor could the army make more than slow advance, from the narrowness of the road and the harassing attack of the Karduchians, who were now assembled in considerable numbers. Their attack was renewed with double vigor on the ensuing day, when the Greeks were forced, from want of provisions, to hasten forward their march, though in the midst of a terrible snowstorm. Both Cheirisophus in the front and Xenophon in the rear, were hard pressed by the Karduchian slingers and bowmen ; the latter, men of consummate skill, having bows three cubits[1] in length, and arrows of more than two cubits, so strong that the Greeks when they took them could dart them as javelins. These archers, amidst the rugged ground and narrow paths, approached so near and drew the bow with such surprising force, resting one extremity of it on the ground, that several Greek warriors were mortally wounded even through both shield and corselet[2] into the reins,[3] and through the brazen helmet into their heads ; among them especially, two distinguished men, a Lacedæmonian named Kleonymus and an Arcadian named Basias. The rear division, more roughly handled than the rest, was obliged continually to halt to repel the enemy, under all the difficulties of the ground, which made it scarcely possible to act against nimble mountaineers. On one occasion, however, a body of these latter were entrapped into an ambush, driven back with loss, and (what was still more fortunate) two of their number were made prisoners.

[1] **Cubit**: a measure of length; the distance from the elbow to the end of the middle finger, or about eighteen inches.
[2] **Corselet**: armor covering the front of the upper part of the body.
[3] **Reins**: the small of the back, or the kidneys.

Thus impeded, Xenophon sent frequent messages entreating Cheirisophus to slacken the march of the van division; but instead of obeying, Cheirisophus only hastened the faster, urging Xenophon to follow him. The march of the army became little better than a rout, so that the rear division reached the halting place in extreme confusion; upon which Xenophon proceeded to remonstrate with Cheirisophus for prematurely hurrying forward and neglecting his comrades behind. But the other — pointing out to his attention the hill before them, and the steep path ascending it, forming their future line of march, which was beset with numerous Karduchians — defended himself by saying that he had hastened forward in hopes of being able to reach this pass before the enemy, in which attempt however he had not succeeded.

To advance farther on this road appeared hopeless; yet the guides declared that no other could be taken. Xenophon then bethought him of the two prisoners whom he had just captured, and proposed that these two should be questioned also. They were accordingly interrogated apart; and the first of them — having persisted in denying, notwithstanding all menaces, that there was any road except that before them — was put to death under the eyes of the second prisoner. This latter, on being then questioned, gave more comfortable intelligence; saying that he knew of a different road, more circuitous, but easier and practicable even for beasts of burden, whereby the pass before them and the occupying enemy might be turned; but that there was one particular high position commanding the road, which it was necessary to master beforehand by surprise, as the Karduchians were already on guard there. Two thousand Greeks, having the guide bound along with them, were accordingly despatched late in the afternoon, to surprise this post by a nightmarch; while Xenophon, in order to distract the attention of the Karduchians in front, made a feint of advancing as if about to force the direct pass. As soon as he was seen crossing the ravine which led to this mountain, the Karduchians on the top immediately began to roll down vast masses of rock, which bounded and dashed down the roadway in such a manner as to render it unapproachable. They continued to do this all night, and the Greeks heard the noise of the descending masses long after they had returned to their camp for supper and rest.

Meanwhile the detachment of 2000, marching by the circuitous road, and reaching in the night the elevated position (though there was another above yet more commanding) held by the Karduchians, surprised and dispersed them, passing the night by their fires. At daybreak, and under favor of a mist, they stole silently towards the position occupied by the other Karduchians in front of the main Grecian army. On coming near they suddenly sounded their trumpets, shouted aloud, and commenced the attack, which proved completely successful. The defenders, taken unprepared, fled with little resistance, and scarcely any loss, from their activity and knowledge of the country; while Cheirisophus and the main Grecian force, on hearing the trumpet which had been previously concerted as the signal, rushed forward and stormed the height in front; some along the regular path; others climbing up as they could and pulling each other up by means of their spears. The two bodies of Greeks thus joined each other on the summit, so that the road became open for farther advance.

Xenophon, however, with the rear-guard marched on the circuitous road taken by the 2000, as the most practicable for the baggage animals, whom he placed in the centre of his division — the whole array covering a great length of ground, since the road was very narrow. During this interval the dispersed Karduchians had rallied, and reoccupied two or three high peaks, commanding the road — from whence it was necessary to drive them. Xenophon's troops stormed successively these three positions, the Karduchians not daring to come to close combat, yet making destructive use of their missiles. A Grecian guard was left on the hindermost of the three peaks, until all the baggage train should have passed by. But the Karduchians, by a sudden and well-timed movement, contrived to surprise this guard, slew two out of the three leaders with several soldiers, and forced the rest to jump down the crags as they could, in order to join their comrades in the road. Encouraged by such success the assailants pressed nearer to the marching army, occupying a crag over against that lofty summit on which Xenophon was posted. As it was within speaking distance, he endeavored to open a negotiation with them in order to get back the bodies of the slain. To this demand the Karduchians at first acceded, on condition that their villages should not be burnt; but finding their numbers every moment increasing, they resumed the offensive. When Xenophon with the army had begun his descent from the last summit, they hurried onward in crowds to occupy it; beginning again to roll down masses of rock, and renew their fire of missiles, upon the Greeks. Xenophon himself was here in some danger, having been deserted by his shield-bearer; but he was rescued by an Arcadian heavy-armed foot-soldier named Eurylochus, who ran to give him the benefit of his own shield as a protection for both in the retreat.

After a march thus painful and perilous, the rear division at length found themselves in safety among their comrades, in villages with well-stocked houses and abundance of corn and wine. So eager however were Xenophon and Cheirisophus to obtain the bodies of the slain for burial, that they consented to purchase them by surrendering the guide, and to march onward without any guide: a heavy sacrifice in this unknown country, attesting their great anxiety about the burial.[1]

For three more days did they struggle and fight their way through the narrow and rugged paths of the Karduchian mountains, beset throughout by these formidable bowmen and slingers; whom they had to dislodge at every difficult turn, and against whom their own Kretan[2] bowmen were found inferior indeed, but still highly useful. Their seven days' march through this country, with its free and warlike inhabitants, were days of the utmost fatigue, suffering, and peril; far more intolerable than any thing which they had experienced from Tissaphernês and the Persians. Right glad were they once more to see a plain, and to find themselves near the banks of the river Kentritês, which divided these mountains from the hillocks and plains of Armenia — enjoying comfortable quarters in villages, with the satisfaction of talking over past miseries.

Such were the apprehensions of Karduchian invasion, that the Armenian side of the Kentritês for a breadth of 15 miles was unpeopled and destitute of villages. But the

---

[1] **Burial:** the Greeks believed that so long as the corpse remained unburied the spirit would roam about restlessly in the dreary under-world or common abode of departed souls.   [2] **Kretan:** or Cretan (from Crete).

approach of the Greeks having become known to Tiribazus, satrap of Armenia, the banks of the river were lined with his cavalry and infantry to oppose their passage; a precaution, which if Tissaphernês had taken at the Great Zab at the moment when he perfidiously seized Klearchus and his colleagues, the Greeks would hardly have reached the northern bank of that river. In the face of such obstacles, the Greeks nevertheless attempted the passage of the Kentritês, seeing a regular road on the other side. But the river was 200 feet in breadth (only half the breadth of the Zab), above their breasts in depth, extremely rapid, and with a bottom full of slippery stones; insomuch that they could not hold their shields in the proper position, from the force of the stream; while if they lifted the shields above their heads, they were exposed defenceless to the arrows of the satrap's troops. After various trials, the passage was found impracticable, and they were obliged to resume their encampment on the left bank. To their great alarm, they saw the Karduchians assembling on the hills in their rear, so that their situation, during this day and night, appeared nearly desperate. In the night Xenophon had a dream — the first which he has told us since his dream on the terrific night after the seizure of the generals — but on this occasion, of augury[1] more unequivocally good. He dreamt that he was bound in chains, but that his chains on a sudden dropt off spontaneously; on the faith of which, he told Cheirisophus at daybreak that he had good hopes of preservation; and when the generals offered sacrifice, the victims were at once favorable. As the army were taking their morning meal, two young Greeks ran to Xenophon with the auspicious news that

---

[1] **Augury**: omen or sign.

they had accidentally found another ford near half a mile up the river, where the water was not even up to their middle, and where the rocks came so close on the right bank that the enemy's horse could offer no opposition. Xenophon, starting from his meal in delight, immediately offered libations [1] to those gods who had revealed both the dream to himself in the night, and the unexpected ford afterwards to these youths; two revelations which he ascribed to the same gods.

Presently they marched in their usual order, Cheirisophus commanding the van and Xenophon the rear, along the river to the newly-discovered ford; the enemy marching parallel with them on the opposite bank. Having reached the ford, halted, and grounded arms, Cheirisophus placed a wreath on his head, took off his clothes, and then resumed his arms, ordering all the rest to resume their arms also. Each company of 100 men was then arranged in column or single file, with Cheirisophus himself in the centre. Meanwhile the prophets were offering sacrifice to the river. So soon as the signs were pronounced to be favorable, all the soldiers shouted the pæan, and all the women joined in chorus with their feminine yell. Cheirisophus then, at the head of the army, entered the river and began to ford it; while Xenophon, with a large portion of the rear division, made a feint of hastening back to the original ford, as if he were about to attempt the passage there. This distracted the attention of the enemy's horse; who became afraid of being attacked on both sides, galloped off to guard the passage at the other point, and opposed no serious resistance to Cheirisophus. As soon as the latter had reached

---

[1] **Libations**: wine or liquor poured out on the ground or on a victim in honor of the gods.

the other side, and put his division into order, he marched up to attack the Armenian infantry, who were on the high banks a little way above; but this infantry, deserted by its cavalry, dispersed without awaiting his approach. The handful of Grecian cavalry, attached to the division of Cheirisophus, pursued and took some valuable spoils.

As soon as Xenophon saw his colleague successfully established on the opposite bank, he brought back his detachment to the ford over which the baggage and attendants were still passing, and proceeded to take precautions against the Karduchians on his own side who were assembling in the rear. He found some difficulty in keeping his rear division together, for many of them, in spite of orders, quitted their ranks and went to look after the women or their baggage in the crossing of the water. The light-armed foot-soldiers and bowmen, who had gone over with Cheirisophus, but whom that general now no longer needed, were directed to hold themselves prepared on both flanks of the army crossing, and to advance a little way in the water in the attitude of men just about to recross. When Xenophon was left with only the diminished rear-guard, the rest having got over, — the Karduchians rushed upon him, and began to shoot and sling. But on a sudden, the Grecian heavy-armed foot-soldiers charged with their accustomed pæan, upon which the Karduchians took to flight — having no arms for close combat on the plain. The trumpet now being heard to sound, they ran away so much the faster; while this was the signal, according to orders before given by Xenophon, for the Greeks to suspend their charge, to turn back, and to cross the river as speedily as possible. By favor of this able manœuvre, the passage was accomplished by the whole army with little or no loss, about midday.

## § 8. March through Armenia. Great suffering from cold and hunger.

They now found themselves in Armenia; a country of even, undulating surface, but very high above the level of the sea, and extremely cold at the season when they entered it — December. Though the strip of land bordering on Karduchia furnished no supplies, one long march brought them to a village, containing abundance of provisions, together with a residence of the satrap Tiribazus; after which, in two farther marches they reached the river Teleboas, with many villages on its banks. Here Tiribazus himself, appearing with a division of cavalry, sent forward his interpreter to request a conference with the leaders; which being held, it was agreed that the Greeks should proceed unmolested through his territory, taking such supplies as they required, — but should neither burn nor damage the villages. They accordingly advanced onward for three days, computed at about 52 miles, or three pretty full days' march; without any hostility from the satrap, though he was hovering within less than two miles of them. They then found themselves amidst several villages, wherein were regal or satrapical residences with a plentiful stock of bread, meat, wine, and all sorts of vegetables. Here, during their nightly bivouac,[1] they were overtaken by so heavy a fall of snow that the generals on the next day distributed the troops into separate quarters among the villages. No enemy appeared near, while the snow seemed to forbid any rapid surprise. Yet at night,

---

[1] **Bivouac** (biv-wak′): an encampment without tents or shelter, or one in which the whole army is on guard against surprise; here, the former is probably meant.

the scouts reported that many fires were discernible, together with traces of military movements around; insomuch that the generals thought it prudent to put themselves on their guard, and again collected the army into one bivouac. Here in the night they were overwhelmed by a second fall of snow still heavier than the preceding; sufficient to cover over the sleeping men and their arms, and to benumb the cattle. The men however lay warm under the snow and were unwilling to rise, until Xenophon himself set the example of rising and employing himself without his arms in cutting wood and kindling a fire. Others followed his example, and great comfort was found in rubbing themselves with pork-fat, oil of almonds or of sesame,[1] or turpentine. Having sent out a clever scout named Demokratês, who captured a native prisoner, they learned that Tiribazus was laying plans to intercept them in a lofty mountain pass lying farther on in their route; upon which they immediately set forth, and by two days of forced march, surprising in their way the camp of Tiribazus, got over the difficult pass in safety. Three days of additional march brought them to the Euphratês river — that is, to its eastern branch, now called Murad. They found a ford and crossed it, without having the water higher than the waist; and they were informed that its sources were not far off.

Their four days of march, next on the other side of the Euphratês, were toilsome and distressing in the extreme; through a plain covered with deep snow (in some places six feet deep), and at times in the face of a north wind so intolerably chilling and piercing, that at length one of the

[1] **Sesame**: an Eastern plant from whose seeds an oil is obtained, which is used for food and other purposes.

prophets urged the necessity of offering sacrifices to Boreas[1]; upon which (says Xenophon), the severity of the wind abated conspicuously, to the evident consciousness of all. Many of the slaves and beasts of burthen, and a few even of the soldiers, perished: some had their feet frost-bitten, others became blinded by the snow, others again were exhausted by hunger. Several of these unhappy men were unavoidably left behind; others lay down to perish, near a warm spring which had melted the snow around, from extremity of fatigue and sheer wretchedness, though the enemy were close upon the rear. It was in vain that Xenophon, who commanded the rear-guard, employed his earnest exhortations, prayers, and threats, to induce them to move forward. The sufferers, miserable and motionless, answered only by entreating him to kill them at once. So greatly was the army disorganized by wretchedness, that we hear of one case in which a soldier, ordered to carry a disabled comrade, disobeyed the order, and was about to bury him alive. Xenophon made a sally, with loud shouts and clatter of spear with shield, in which even the exhausted men joined, — against the pursuing enemy. He was fortunate enough to frighten them away, and drive them to take shelter in a neighboring wood. He then left the sufferers lying down, with assurance that relief should be sent to them on the next day, — and went forward; seeing all along the line of march the exhausted soldiers lying on the snow, without even the protection of a watch. He and his rear-guard as well as the rest were obliged thus to pass the night without either food or fire, distributing scouts in the best way that the case admitted. Meanwhile Cheirisophus with the van division had got into a village,

---

[1] **Boreas**: the god of the north wind.

which they reached so unexpectedly, that they found the women fetching water from a fountain outside the wall, and the head-man of the village in his house within. This division here obtained rest and refreshment, and at daybreak some of their soldiers were sent to look after the rear. It was with delight that Xenophon saw them approach, and sent them back to bring up in their arms, into the neighboring village, those exhausted soldiers who had been left behind.

Repose was now indispensable after the recent sufferings. There were several villages near at hand, and the generals, thinking it no longer dangerous to divide the army, quartered the different divisions among them according to lot. Polykratês an Athenian, one of the captains in the division of Xenophon, requested his permission to go at once and take possession of the village assigned to him, before any of the inhabitants could escape. Accordingly, running at speed with a few of the swiftest soldiers, he came upon the village so suddenly as to seize the head-man with his newly-married daughter, and several young horses intended as a tribute for the king. This village, as well as the rest, was found to consist of houses excavated in the ground (as the Armenian villages are at the present day), spacious within, but with a narrow mouth like a well, entered by a descending ladder. A separate entrance was dug for conveniently admitting the cattle. All of them were found amply stocked with live cattle of every kind, wintered upon hay ; as well as with wheat, barley, vegetables, and a sort of barley-wine or beer in tubs, with the grains of barley on the surface. Reeds or straws without any joint in them, were lying near, through which they sucked the liquid: Xenophon did his utmost to conciliate the head-man (who spoke Persian, and with whom he communicated through the Perso-Grecian interpreter of the army), promising him that not one of his relations should be maltreated, and that he should be fully remunerated if he would conduct the army safely out of the country, into that of the Chalybes which he described as being adjacent. By such treatment the head-man was won over, promised his aid, and even revealed to the Greeks the subterranean cellars wherein the wine was deposited; while Xenophon, though he kept him constantly under watch, and placed his youthful son as a hostage under the care of Episthenês, yet continued to treat him with studied attention and kindness. For seven days did the fatigued soldiers remain in these comfortable quarters, refreshing themselves and regaining strength. They were waited upon by the native youths, with whom they communicated by means of signs. The uncommon happiness which all of them enjoyed after their recent sufferings, stands depicted in the lively details given by Xenophon, who left here his own exhausted horse, and took young horses in exchange, for himself and the other officers.

After this week of repose, the army resumed its march through the snow. The head-man, whose house they had replenished as well as they could, accompanied Cheirisophus in the van as guide, but was not put in chains or under guard: his son remained as an hostage with Episthenês, but his other relations were left unmolested at home. As they marched for three days, without reaching a village, Cheirisophus began to suspect his fidelity, and even became so out of humor, though the man affirmed that there were no villages in the track, as to beat him — yet without the precaution of putting him afterwards in fetters. The next night, accordingly, this head-man made his escape; much to the displeasure of Xenophon, who severely reproached Cheirisophus first for his harshness, and next for his neglect. This was the only point of difference between the two (says Xenophon) during the whole march; a fact very honorable to both, considering the numberless difficulties against which they had to contend. Episthenês retained the head-man's youthful son, carried him home in safety, and became much attached to him.

Condemned thus to march without a guide, they could do no better than march up the course of the river; and thus, from the villages which had proved so cheering and restorative, they proceeded seven days' march all through snow, up the river Phasis; a river not verifiable, but certainly not the same as is commonly known under that name by Grecian geographers: it was 100 feet in breadth. Two more days' march brought them from this river to the foot of a range of mountains near a pass occupied by an armed body of Chalybes, Taochi, and Phasiani.

Observing the enemy in possession of this lofty ground, Cheirisophus halted until all the army came up, in order that the generals might take counsel. Here Kleanor began by advising that they should storm the pass with no greater delay than was necessary to refresh the soldiers. But Xenophon suggested that it was far better to avoid the loss of life which must be incurred, and to amuse the enemy by feigned attack, while a detachment should be sent by stealth at night to ascend the mountain at another point and turn the position. "However (continued he, turning to Cheirisophus), stealing a march upon the enemy is more your trade than mine. For I understand that you the full citizens and peers at Sparta, practise stealing from your boyhood upward; and that it is held noway base, but even honorable, to steal such things as the law does not distinctly forbid. And to the end that you may steal with the greatest effect, and take pains to do it in secret, the custom is, to flog you if you are found out. Here then, you have an excellent opportunity of displaying your training. Take good care that we be not found out in stealing an occupation of the mountain now before us; for if we *are* found out, we shall be well beaten."

"Why, as for that (replied Cheirisophus), you Athenians also, as I learn, are capital hands at stealing the public money — and that too in spite of prodigious peril to the thief: nay, your most powerful men steal most of all — at least if it be the most powerful men among you who are raised to official command. So that this is a time for *you* to exhibit *your* training, as well as for me to exhibit mine."

We have here an interchange of raillery between the two Grecian officers, which is not an uninteresting feature in the history of the expedition. The remark of Cheirisophus, especially, illustrates that which I noted in a former chapter as true both of Sparta and Athens — the readiness to take bribes, so general in individuals clothed with official power; and the readiness, in official Athenians, to commit such peculation, in spite of serious risk of punishment. Now this chance of punishment proceeded altogether from those accusing orators commonly called demagogues,[1] and from the popular judicature whom they addressed. The joint working of both greatly abated the evil, yet was

---

[1] **Demagogues**: leaders of the people, popular orators. (The word now means those who mislead the people or who pretend to be interested in public affairs and reforms merely to gain their own ends.) In Greece these orators usually addressed assemblies or bodies of citizens who acted as judges.

incompetent to suppress it. But according to the pictures commonly drawn of Athens, we are instructed to believe that the crying public evil was,—too great a license of accusation, and too much judicial trial. Assuredly such was not the conception of Cheirisophus; nor shall we find it borne out by any fair appreciation of the general evidence. When the peculation of official persons was thus notorious in spite of serious risks, what would it have become if the door had been barred to accusing demagogues, and if the numerous popular judges[1] had been exchanged for a select few judges of the same stamp and class as the official men themselves?

Enforcing his proposition, Xenophon now informed his colleagues that he had just captured a few guides, by laying an ambush for certain native plunderers who beset the rear; and that these guides acquainted him that the mountain was not inaccessible, but pastured by goats and oxen. He farther offered himself to take command of the marching detachment. But this being overruled by Cheirisophus, some of the best among the captains, Aristonymus, Aristeas, and Nikomachus, volunteered their services and were accepted. After refreshing the soldiers, the generals marched with the main army near to the foot of the pass, and there took up their night-station, making demonstrations of a purpose to storm it the next morning. But as soon as it was dark, Aristonymus and his detachment started, and ascending the mountain at another point, obtained without resistance a high position on the flank of the enemy, who soon however saw them and despatched a

[1] **Judges** (dicasts): these sometimes, as in the case of the trial of Socrates, numbered five and six hundred persons, who acted as judge and jury combined.

force to keep guard on that side. At daybreak those two detachments came to conflict on the heights, in which the Greeks were completely victorious; while Cheirisophus was marching up the pass to attack the main body. His light troops, encouraged by seeing this victory of their comrades, hastened on to the charge faster than their heavy-armed foot-soldiers could follow. But the enemy were so dispirited by seeing themselves turned, that they fled with little or no resistance. Though only a few were slain, many threw away their light shields of wicker or wood-work, which became the prey of the conquerors.

Thus masters of the pass, the Greeks descended to the level ground on the other side, where they found themselves in some villages well-stocked with provisions and comforts; the first in the country of the Taochi. Probably they halted here some days; for they had seen no villages, either for rest or for refreshment, during the last nine days' march, since leaving those Armenian villages in which they had passed a week so eminently restorative, and which apparently had furnished them with a stock of provisions for the onward journey. Such halt gave time to the Taochi to carry up their families and provisions into inaccessible strongholds, so that the Greeks found no supplies, during five days' march through the territory. Their provisions were completely exhausted, when they arrived before one of these strongholds, a rock on which were seen the families and the cattle of the Taochi; without houses or fortification, but nearly surrounded by a river, so as to leave only one narrow ascent, rendered unapproachable by vast rocks which the defenders hurled or rolled from the summit. By an ingenious combination of bravery and stratagem, in which some of the captains much distinguished themselves, the Greeks overcame this difficulty, and took the height. The scene which then ensued was awful. The Taochian women seized their children, flung them over the precipice, and then cast themselves headlong also, followed by the men. Almost every soul thus perished, very few surviving to become prisoners. An Arcadian captain named Æneas, seeing one of them in a fine dress about to precipitate himself with the rest, seized him with a view to prevent it. But the man in return grasped him firmly, dragged him to the edge of the rock, and leaped down to the destruction of both. Though scarcely any prisoners were taken, however, the Greeks obtained abundance of oxen, asses, and sheep, which fully supplied their wants.

They now entered into the territory of the Chalybes, which they were seven days in passing through. These were the bravest warriors whom they had seen in Asia. Their equipment was a spear of fifteen cubits long, with only one end pointed — a helmet, greaves,[1] stuffed corselet, with a kilt or dependent flaps — a short sword which they employed to cut off the head of a slain enemy, displaying the head in sight of their surviving enemies with triumphant dance and song. They carried no shield; perhaps because the excessive length of the spear required the constant employment of both hands — yet they did not shrink from meeting the Greeks occasionally in regular, stand-up fight. As they had carried off all their provisions into hill-forts, the Greeks could obtain no supplies, but lived all the time upon the cattle which they had acquired from the Taochi. After seven days of march and combat — the Chalybes perpetually attacking their rear — they

[2] **Greaves**: armor for the front of the lower part of the leg.

reached the river Harpasus (400 feet broad), where they passed into the territory of the Skythini. It rather seems that the territory of the Chalybes was mountainous; that of the Skythini was level, and contained villages, wherein they remained three days, refreshing themselves, and stocking themselves with provisions.

### § 9. The Greeks come in sight of the Black Sea.

Four days of additional march brought them to a sight, the like of which they had not seen since Opis and Sittakê on the Tigris in Babylonia — a large and flourishing city called Gymnias; an indication of the neighborhood of the sea, of commerce, and of civilization. The chief of this city received them in a friendly manner, and furnished them with a guide, who engaged to conduct them, after five days' march, to a hill from whence they would have a view of the sea. This was by no means their nearest way to the sea, for the chief of Gymnias wished to send them through the territory of some neighbors to whom he was hostile; which territory, as soon as they reached it, the guide desired them to burn and destroy. However, the promise was kept, and on the fifth day, marching still apparently through the territory of the Skythini, they reached the summit of a mountain called Thêchês, from whence the Euxine Sea was visible.

An animated shout from the soldiers who formed the van-guard testified the impressive effect of this long-deferred spectacle, assuring, as it seemed to do, their safety and their return home. To Xenophon and to the rear-guard — engaged in repelling the attack of natives who had come forward to revenge the plunder of their territory — the shout was unintelligible. They at first imagined that the natives had commenced attack in front as well as in the rear, and that the van-guard was engaged in battle. But every moment the shout became louder, as fresh men came to the summit and gave vent to their feelings; so that Xenophon grew anxious, and galloped up to the van with his handful of cavalry to see what had happened. As he approached, the voice of the overjoyed crowd was heard distinctly crying out *Thalatta! Thalatta!* (The sea! the sea!), and congratulating each other in ecstasy. The main body, the rear-guard, the baggage-soldiers driving up their horses and cattle before them, became all excited by the sound, and hurried up breathless to the summit. The whole army, officers and soldiers, were thus assembled, manifesting their joyous emotions by tears, embraces, and outpourings of enthusiastic sympathy. With spontaneous impulse they heaped up stones to decorate the spot by a monument and commemorative trophy; putting on the stones such homely offerings as their means afforded— sticks, hides, and a few of the wicker shields just taken from the natives. To the guide, who had performed his engagement of bringing them in five days within sight of the sea, their gratitude was unbounded. They presented him with a horse, a silver bowl, a Persian costume, and ten darics[1] in money; besides several of the soldiers' rings, which he especially asked for. Thus loaded with presents, he left them, having first shown them a village wherein they could find quarters — as well as the road which they were to take through the territory of the Makrônes.

When they reached the river which divided the land of the Makrônes from that of the Skythini, they perceived the

[1] **Daric**: a Persian gold coin worth about $5.00.

former assembled in arms on the opposite side to resist their passage. The river not being fordable, they cut down some neighboring trees to provide the means of crossing. While these Makrônes were shouting and encouraging each other aloud, a light-armed foot-soldier in the Grecian army came to Xenophon, saying that he knew their language, and that he believed this to be his country. He had been a slave at Athens, exported from home during his boyhood — he had then made his escape (probably during the Peloponnesian War, to the garrison of Dekeleia), and afterwards taken military service. By this fortunate accident, the generals were enabled to open negotiations with the Makrônes, and to assure them that the army would do them no harm, desiring nothing more than a free passage and a market to buy provisions. The Makrônes, on receiving such assurances in their own language from a countryman, exchanged pledges of friendship with the Greeks, assisted them to pass the river, and furnished the best market in their power during the three days' march across their territory.

The army now reached the borders of the Kolchians, who were found in hostile array, occupying the summit of a considerable mountain which formed their frontier. Here Xenophon, having marshalled the soldiers for attack, with each company of 100 men in single file, instead of marching up the hill in phalanx, or continuous front with only a scanty depth — addressed to them the following pithy encouragement — " Now, fellow-soldiers, these enemies before us are the only impediment that keeps us away from reaching the point at which we have been so long aiming. We must even eat them raw, if in any way we can do so."

Eighty of these formidable companies of heavy-armed

foot-soldiers, each in single file, now began to ascend the hill; the light-armed foot-soldiers and bowmen being partly distributed among them, partly placed on the flanks. Cheirisophus and Xenophon, each commanding on one wing, spread their light-armed foot-soldiers in such a way as to outflank the Kolchians, who accordingly weakened their centre in order to strengthen their wings. Hence the Arcadian light-armed foot-soldiers and heavy-armed footsoldiers in the Greek centre were enabled to attack and disperse the centre with little resistance; and all the Kolchians presently fled, leaving the Greeks in possession of their camp, as well as of several well-stocked villages in their rear. Amidst these villages the army remained to refresh themselves for several days. It was here that they tasted the grateful, but unwholesome honey, which this region still continues to produce — unaware of its peculiar properties. Those soldiers who ate little of it were like men greatly intoxicated with wine; those who ate much, were seized with the most violent vomiting and diarrhœa, lying down like madmen in a state of delirium. From this terrible distemper some recovered on the ensuing day, others two or three days afterwards. It does not appear that any one actually died.

Two more days' march brought them to the sea, at the Greek maritime city of Trapezus or Trebizond, founded by the inhabitants of Sinôpê on the coast of the Kolchian territory. Here the Trapezuntines received them with kindness and hospitality, sending them presents of bullocks, barley-meal, and wine. Taking up their quarters in some Kolchian villages near the town, they now enjoyed, for the first time since leaving Tarsus, a safe and undisturbed repose during thirty days, and were enabled to recover in some degree from the severe hardships which they had undergone. While the Trapezuntines brought produce for sale into the camp, the Greeks provided the means of purchasing it by predatory incursions against the Kolchians on the hills. Those Kolchians who dwelt under the hills and on the plain were in a state of semi-dependence upon Trapezus; so that the Trapezuntines mediated on their behalf and prevailed on the Greeks to leave them unmolested, on condition of a contribution of bullocks.

These bullocks enabled the Greeks to discharge the vow which they had made, on the proposition of Xenophon, to Zeus the Preserver, during that moment of dismay and despair which succeeded immediately on the massacre of their generals by Tissaphernês. To Zeus the Preserver, to Heraklês[1] the Conductor, and to various other gods, they offered an abundant sacrifice on their mountain camp overhanging the sea; and after the festival ensuing, the skins of the victims were given as prizes to competitors in running, wrestling, boxing, and other contests. The superintendence of such festival games, so fully accordant with Grecian usage and highly interesting to the army, was committed to a Spartan named Drakontius; a man whose destiny recalls that of Patroklus and other Homeric heroes — for he had been exiled as a boy, having unintentionally killed another boy with a short sword. Various departures from Grecian customs however were admitted. The matches took place on the steep and stony hill-side overhanging the sea, instead of on a smooth plain; and the numerous hard falls of the competitors afforded increased interest to the by-standers. The captive non-Hellenic boys

---

[1] Heraklês (Hercules): the exploits of this god in his numerous encounters with wild beasts and robbers led to his worship on perilous journeys.

were admitted to run for the prize, since otherwise a boy-race could not have been obtained. ["Horses also ran; and they had to gallop down the steep, and, turning round in the sea, to come up again to the altar.[1] In the descent, many rolled down; but in the ascent, against the exceedingly steep ground, the horses could scarcely get up at a walking pace. There was consequently great shouting, and laughter, and cheering from the people."[2]] Lastly, the animation of the scene, as well as the ardor of the competitors, was much enhanced by the number of the women present.

§ 10. **The Greek cities on the Black Sea; their feelings toward the Ten Thousand.**

We now commence a third act in the history of this memorable body of men. After having followed them from Sardis to Kunaxa as mercenaries[1] to procure the throne for Cyrus — then from Kunaxa to Trapezus as men anxious only for escape, and purchasing their safety by marvellous bravery, endurance, and organization — we shall now track their proceedings among the Greek colonies on the Euxine and at the Bosphorus of Thrace, succeeded by their struggles against the meanness of the Thracian prince Seuthês, as well as against the treachery and arbitrary harshness of the Lacedæmonian commanders Anaxibius and Aristarchus.

Trapezus, now Trebizond, where the army had recently found repose, was a colony from Sinôpê, as were also Kerasus and Kotyôra farther westward; each of them receiving a governor from the mother-city, and paying to her an annual tribute. All these three cities were planted on the narrow strip of land dividing the Euxine from the

---

[1] **The altar:** probably that where they had been sacrificing.
[2] Xenophon.  [3] **Mercenaries:** hired soldiers.

elevated mountain range which so closely borders on its southern coast. At Sinôpê itself, the land stretches out into a defensible peninsula, with a secure harbor, and a large breadth of adjacent fertile soil. So tempting a site invited the Milesians,[1] even before the year 600 B.C., to plant a colony there, and enabled Sinôpê to attain much prosperity and power. Farther westward, not more than a long day's journey for a rowing vessel from Byzantium, was situated the Megarian[2] colony of Herakleia, in the territory of the Mariandyni.

The native tenants of this line of coast, upon which the Greek settlers intruded themselves (reckoning from the westward), were the Bythynian Thracians, the Mariandyni, the Paphlagonians, the Tibarêni, Chalybes, Mosynœki, Drilæ, and Kolchians. Here as elsewhere, these natives found the Greek seaports useful, in giving a new value to inland produce, and in furnishing the great men with ornaments and luxuries to which they would otherwise have had no access. The citizens of Herakleia had reduced into dependence a considerable portion of the neighboring Mariandyni, and held them in a relation resembling that of the natives of Esthonia and Lavonia to the German colonies in the Baltic. Some of the Kolchian villages were also subject in the same manner to the Trapezuntines; and Sinôpê doubtless possessed a similar inland dominion of greater or less extent. But the principal wealth of this important city arose from her navy and maritime commerce; from the rich thunny fishery[3] at-

[1] **Milesians**: inhabitants of Miletus, Asia Minor.

[2] **Megarian**: pertaining to Megara, a district of Greece northwest of Athens. It was famous for its commerce.

[3] **Thunny fishery**: the thunny, or tunny, a large fish abundant in the Mediterranean and highly esteemed both for food and for the oil which it yields.

tached to her promontory; from the olives in her immediate neighborhood, which was a cultivation not indigenous, but only naturalized by the Greeks on the seaboard; from the varied produce of the interior, comprising abundant herds of cattle, mines of silver, iron, and copper, in the neighboring mountains, wood for ship-building, as well as for house-furniture, and native slaves. The case was similar with the three colonies of Sinôpê, more to the eastward — Kotyôra, Kerasus, and Trapezus; except that the mountains which border on the Euxine, gradually approaching nearer and nearer to the shore, left to each of them a more confined strip of cultivable land. For these cities the time had not yet arrived to be conquered and absorbed by the inland monarchies around them, as Miletus and the cities on the western coast of Asia Minor had been. The Paphlagonians were at this time the only native people in those regions who formed a considerable aggregated force, under a prince named Korylas; a prince tributary to Persia, yet half independent — since he had disobeyed the summons of Artaxerxês to come up and help in repelling Cyrus — and now on terms of established alliance with Sinôpê, though not without secret designs, which he wanted only force to execute, against that city. The other native tribes to the eastward were mountaineers both ruder and more divided; warlike on their own heights, but little capable of any aggressive combinations.

Though we are told that Periklês had once despatched a detachment of Athenian colonists to Sinôpê, and had expelled from thence the despot Timesilaus, — yet neither that city nor any of her neighbors appear to have taken part in the Peloponnesian war, either for or against Athens; nor were they among the number of tributaries to Persia.

They doubtless were acquainted with the upward march of Cyrus, which had disturbed all Asia; and probably were not ignorant of the perils and critical state of his Grecian army. But it was with a feeling of mingled surprise, admiration, and alarm, that they saw that army descend from the mountainous region, hitherto only recognized as the abode of Kolchians, Makrônes, and other analogous tribes, among whom was perched the mining city of Gymnias.

Even after all the losses and extreme sufferings of the retreat the Greeks still numbered, when mustered at Kerasus, 8600 heavy-armed foot-soldiers, with light-armed foot-soldiers, bowmen, and slingers, making a total of above 10,000 military persons. Such a force had never before been seen in the Euxine. Considering both the numbers and the now-acquired discipline and self-confidence of the Cyreians, even Sinôpê herself could have raised no force capable of meeting them in the field. Yet they did not belong to any city, nor receive orders from any established government. They were like those mercenary armies which marched about in Italy during the fourteenth century, under the generals called Condottieri, taking service sometimes with one city, sometimes with another. No one could predict what schemes they might conceive, or in what manner they might deal with the established communities on the shores of the Euxine. If we imagine that such an army had suddenly appeared in Sicily, a little time before the Athenian expedition against Syracuse, it would have been probably enlisted by Leontini and Katana in their war against Syracuse. If the inhabitants of Trapezus had wished to throw off the dominion of Sinôpê, — or if Korylas the Paphlagonian were meditating war against that city — here were formidable auxiliaries to second their wishes. Moreover there were various tempting sites, open to the formation of a new colony, which, with so numerous a body of original Greek settlers, would probably have overtopped Sinôpê herself. There was no restraining cause to reckon upon, except the general Hellenic sympathies and education of the Cyreian army; and what was of not less importance, the fact that they were not mercenary soldiers by permanent profession, such as became so formidably multiplied in Greece during the next generation — but established citizens who had come out on a special service under Cyrus, with the full intention, after a year of lucrative enterprise, to return to their homes and families. We shall find such gravitation towards home steadily operative throughout the future proceedings of the army. But at the moment when they first emerged from the mountains, no one could be sure that it would be so. There was ample ground for uneasiness among the Euxine Greeks, especially the Sinopians, whose supremacy had never before been endangered.

### § 11. Plans of the army for the future.

An undisturbed repose of thirty days enabled the Cyreians to recover from their fatigues, to talk over their past dangers, and to take pride in the anticipated effect which their unparalleled achievement could not fail to produce in Greece. Having discharged their vows and celebrated their festival to the gods, they held an assembly to discuss their future proceedings; when a Thurian [1] soldier named

---

[1] Thurian: an inhabitant of Thurii, a city of Lower Italy, founded by a colony from Athens.

Antileon exclaimed — "Comrades, I am already tired of packing up, marching, running, carrying arms, falling into line, keeping watch, and fighting. Now that we have the sea here before us, I desire to be relieved from all these toils, to sail the rest of the way, and to arrive in Greece outstretched and asleep, like Odysseus."[1] This pithy address being received with vehement acclamations, and warmly responded to by all, Cheirisophus offered, if the army chose to empower him, to sail forthwith to Byzantium,[2] where he thought he could obtain from his friend the Lacedæmonian admiral Anaxibius, sufficient vessels for transport. His proposition was gladly accepted; and he departed to execute the project.

Xenophon then urged upon the army various resolutions and measures, proper for the regulation of affairs during the absence of Cheirisophus. The army would be forced to maintain itself by marauding expeditions among the hostile tribes in the mountains. Such expeditions accordingly must be put under regulation: neither individual soldiers, nor small companies, must be allowed to go out at pleasure, without giving notice to the generals; moreover, the camp must be kept under constant guard and scouts, in the event of surprise from a retaliating enemy. It was prudent also to take the best measures in their power for procuring vessels; since, after all, Cheirisophus might possibly fail in bringing an adequate number. They ought to borrow a few ships of war from the Trapezuntines, and detain all the merchant ships[3] which they saw;

---

[1] **Odysseus**: as Homer in the "Odyssey" represents Odysseus, or Ulysses, to have done.    [2] **Byzantium**: the modern Constantinople.

[3] **Merchant ships**: small, one-masted vessels, not larger than our fishing-smacks.

unshipping the rudders, placing the cargoes under guard, and maintaining the crew during all the time that the ships might be required for transport of the army. Many such merchant vessels were often sailing by; so that they would thus acquire the means of transport, even though Cheirisophus should bring few or none from Byzantium. Lastly, Xenophon proposed to require the Grecian cities to repair and put in order the road along the coast, for a land-march; since, perhaps, with all their efforts, it would be found impossible to get together a sufficient stock of transports.

All the propositions of Xenophon were readily adopted by the army, except the last. But the mere mention of a renewed land-march excited such universal murmurs of repugnance, that he did not venture to put that question to the vote. He took upon himself however to send messages to the Grecian cities, on his own responsibility; urging them to repair the roads, in order that the departure of the army might be facilitated. And he found the cities ready enough to carry his wishes into effect, as far as Kotyôra.

The wisdom of these precautionary suggestions of Xenophon soon appeared; for Cheirisophus not only failed in his object, but was compelled to stay away for a considerable time. An armed ship with fifty oars was borrowed from the Trapezuntines, and committed to the charge of a Lacedæmonian provincial, named Dexippus, for the purpose of detaining the merchant vessels passing by. This man having violated his trust, and employed the ship to make his own escape out of the Euxine, a second was obtained and confided to an Athenian, Polykratês; who brought in successively several merchant vessels. These the Greeks did not plunder, but secured the cargoes under adequate guard, and only reserved the vessels for transports. It became however gradually more and more difficult to supply the camp with provisions. Though the army was distributed into suitable detachments for plundering the Kolchian villages on the hills, and seizing cattle and prisoners for sale, yet these expeditions did not always succeed; indeed on one occasion, two Grecian companies got entangled in such difficult ground, that they were destroyed to a man. The Kolchians united on the hills in increased and menacing numbers, insomuch that a larger guard became necessary for the camp; while the Trapezuntines — tired of the protracted stay of the army, as well as desirous of exempting from pillage the natives in their own immediate neighborhood — conducted the detachments only to villages alike remote and difficult of access. It was in this manner that a large force under Xenophon himself, attacked the lofty and rugged stronghold of the Drilæ — the most warlike nation of mountaineers in the neighborhood of the Euxine, well-armed, and troublesome to Trapezus by their incursions. After a difficult march and attack, which Xenophon describes in interesting detail, and wherein the Greeks encountered no small hazard of ruinous defeat — they returned, in the end completely successful, and with a plentiful booty.

§ 12. **The Ten Thousand begin their march westward.**

At length, after long awaiting in vain the reappearance of Cheirisophus, increasing scarcity and weariness determined them to leave Trapezus. A sufficient number of vessels had been collected to serve for the transport of the women, of the sick and wounded, and of the baggage. All these were accordingly placed on board under the command of Philesius and Sophænetus, the two oldest generals; while the remaining army marched by land, along a road which had been just made good under the representations of Xenophon. In three days they reached Kerasus,[1] another maritime colony of the Sinopians, still in the territory called Kolchian; there they halted ten days, mustered and numbered the army, and divided the money acquired by the sale of their prisoners. Eight thousand six hundred heavy-armed foot-soldiers, out of a total probably greater than eleven thousand, were found still remaining; besides targeteers[2] and various light troops.

During the halt at Kerasus, the declining discipline of the army became manifest as they approached home. Various acts of outrage occurred, originating now, as afterwards, in the intrigues of treacherous officers. A captain named Klearetus persuaded his company to attempt the plunder of a Kolchian village near Kerasus, which had furnished a friendly market to the Greeks, and which rested secure on the faith of peaceful relations. He intended to make off separately with the booty in one of the vessels: but his attack was repelled, and he himself slain. The injured villagers despatched three elders as heralds, to remonstrate with the Grecian authorities; but these heralds, being seen in Kerasus by some of the repulsed plunderers, were slain. A partial tumult then ensued, in which even the magistrates of Kerasus were in great danger, and only escaped the pursuing soldiers by running

---

[1] **Kerasus**: this place is the native home of the cherry, and the origin of its name. The fruit was introduced into Italy from Kerasus about 70 B.C., and thence to England, France, and other countries conquered by the Romans.

[2] **Targeteers**: troops carrying a light target, or shield.

into the sea. This enormity, though it occurred under the eyes of the generals, immediately before their departure from Kerasus, remained without inquiry or punishment, from the numbers concerned in it.

Between Kerasus and Kotyôra, there was not then (nor is there now) any regular road. This march cost the Cyreian army not less than ten days, by an inland track departing from the sea-shore, and through the mountains inhabited by the native tribes Mosynœki and Chalybes. The latter, celebrated for their iron works, were under dependence to the former. As the Mosynœki refused to grant a friendly passage across their territory, the army were compelled to fight their way through it as enemies, with the aid of one section of these people themselves; which alliance was procured for them by the Trapezuntine Timesitheus, who was consul or agent of the Mosynœki and understood their language. The Greeks took the mountain fastnesses of this people, and plundered the wooden turrets [1] which formed their abodes. Of their peculiar fashions Xenophon gives an interesting description which I have not space to copy. The territory of the Tibarêni was more easy and accessible. This people met the Greeks with presents, and tendered a friendly passage. But the generals at first declined the presents, preferring to treat them as enemies and plunder them; which in fact they would have done, had they not been deterred by unfavorable sacrifices.

Near Kotyôra, which was situated on the coast of the Tibarêni, yet on the borders of Paphlagonia, they remained forty-five days, still awaiting the appearance of Cheirisophus

[1] **Turrets** (or small towers): the name of the people — Mosynœki — means the "tower-dwellers."

with the transports to carry them away by sea. The Sinopian governor did not permit them to be welcomed in so friendly a manner as at Trapezus. No market was provided for them, nor were their sick admitted within the walls. But the fortifications of the town were not so constructed as to resist a Greek force, the like of which had never before been seen in those regions. The Greek generals found a weak point, made their way in, and took possession of a few houses for the accommodation of their sick; keeping a guard at the gate to secure free egress, but doing no farther violence to the citizens. They obtained their victuals partly from the Kotyôrite villages, partly from the neighboring territory of Paphlagonia, until at length envoys arrived from Sinôpê to remonstrate against their proceedings.

These envoys presented themselves before the assembled soldiers in the camp, when Hekatonymus, the chief and most eloquent among them, began by complimenting the army upon their gallant exploits and retreat. He then complained of the injury which Kotyôra, and Sinôpê as the mother-city of Kotyôra, had suffered at their hands, in violation of common Hellenic kinship. If such proceedings were continued, he intimated that Sinôpê would be compelled in her own defence to seek alliance with the Paphlagonian prince Korylas, or any other barbaric auxiliary who would lend them aid against the Greeks. Xenophon replied that if the Kotyôrites had sustained any damage, it was owing to their own ill-will and to the Sinopian governor in the place; that the generals were under the necessity of procuring subsistence for the soldiers, with house-room for the sick, and that they had taken nothing more; that the sick men were lying within the town, but at their own cost, while the other soldiers were all encamped without; that they had maintained cordial friendship with the Trapezuntines, and requited all their good offices; that they sought no enemies except through necessity, being anxious only again to reach Greece; and that as for the threat respecting Korylas, they knew well enough that that prince was eager to become master of the wealthy city of Sinôpê, and would speedily attempt some such enterprise if he could obtain the Cyreian army as his auxiliaries.

This judicious reply shamed the colleagues of Hekatonymus so much, that they went the length of protesting against what he had said, and of affirming that they had come with propositions of sympathy and friendship to the army, as well as with promises to give them an hospitable reception at Sinôpê, if they should visit that town on their way home. Presents were at once sent to the army by the inhabitants of Kotyôra, and a good understanding established.

Such an interchange of goodwill with the powerful city of Sinôpê was an unspeakable advantage to the army — indeed an essential condition to their power of reaching home. If they continued their march by land, it was only through Sinopian guidance and mediation that they could obtain or force a passage through Paphlagonia; while for a voyage by sea, there was no chance of procuring a sufficient number of vessels except from Sinôpê, since no news had been received of Cheirisophus. On the other hand, that city had also a strong interest in facilitating their transit homeward, and thus removing formidable neighbors, for whose ulterior purposes there could be no guarantee. After some preliminary conversation with the Sinopian envoys, the generals convoked the army in assembly, and entreated

Hekatonymus and his companions to advise them as to the best mode of proceeding westward to the Bosphorus. Hekatonymus, after apologizing for the menacing insinuations of his former speech, and protesting that he had no other object in view except to point out the safest and easiest plan of route for the army, began to unfold the insuperable difficulties of a march through Paphlagonia. The very entrance into the country must be achieved through a narrow aperture in the mountains, which it was impossible to force if occupied by the enemy. Even assuming this difficulty to be surmounted, there were spacious plains to be passed over, wherein the Paphlagonian horse,[1] the most numerous and bravest in Asia, would be found almost irresistible. There were also three or four great rivers, which the army would be unable to pass — the Thermôdôn and the Iris, each 300 feet in breadth — the Halys, nearly a quarter of a mile in breadth — the Parthenius, also very considerable. Such an array of obstacles (he affirmed) rendered the project of marching through Paphlagonia impracticable; whereas the voyage by sea from Kotyôra to Sinôpê, and from Sinôpê to Herakleia, was easy; and the transit from the latter place either by sea to Byzantium, or by land across Thrace, yet easier.

Difficulties like these, apparently quite real, were more than sufficient to determine the vote of the army, already sick of marching and fighting, in favor of the sea voyage; though there were not wanting suspicions of the sincerity of Hekatonymus. But Xenophon, in communicating to the latter the decision of the army, distinctly apprised him that they would on no account permit themselves to be divided; that they would either depart or remain all in a

[1] **Paphlagonian horse**: meaning the Paphlagonian cavalry.

body; and that vessels must be provided sufficient for the transport of all. Hekatonymus desired them to send envoys of their own to Sinôpê to make the necessary arrangements. Three envoys were accordingly sent — Ariston, an Athenian, Kallimachus, an Arcadian, and Samolas, an Achæan; the Athenian, probably, as possessing the talent of speaking in the Sinopian senate or assembly.

During the absence of the envoys, the army still continued near Kotyôra, with a market provided by the town, and with traders from Sinôpê and Herakleia in the camp. Such soldiers as had no money wherewith to purchase, subsisted by pillaging the neighboring frontier of Paphlagonia. But they were receiving no pay; every man was living on his own resources; and instead of carrying back a handsome purse to Greece, as each soldier had hoped when he first took service under Cyrus, there seemed every prospect of their returning poorer than when they left home. Moreover, the army was now moving onward without any definite purpose, with increasing dissatisfaction and decreasing discipline; insomuch that Xenophon foresaw the difficulties which would beset the responsible commanders when they should come within the stricter restraints and obligations of the Grecian world.

§ 13. **Plans of Xenophon for founding a city on the Black Sea.**

It was these considerations which helped to suggest to him the idea of employing the army on some enterprise of conquest and colonization on the Euxine itself; an idea highly flattering to his personal ambition, especially as the army was of unrivalled efficiency against an enemy, and no such second force could ever be got together in those distant regions. His patriotism as a Greek was inflamed with the thoughts of procuring for Hellas[1] a new self-governing city, occupied by a considerable Hellenic population, possessing a spacious territory, and exercising dominion over many neighboring natives. He seems to have thought first of attacking and conquering some established non-Hellenic city; an act which his ideas of international morality did not forbid, in a case where he had contracted no special convention with the inhabitants — though he (as well as Cheirisophus) strenuously protested against doing wrong to any innocent Hellenic community. He contemplated the employment of the entire force in capturing Phasis or some other native city; after which, when the establishment was once safely effected, those soldiers who preferred going home to remaining as settlers, might do so without emperiling those who stayed, and probably with their own purses filled by plunder and conquest in the neighborhood. To settle as one of the richest proprietors and chiefs, — perhaps even the recognized founder, like Agnon at Amphipolis, — of a new Hellenic city such as could hardly fail to become rich, powerful, and important — was a tempting prospect for one who had now acquired the habits of command. Moreover, the sequel will prove how correctly Xenophon appreciated the discomfort of leading the army back to Greece without pay and without certain employment.

It was the practice of Xenophon, and the advice of his master, Sokratês,[2] in grave and doubtful cases where the

[1] Hellas: Greece.

[2] "The gods (says Euripidês, in the Sokratic vein) have given us wisdom to understand and appropriate to ourselves the ordinary comforts of life; in obscure or unintelligible cases we are enabled to inform ourselves by looking at

most careful reflection was at fault, to recur to the inspired authority of an oracle or a prophet, and to offer sacrifice, in full confidence that the gods would vouchsafe to communicate a special revelation to such persons as they favored. Accordingly Xenophon, previous to any communication with the soldiers respecting his new project, was anxious to ascertain the will of the gods by a special sacrifice; for which he invoked the presence of Silanus, the chief prophet in the army. This prophet (as I have already mentioned), before the battle of Kunaxa, had assured Cyrus that Artaxerxês would not fight for ten days — and the prophecy came to pass; which made such an impression on Cyrus, that he rewarded him with the prodigious present of 3000 darics or ten Attic talents. While others were returning poor, Silanus, having contrived to preserve this sum through all the hardships of the retreat, was extremely rich, and anxious only to hasten home with his treasure in safety. He heard with strong repugnance the project of remaining on the Euxine, and determined to traverse[1] it by intrigue. As far as concerned the sacrifices, indeed, which he offered apart with Xenophon he was obliged to admit that the indications of the victims

the blaze of the fire, or by consulting prophets who understand the livers of sacrificial victims and the flight of birds. When they have thus furnished so excellent a provision for life, who but spoilt children can be discontented and ask for more? Yet still human prudence, full of self-conceit, will struggle to be more powerful, and will presume itself to be wiser, than the gods."

It will be observed that this constant outpouring of special revelations, through prophets, omens, &c., was (in view of these Sokratic thinkers) an essential part of divine government; indispensable to satisfy their ideas of the benevolence of the gods; since rational and scientific prediction was so habitually at fault and unable to fathom the phenomena of the future. (Grote.)

[1] **Traverse:** thwart.

were favorable; Xenophon himself being too familiar with the process to be imposed upon. But he at the same time tried to create alarm by declaring that a nice inspection disclosed evidence of treacherous snares laid for Xenophon; which latter indications he himself began to realize by spreading reports among the army that the Athenian general was laying clandestine plans for keeping them away from Greece without their own concurrence.[1]

Thus prematurely and insidiously divulged, the scheme found some supporters, but a far larger number of opponents; especially among those officers who were jealous of the ascendency of Xenophon. Timasion and Thorax employed it as a means of alarming the Herakleotic and Sinopian traders in the camp; telling them that unless they provided not merely transports, but also pay for the soldiers, Xenophon would find means to detain the army in the Euxine, and would employ the transports when they arrived not for the homeward voyage, but for his own projects of acquisition. This news spread so much terror both at Sinôpê and Herakleia that large offers of money were made from both cities to Timasion, on condition that he would ensure the departure of the army, as soon as the vessels should be assembled at Kotyôra. Accordingly these officers, convening an assembly of the soldiers, protested against the duplicity of Xenophon in thus preparing momentous schemes without any public debate or decision. And Timasion, seconded by Thorax, not only strenuously

[1] Though Xenophon accounted sacrifice to be an essential preliminary to any action of dubious result, and placed great faith in the indications which the victims offered, as signs of the future purposes of the gods,—he nevertheless had very little confidence in the professional prophets. He thought them quite capable of gross deceit. (Grote.) Thus Silanus (see p. 92) pretends to find some unfavorable indications in sacrifices which supported Xenophon.

urged the army to return, but went so far as to promise to them, on the faith of the assurances from Herakleia and Sinôpê, future pay on a liberal scale, to commence from the first new moon after their departure; together with a hospitable reception in his native city of Dardanus on the Hellespont, from whence they could make incursions on the rich neighboring satrapy of Pharnabazus.

It was not, however, until these attacks were repeated from more than one quarter — until the Achæans Philêsius and Lykon had loudly accused Xenophon of underhand manœuvring to cheat the army into remaining against their will — that the latter rose to repel the imputation; saying that all he had done was, to consult the gods whether it would be better to lay his project before the army or keep it in his own bosom. The encouraging answer of the gods, as conveyed through the victims and testified even by Silanus himself, proved that the scheme was not ill-conceived; nevertheless (he remarked) Silanus had begun to lay snares for him, obtaining by his own proceedings a collateral indication which he had announced to be visible in the victims. "If (added Xenophon) you had continued as destitute and unprovided, as you were just now — I should still have looked out for a resource in the capture of some city which would have enabled such of you as chose, to return at once; while the rest stay behind to enrich themselves. But now there is no longer any necessity; since Herakleia and Sinôpê are sending transports, and Timasion promises pay to you from the next new moon. Nothing can be better; you will go back safely to Greece, and will receive pay for going thither. I desist at once from my scheme, and call upon all who were favorable to it to desist also. Only let us all keep together until we are on safe ground; and let the man who lags behind or runs off, be condemned as a wrongdoer."

Xenophon immediately put this question to the vote, and every hand was held up in its favor. There was no man more disconcerted with the vote than the prophet Silanus, who loudly exclaimed against the injustice of detaining any one desirous to depart. But the soldiers put him down with vehement disapprobation, threatening that they would assuredly punish him if they caught him running off. His intrigue against Xenophon thus recoiled upon himself, for the moment. But shortly afterwards, when the army reached Herakleia, he took his opportunity for clandestine flight, and found his way back to Greece with the 3000 darics.

If Silanus gained little by his manœuvre, Timasion and his partners gained still less. For so soon as it became known that the army had taken a formal resolution to go back to Greece, and that Xenophon himself had made the proposition, the Sinopians and the Herakleots felt at their ease. They sent the transport vessels, but withheld the money which they had promised to Timasion and Thorax. Hence these officers were exposed to dishonor and peril; for having positively engaged to find pay for the army, they were now unable to keep their word. So keen were their apprehensions, that they came to Xenophon and told him that they had altered their views, and that they now thought it best to employ the newly-arrived transports in conveying the army, not to Greece, but against the town and territory of Phasis[1] at the eastern extremity of the

---

[1] **Phasis**: on the Euxine; means the town of that name, not the river. (Grote.)

Euxine. Xenophon replied, that they might convene the soldiers and make the proposition, if they chose; but that he would have nothing to say to it. To make the very proposition themselves, for which they had so much inveighed against Xenophon, was impossible without some preparation; so that each of them began individually to sound his captains, and get the scheme suggested by them. During this interval, the soldiery obtained information of the manœuvre, much to their discontent and indignation; of which Neon (the lieutenant of the absent Cheirisophus) took advantage, to throw the whole blame upon Xenophon; alleging that it was he who had converted the other officers to his original project, and that he intended, as soon as the soldiers were on shipboard, to convey them fraudulently to Phasis instead of to Greece. There was something so plausible in this glaring falsehood, which represented Xenophon as the author of the renewed project, once his own — and something so improbable in the fact that the other officers should spontaneously have renounced their own strong opinions to take up his — that we can hardly be surprised at the ready credence which Neon's calumny found among the army. Their exasperation against Xenophon became so intense, that they collected in fierce groups; and there was even a fear that they would break out into mutinous violence, as they had before done against the magistrates of Kerasus.

Well knowing the danger of such spontaneous and informal assemblages, and the importance of the habitual solemnities of convocation and arrangement, to ensure either discussion or legitimate defence — Xenophon immediately sent round the herald to summon the army into the regular place of assembly with customary method and ceremony. The summons was obeyed with unusual alacrity, and Xenophon then addressed them — refraining, with equal generosity and prudence, from saying anything about the last proposition which Timasion and others had made to him. Had he mentioned it, the question would have become one of life and death between him and those other officers.

### § 14. Xenophon defends himself against false accusations.

"Soldiers (said he), I understand that there are some men here calumniating me, as if I were intending to cheat you and carry you to Phasis. Hear me then, in the name of the gods. If I am shown to be doing wrong, let me not go from hence unpunished; but if, on the contrary, my calumniators are proved to be the wrong-doers, deal with them as they deserve. You surely well know where the sun rises and where he sets; you know that if a man wishes to reach Greece, he must go westward — if to the barbaric territories, he must go eastward. Can any one hope to deceive you on this point, and persuade you that the sun rises on *this* side, and sets on *that?* Can any one cheat you into going on shipboard with a wind which blows you away from Greece? Suppose even that I put you aboard when there is no wind at all. How am I to force you to sail with me against your own consent — I being only in one ship, you in a hundred and more? Imagine however that I could even succeed in deluding you to Phasis. When we land there, you will know at once that we are not in Greece; and what fate can I then expect — a detected impostor in the midst of ten thousand men with arms in their hands? No — these stories all proceed from foolish men, who are jealous of my influence with you; jealous, too, without reason — for I neither hinder *them* from outstripping me in your favor, if they can render you greater service — nor *you* from electing them commanders, if you think fit. Enough of this now: I challenge any one to come forward and say how it is possible either to cheat, or to be cheated, in the manner laid to my charge."

Having thus grappled directly with the calumnies of his enemies, and dissipated them in such manner as doubtless to create a reaction in his own favor, Xenophon made use of the opportunity to denounce the growing disorders in the army; which he depicted as such, that if no corrective were applied, disgrace and contempt must fall upon all. As he paused after this general remonstrance, the soldiers loudly called upon him to go into particulars; upon which he proceeded to recall, with lucid and impressive simplicity, the outrages which had been committed at and near Kerasus — the unauthorized and unprovoked attack made by Klearetus and his company on a neighboring village which was in friendly commerce with the army — the murder of the three elders of the village, who had come as heralds to complain to the generals about such wrong — the mutinous attack made by disorderly soldiers even upon the magistrates of Kerasus, at the very moment when they were remonstrating with the generals on what had occurred; exposing these magistrates to the utmost peril, and putting the generals themselves to ignominy "If such are to be our proceedings (continued Xenophon), look you well into what condition the army will fall. You, the aggregate body, will no longer be the sovereign authority to make war or peace with whom you please; each individual among you will conduct the army against any point which he may choose. And even if men should come to you as envoys, either for peace or for other purposes, they may be slain by any single enemy; so that you will be debarred from all public communications whatever. Next, those whom your universal suffrage shall have chosen commanders, will have no authority; while any self-elected general who chooses to give the word, Cast, Cast (*i.e.* darts or stones), may put to death without trial either officer or soldier as it suits him; that is, if he finds you ready to obey him, as it happened near Kerasus. Look now what these self-elected leaders have done for you. The magistrate of Kerasus, if he was really guilty of wrong towards you, has been enabled to escape with impunity; if he was innocent, he has been obliged to run away from you, as the only means of avoiding death without pretence of trial. Those who stoned the heralds to death have brought matters to such a pass, that you alone, of all Greeks, cannot enter the town of Kerasus in safety, unless in commanding force; and that we cannot even send in a herald to take up our dead (Klearetus and those who were slain in the attack on the Kerasuntine village) for burial; though at first those who had slain them in self-defence were anxious to give up the bodies to us. For who will take the risk of going in as herald, from those who have set the example of putting heralds to death? We generals were obliged to entreat the Kerasuntines to bury the bodies for us."

Continuing in this emphatic protest against the recent disorders and outrages, Xenophon at length succeeded in impressing his own sentiment, heartily and unanimously, upon the soldiers. They passed a vote that the ringleaders of the mutiny at Kerasus should be punished; that if any one was guilty of similar outrages in future, he should be put upon his trial by the generals, before the captains as judges, and if condemned by them, put to death; and that trial should be had before the same persons, for any other wrong committed since the death of Cyrus. A suitable religious ceremony was also directed to be performed, at the instance of Xenophon and the prophets, to purify the army.

This speech affords an interesting specimen of the political morality universal throughout the Grecian world, though deeper and more predominant among its better sections. In the miscellaneous aggregate, and temporary society, now mustered at Kotyôra, Xenophon insists on the universal suffrage of the whole body, as the legitimate sovereign authority for the guidance of every individual will; the decision of the majority, fairly and formally collected, as carrying a title to prevail over every dissentient minority; the generals chosen by the majority of votes, as the only persons entitled to obedience. This is the cardinal principle to which he appeals, as the anchorage of political obligation in the mind of each separate man or fraction; as the condition of all success, all safety, and all conjoint action; as the only condition either for punishing wrong or protecting right; as indispensable to keep up their sympathies with the Hellenic communities, and their dignity either as soldiers or as citizens. The complete success of his speech proves that he knew how to touch the right chord of Grecian feeling. No serious acts of individual insubordination occurred afterwards, though the army collectively went wrong on more than one occasion. And what is not less important to notice — the influence of Xenophon himself, after his unreserved and courageous remonstrance, seems to have been sensibly augmented — certainly noway diminished.

The circumstances which immediately followed were

indeed well calculated to augment it. For it was resolved, on the proposition of Xenophon himself, that the generals themselves should be tried before the newly-constituted tribunal of the captains, in case anyone had complaint to make against them for past matters; agreeably to the Athenian habit of subjecting every magistrate to a trial of accountability on laying down his office. In the course of this investigation, Philesius and Xanthiklês were fined twenty minæ,[1] to make good an assignable deficiency of that amount, in the cargoes of those merchantmen which had been detained at Trapezus for the transport of the army: Sophænetus, who had the general superintendence of this property, but had been negligent in that duty, was fined ten minæ. Next, the name of Xenophon was put up, when various persons stood forward to accuse him of having beaten and ill-used them. As commander of the rear-guard, his duty was by far the severest and most difficult, especially during the intense cold and deep snow; since the sick and wounded, as well as the laggards and plunderers, all fell under his inspection. One man especially was loud in complaints against him, and Xenophon questioned him, as to the details of his case, before the assembled army. It turned out that he had given him blows, because the man, having been entrusted with the task of carrying a sick soldier, was about to evade the duty by burying the dying man alive. This interesting debate ended by a full approbation on the part of the army of Xenophon's conduct, accompanied with regret that he had not handled the man yet more severely.

The statements of Xenophon himself give us a vivid

[1] **Minæ**: the mina was about one pound by weight of silver, or $20. Twenty minæ would be therefore $400.

idea of the internal discipline of the army, even as managed by a discreet and well-tempered officer. "I acknowledge (said he to the soldiers) to have struck many men for disorderly conduct; men who were content to owe their preservation to your orderly march and constant fighting, while they themselves ran about to plunder and enrich themselves at your cost. Had we all acted as they did, we should have perished to a man. Sometimes too I struck men who were lagging behind with cold and fatigue, or were stopping the way so as to hinder others from getting forward: I struck them with my fist, in order to save them from the spear of the enemy. You yourselves stood by and saw me: you had arms in your hands, yet none of you interfered to prevent me. I did it for their good as well as for yours, not from any insolence of disposition; for it was a time when we were all alike suffering from cold, hunger, and fatigue; whereas I now live comparatively well, drink more wine and pass easy days — and yet I strike no one. You will find that the men who failed most in those times of hardship, are now the most outrageous offenders in the army. There is Boïskus, the Thessalian pugilist, who pretended sickness during the march, in order to evade the burden of carrying his shield — and now, as I am informed, he has stripped several citizens of Kotyôra of their clothes. If (he concluded) the blows which I have occasionally given, in cases of necessity, are now brought in evidence — I call upon those among you also, to whom I have rendered aid and protection, to stand up and testify in my favor."

Many individuals responded to this appeal, insomuch that Xenophon was not merely acquitted, but stood higher than before in the opinion of the army. We learn from his defence that for a commanding officer to strike a soldier with his fist, if wanting in duty, was not considered improper; at least under such circumstances as those of the retreat. But what deserves notice still more, is, the extraordinary influence which Xenophon's powers of speaking gave him over the minds of the army. He stood distinguished from the other generals, Lacedæmonian, Arcadian, Achæan, and the rest, by his power of working on the minds of the soldiers collectively; and we see that he had the good sense, as well as the spirit, not to shrink from telling them unpleasant truths. In spite of such frankness — or rather, partly by means of such frankness — his ascendency as commander not only remained unabated, as compared with that of the others, but went on increasing. For whatever may be said about the flattery of orators as a means of influence over the people, — it will be found that though particular points may be gained in this way, yet wherever the influence of an orator has been steady and long-continued (like that of Periklês or Demosthenês) it is owing in part to the fact that he has an opinion of his own, and is not willing to accommodate himself constantly to the prepossessions of his hearers. Without the oratory of Xenophon, there would have existed no engine for kindling or sustaining the common sense or feeling of the ten thousand Cyreians assembled at Kotyôra, or for keeping up the moral authority of the aggregate over the individual members and fractions. The other officers could doubtless speak well enough to address short encouragements, or give simple explanations, to the soldiers: without this faculty, no man was fit for military command over Greeks. But the oratory of Xenophon was something of a higher order. Whoever will study the discourse pronounced by him at Kotyôra will perceive a dexterity in dealing with assembled multitudes — a discriminating use sometimes of the plainest and most direct appeal, sometimes of indirect insinuation or circuitous transitions to work round the minds of the hearers — a command of those fundamental political convictions which lay deep in the Grecian mind, but were often so overlaid by the fresh impulses arising out of each successive situation, as to require some positive friction to draw them out from their latent state — lastly, a power of expansion and varied repetition — such as would be naturally imparted both by the education and the practice of an intelligent Athenian, but would rarely be found in any other Grecian city. The energy and judgment displayed by Xenophon in the retreat were doubtless not less essential to his influence than his power of speaking; but in these points we may be sure that other officers were more nearly his equals.

The important public proceedings above described not only restored the influence of Xenophon, but also cleared off a great amount of bad feeling, and sensibly abated the bad habits, which had grown up in the army. A scene which speedily followed was not without effect in promoting cheerful and amicable sympathies. The Paphlagonian prince Korylas, weary of the desultory warfare carried on between the Greeks and the border inhabitants, sent envoys to the Greek camp with presents of horses and fine robes, and with expressions of a wish to conclude peace. The Greek generals accepted the presents, and promised to submit the proposition to the army. But first, they entertained the envoys at a banquet, providing at the same time games and dances, with other recreations amusing not only to them but also to the soldiers generally. [Xenophon thus describes them — "As soon as the libations were over, and they had sung the pæan, two Thracians rose up and danced in full armor, to the sound of a pipe;[1] they leaped very high, and with great agility, and wielded their swords; and at last one struck the other, in such a manner that every one thought he had killed him. He fell, however, artfully, and the Paphlagonians cried out; the other having stripped him of his arms, went out singing; while other Thracians carried off the man as if he had been dead; though indeed he had suffered no hurt. Afterward some others stood up and danced what they called the Carpæan dance[2] in heavy arms. The nature of the dance was as follows: one man having laid aside his arms, sows, and drives a yoke of oxen, frequently turning to look back as if he were afraid. A robber then approaches, and the plowman when he perceives him, snatches up his arms and runs to meet him, and fights with him in defence of his oxen (and the dancers acted all this, keeping time to the music); but at last the robber binding the ox driver, leads him off with his oxen. Sometimes, however, the plowman binds the robber, and then having fastened him to his oxen, drives him off with his hands tied behind him.

"Next came forward a man with a light shield in each hand, and danced, sometimes acting as if two adversaries were attacking him; sometimes he used his shields as if engaged with only one; sometimes he whirled about, and threw a somersault, still keeping the shields in his hands, presenting an interesting spectacle. At last he danced the

---

[1] **Pipe:** a fife or flute-like instrument.

[2] **Carpæan dance:** perhaps because one of the dancers represented a sower of grain (from *karpos*, fruit), or possibly from *karpos*, wrist, the wrists of one being bound.

Persian dance (frequently bending the knee), clashing his shields together, sinking on his knees, and rising again; and all this he performed in time to the pipe.

"After him some of the Arcadians coming forward and taking their stand, armed as handsomely as they could equip themselves, moved along in time, accompanied by a pipe tuned for the war-movement, and sung the pæan, and danced in the same manner as in the procession to the gods. The Paphlagonians, looking on, testified their astonishment that all the dances were performed in armor. The Mysian,[1] observing that they were surprised at the exhibition, and prevailing on one of the Arcadians, who had a female dancer, to let her come in, brought her forward, equipping her as handsomely as he could, and giving her a light shield. She danced the Pyrrhic[2] dance with great agility, and a general clapping of hands followed; and the Paphlagonians asked whether the women fought along with the men; when they replied that it was the women who had driven the King from his camp.[3] This was the conclusion of the entertainment for that night."[4] They were followed on the next day by an amicable convention concluded between the army and the Paphlagonians.

### § 15. The army passes by sea to Sinôpê.

Not long afterwards — a number of transports, sufficient for the whole army, having been assembled from Herakleia and Sinôpê — all the soldiers were conveyed by sea to the

---

[1] Mysian: from Mysia, Asia Minor.

[2] Pyrrhic dance: a kind of dance accompanied with every gesture of the body used in giving and avoiding blows.

[3] This appears to have been said jocosely in reference to the Persian King.

[4] Xenophon.

latter place, passing by the mouth of the rivers Thermodon, Iris, and Halys, which they would have found impracticable to cross in a land-march through Paphlagonia. Having reached Sinôpê after a day and a night of sailing with a fair wind, they were hospitably received, and lodged in the neighboring seaport of Armênê, where the Sinopians sent to them a large present of barley-meal and wine, and where they remained for five days.

It was here that they were joined by Cheirisophus, whose absence had been so unexpectedly prolonged. But he came with only a single trireme,[1] bringing nothing except a message from Anaxibius, the Lacedæmonian general in the Bosphorus; who complimented the army, and promised that they should be taken into pay as soon as they were out of the Euxine. The soldiers, severely disappointed on seeing him arrive thus empty-handed, became the more strongly bent on striking some blow to fill their own purses before they reached Greece. Feeling that it was necessary to the success of any such project that it should be prepared not only skilfully, but secretly, they resolved to elect a single general in place of that board of six (or perhaps more) who were still in function. Such was now the ascendency of Xenophon, that the general sentiment of the army at once turned towards him; and the captains, communicating to him what was in contemplation, intimated to him their own anxious hopes that he would not decline the offer. Tempted by so flattering a proposition, he hesitated at first what answer he should give. But at length the uncertainty of being able to satisfy the exigencies of the army, and the fear of thus compromising the

---

[1] **Trireme:** a war-vessel propelled by three ranks of rowers placed one above the other.

reputation which he had already realized, outweighed the opposite inducements. As in other cases of doubt, so in this — he offered sacrifice to Zeus the King; and the answer returned by the victims was such as to determine him to refusal. Accordingly, when the army assembled, with predetermination to choose a single chief, and proceeded to nominate him — he respectfully and thankfully declined, on the ground that Cheirisophus was a Lacedæmonian, and that he himself was not; adding that he should cheerfully serve under any one whom they might name. His excuse however was repudiated; especially by the captains. Several of these latter were Arcadians; and one of them, Agasias, cried out, with full sympathy of the soldiers, that, if that principle were admitted, he as an Arcadian ought to resign his command. Finding that his former reason was not approved, Xenophon acquainted the army that he had sacrificed to know whether he ought to accept the command, and that the gods had peremptorily forbidden him to do so.

Cheirisophus was then elected sole commander, and undertook the duty; saying that he would have willingly served under Xenophon, if the latter had accepted the office, but that it was a good thing for Xenophon himself to have declined — since Dexippus had already poisoned the mind of Anaxibius against him, though he (Cheirisophus) had emphatically contradicted the calumnies.

On the next day, the army sailed forward under the command of Cheirisophus, to Herakleia; near which town they were hospitably entertained, and gratified with a present of meal, wine, and bullocks, even greater than they had received at Sinôpê. It now appeared that Xenophon had acted wisely in declining the sole command; and also that Cheirisophus, though elected commander, yet having been very long absent, was not really of so much importance in the eyes of the soldiers as Xenophon. In the camp near Herakleia, the soldiers became impatient that their generals (for the habit of looking upon Xenophon as one of them still continued) took no measures to procure money for them. The Achæan Lykon proposed that they should extort a contribution of no less than 3000 staters[1] of Kyzikus from the inhabitants of Herakleia: another man immediately outbid this proposition, and proposed that they should require 10,000 staters[1] — a full month's pay for the army. It was moved that Cheirisophus and Xenophon should go to the Herakleots as envoys with this demand. But both of them indignantly refused to be concerned in so unjust an extortion, from a Grecian city which had just received the army kindly and sent handsome presents. Accordingly Lykon with two Arcadian officers undertook the mission, and intimated the demand, not without threats in case of non-compliance, to the Herakleots. The latter replied that they would take it into consideration. But they waited only for the departure of the envoys, and then immediately closed their gates, manned their walls, and brought in their outlying property.

The project being thus baffled, Lykon and the rest turned their displeasure upon Cheirisophus and Xenophon, whom they accused of having occasioned its miscarriage. And they now began to exclaim that it was disgraceful to the Arcadians and Achæans, who formed more than one

---

[1] **Three thousand staters:** about $11,500; ten thousand staters would be in round numbers about $38,000. The stater was a Greek gold coin; its value is usually given at about $5.00, but Grote here makes it considerably less.

numerical half of the army and endured all the toil — to obey as well as to enrich generals from other Hellenic cities; especially a single Athenian who furnished no contingent to the army. Here again it is remarkable that the personal importance of Xenophon caused him to be still regarded as a general, though the sole command had been vested by formal vote in Cheirisophus. So vehement was the dissatisfaction, that all the Arcadian and Achæan soldiers in the army, more than 4500 heavy-armed foot-soldiers in number, renounced the authority of Cheirisophus, formed themselves into a distinct division, and chose ten commanders from out of their own numbers. The whole army thus became divided into three portions — first the Arcadians and Achæans: secondly, 1400 heavy-armed foot-soldiers and 700 Thracian light-armed foot-soldiers, who adhered to Cheirisophus: lastly, 1700 heavy-armed foot-soldiers, 300 light-armed foot-soldiers, and 40 horsemen (all the horsemen in the army), attaching themselves to Xenophon; who however was taking measures to sail away individually from Herakleia and quit the army altogether, which he would have done had he not been restrained by unfavorable sacrifices.

The Arcadian division, departing first, in vessels from Herakleia, landed at Kalpê; an untenanted promontory of the Bithynian or Asiatic Thrace, midway between Herakleia and Byzantium. From thence they marched at once into the interior of Bithynia, with the view of surprising the villages and acquiring plunder. But through rashness and bad management, they first sustained several partial losses, and ultimately became surrounded upon an eminence, by a large muster of the native Bithynians from all the territory around. They were only rescued from destruction by the unexpected appearance of Xenophon with his division ; who had left Herakleia somewhat later, but heard by accident, during their march, of the danger of their comrades. The whole army thus became re-assembled at Kalpê, where the Arcadians and Achæans, disgusted at the ill-success of their separate expedition, again established the old union and the old generals. They chose Neon in place of Cheirisophus, who — afflicted by the humiliation put upon him, in having been first named sole commander and next deposed within a week — had fallen sick of a fever and died. The elder Arcadian captains farther moved a resolution, that if any one henceforward should propose to separate the army into fractions, he should be put to death.

The locality of Kalpê was well-suited for the foundation of a colony, which Xenophon evidently would have been glad to bring about, though he took no direct measures tending towards it; while the soldiers were so bent on returning to Greece, and so jealous lest Xenophon should entrap them into remaining, that they almost shunned the encampment. It so happened that they were detained there for some days without being able to march forth even in quest of provisions, because the sacrifices were not favorable. Xenophon refused to lead them out, against the warning of the sacrifices — although the army suspected him of a deliberate manœuvre for the purpose of detention. Neon however, less scrupulous, led out a body of 2000 men who chose to follow him, under severe distress for want of provisions. But being surprised by the native Bithynians, with the aid of some troops of the Persian satrap Pharnabazus, he was defeated with the loss of no less than 500 men ; a misfortune which Xenophon regards as the natural retribution for contempt of the sacrificial warning. The dangerous position of Neon with the remainder of the detachment was rapidly made known at the camp: upon which Xenophon, unharnessing a wagon-bullock as the only animal near at hand, immediately offered sacrifice. On this occasion the victim was at once favorable; so that he led out without delay the greater part of the force, to the rescue of the exposed detachment, which was brought back in safety to the camp. So bold had the enemy become, that in the night the camp was attacked. The Greeks were obliged on the next day to retreat into stronger ground, surrounding themselves with a ditch and a palisade. Fortunately a vessel arrived from Herakleia, bringing to the camp at Kalpê a supply of barley-meal, cattle, and wine; which restored the spirits of the army, enabling them to go forth on the ensuing morning and assume the aggressive against the Bithynians, and the troops of Pharnabazus. These troops were completely defeated and dispersed, so that the Greeks returned to their camp at Kalpê in the evening both safe and masters of the country.

At Kalpê they remained some time awaiting the arrival of Kleander from Byzantium, who was said to be about to bring vessels for their transport. They were now abundantly provided with supplies, not merely from the undisturbed plunder of the neighboring villages, but also from the visits of traders who came with cargoes. Indeed the impression — that they were preparing, at the instance of Xenophon, to found a new city at Kalpê — became so strong that several of the neighboring native villages sent envoys to ask on what terms alliance would be granted to them. At length Kleander came, but with two triremes only.

Kleander was the Lacedæmonian governor of Byzantium. His appearance opens to us a new phase in the eventful history of this gallant army, as well as an insight into the state of the Grecian world under the Lacedæmonian empire. He came attended by the Lacedæmonian Dexippus, who had served in the Cyreian army until their arrival at Trapezus, and who had there been entrusted with an armed vessel for the purpose of detaining transports to convey the troops home but had abused the confidence reposed in him, by running away with the ship to Byzantium.

It so happened that at the moment when Kleander arrived, the whole army was out on a marauding excursion. Orders had already been promulgated, that whatever was captured by every one when the whole army was out, should be brought in and dealt with as public property; though on days when the army was collectively at rest, any soldier might go out individually and take to himself whatever he could pillage. On the day when Kleander arrived, and found the whole army out, some soldiers were just coming back with a lot of sheep which they had seized. By right, the sheep ought to have been handed into the public store. But these soldiers, desirous to appropriate them wrongfully, addressed themselves to Dexippus, and promised him a portion if he would enable them to retain the rest. Accordingly the latter interfered, drove away those who claimed the sheep as public property, and denounced them as thieves to Kleander; who desired him to bring them before him. Dexippus arrested one of them, a soldier belonging to the company of one of the best friends of Xenophon — the Arcadian Agasias. The latter took the man under his protection; while the soldiers around incensed not less at the past than at the present conduct of Dexippus, broke out into violent manifestations, called him a traitor, and pelted him with stones. Such was their wrath, that not Dexippus alone, but the crew of the triremes also, and even Kleander himself fled, in alarm; in spite of the intervention of Xenophon, and the other generals, who on the one hand explained to Kleander, that it was an established army-order which these soldiers were seeking to enforce — and on the other hand controlled the mutineers. But the Lacedæmonian governor was so incensed as well by his own fright as by the calumnies of Dexippus, that he threatened to sail away at once, and proclaim the Cyreian army enemies to Sparta, so that every Hellenic city should be interdicted from giving them reception. It was in vain that the generals, well knowing the formidable consequences of such an interdict, entreated him to relent. He would consent only on condition that the soldiers who had begun to throw stones as well as Agasias the interfering officer, should be delivered up to him. This latter demand was especially insisted upon by Dexippus, who hating Xenophon, had already tried to prejudice Anaxibius against him, and believed that Agasias had acted by his order.

The situation now became extremely critical; since the soldiers would not easily be brought to surrender their comrades — who had a perfectly righteous cause, though they had supported it by undue violence — to the vengeance of a traitor like Dexippus. When the army was convened in assembly, several of them went so far as to treat the menace of Kleander with contempt. But Xenophon took pains to set them right upon this point. "Soldiers (said he) it will be no slight misfortune if Kleander shall depart as he threatens to do, in his present temper toward us. We are here close upon the cities of Greece: now the Lacedæmonians are the imperial power in Greece, and not merely their authorized officers, but even each one of their individual citizens, can accomplish what he pleases in the various cities. If then Kleander begins by shutting us out from Byzantium, and next enjoins the Lacedæmonian governors in the other cities [1] to do the same, proclaiming us lawless and disobedient to Sparta — if, besides, the same representation should be conveyed to the Lacedæmonian admiral of the fleet, Anaxibius — we shall be hard pressed either to remain or to sail away; for the Lacedæmonians are at present masters both on land and at sea. We must not, for the sake of any one or two men, suffer the whole army to be excluded from Greece. We must obey whatever the Lacedæmonians command, especially as our cities, to which we respectively belong, now obey them. As to what concerns myself, I understand that Dexippus has told Kleander that Agasias would never have taken such a step except by my orders. Now, if Agasias himself states this, I am ready to exonerate both him and all of you, and to give myself up to any extremity of punishment. I maintain too that any other man whom Kleander arraigns ought in like manner to give himself up for trial, in order that you collectively may be discharged from the imputation. It will be hard indeed, if just as we are reaching Greece, we should not only be debarred from the praise and honor which we anticipated, but should be degraded even below the level of others, and shut out from the Grecian cities."

After this speech from the philo-Laconian [2] Xenophon —

[1] **Cities**: cities then were generally built with walls and gates, so that it was easy to exclude any whom they did not wish should enter.

[2] **Philo-Laconian**: Sparta-loving (Sparta being in the district of Laconia). Compare what is said of Xenophon on p. 41.

so significant a testimony of the unmeasured ascendency and interference of the Lacedæmonians throughout Greece — Agasias rose, and proclaimed, that what he had done was neither under the orders, nor with the privity, of Xenophon; that he had acted on a personal impulse of wrath, at seeing his own honest and innocent soldier dragged away by the traitor Dexippus; but that he now willingly gave himself up as a victim, to avert from the army the displeasure of the Lacedæmonians. This generous self-sacrifice, which at the moment promised nothing less than a fatal result to Agasias, was accepted by the army: and the generals conducted both him and the soldier whom he had rescued, as prisoners to Kleander. Presenting himself as the responsible party, Agasias at the same time explained to Kleander the infamous behavior of Dexippus to the army, and said that towards no one else would he have acted in the same manner; while the soldier whom he had rescued, and who was given up at the same time, also affirmed that he had interfered merely to prevent Dexippus and some others from overruling, for their own individual benefit, a proclaimed order of the entire army. Kleander, having observed that if Dexippus had done what was affirmed, he would be the last to defend him, but that no one ought to have been stoned without trial — desired that the persons surrendered might be left for his consideration, and at the same time retracted his expressions of displeasure as regarded all the others.

The generals then retired, leaving Kleander in possession of the prisoners, and on the point of taking his dinner. But they retired with mournful feelings, and Xenophon presently convened the army to propose that a general deputation should be sent to Kleander to implore his lenity towards their two comrades. This being cordially adopted, Xenophon, at the head of a deputation comprising Drakontius the Spartan as well as the chief officers, addressed an earnest appeal to Kleander, representing that his honor had been satisfied with the unconditional surrender of the two persons required; that the army, deeply concerned for two meritorious comrades, entreated him now to show mercy and spare their lives; that they promised him in return the most explicit obedience, and entreated him to take the command of them, in order that he might have personal cognizance of their exact discipline, and compare their worth with that of Dexippus. Kleander was not merely soothed, but completely won over, by this address; and said in reply that the conduct of the generals belied altogether the representations made to him (doubtless by Dexippus), that they were seeking to alienate the army from the Lacedæmonians. He not only restored the two men in his power, but also accepted the command of the army, and promised to conduct them back into Greece.

The prospects of the army appeared thus greatly improved; the more so, as Kleander, on entering upon his new functions as commander, found the soldiers so cheerful and orderly, that he was highly gratified, and exchanged personal tokens of friendship and hospitality with Xenophon. But when sacrifices came to be offered, for beginning the march homeward, the signs were so unpropitious, for three successive days, that Kleander could not bring himself to brave such auguries at the outset of his career. Accordingly, he told the generals, that the gods plainly forbade him, and reserved it for them, to conduct the army into Greece; that he should therefore sail back to Byzantium, and would receive the army in the best way he could, when they reached the Bosphorus. After an interchange of presents with the soldiers, he then departed with his two triremes.

The favorable sentiment now established in the bosom of Kleander will be found very serviceable hereafter to the Cyreians at Byzantium; but they had cause for deeply regretting the unpropitious sacrifices which had deterred him from assuming the actual command at Kalpê. In the request preferred to him by them that he would march as their commander to the Bosphorus, we may recognize a scheme, and a very well-contrived scheme, of Xenophon; who had before desired to leave the army at Herakleia, and who saw plainly that the difficulties of a commander, unless he were a Lacedæmonian of station and influence, would increase with every step of their approach to Greece. Had Kleander accepted the command, the soldiers would have been better treated, while Xenophon himself might either have remained as his adviser, or might have gone home. He would probably have chosen the latter course.

§ 16. **The army crosses the Bosphorus to Byzantium; false promises of Anaxibius and their results.**

Under the command of their own officers, the Cyreians now marched from Kalpê across Bithynia to Chrysopolis (in the territory of Chalkêdon on the Asiatic edge of the Bosphorus, immediately opposite to Byzantium,[1] as Scutari now is to Constantinople), where they remained seven days, turning into money the slaves and plunder which they had collected. Unhappily for them, the Lacedæ-

---
[1] **Byzantium**: this city (the modern Constantinople) was founded by a Greek colony B.C. 657. It had a mixed population, and was at this time under the rule of a Lacedæmonian or Spartan governor.

monian admiral Anaxibius was now at Byzantium, so that their friend Kleander was under his superior command. And Pharnabazus, the Persian satrap of the north-western regions of Asia Minor, becoming much alarmed lest they should invade his satrapy, despatched a private message to Anaxibius; whom he prevailed upon, by promise of large presents, to transport the army forthwith across to the European side of the Bosphorus. Accordingly, Anaxibius, sending for the generals and the captains across to Byzantium, invited the army to cross, and gave them his assurance that as soon as the soldiers should be in Europe, he would provide pay for them. The other officers told him that they would return with this message and take the sense of the army; but Xenophon on his own account said that he should not return; that he should now retire from the army, and sail away from Byzantium. It was only on the pressing instance of Anaxibius that he was induced to go back to Chrysopolis and conduct the army across; on the understanding that he should depart immediately afterwards.

Here at Byzantium, he received his first communication from the Thracian prince Seuthês; who sent Medosadês to offer him a reward if he would bring the army across. Xenophon replied that the army would cross; that no reward from Seuthês was needful to bring about that movement; but that he himself was about to depart, leaving the command in other hands. In point of fact, the whole army crossed with little delay, landed in Europe, and found themselves within the walls of Byzantium. Xenophon, who had come along with them, paid a visit shortly afterwards to his friend the governor Kleander, and took leave of him as about to depart immediately. But Kleander told him that he must not think of departing until the army was out of the city, and that he would be held responsible if they stayed. In truth Kleander was very uneasy so long as the soldiers were within the walls, and was well aware that it might be no easy matter to induce them to go away. For Anaxibius had practised a gross fraud in promising them pay, which he had neither the ability nor the inclination to provide. Without handing to them either pay or even means of purchasing supplies, he issued orders that they must go forth with arms and baggage, and muster outside of the gates, there to be numbered for an immediate march; any one who stayed behind being held as punishable. This proclamation was alike unexpected and offensive to the soldiers, who felt that they had been deluded, and were very backward in obeying. Hence Kleander, while urgent with Xenophon to defer his departure until he had conducted the army outside of the walls, added — "Go forth as if you were about to march along with them; when you are once outside, you may depart as soon as you please;" Xenophon replied that this matter must be settled with Anaxibius, to whom accordingly both of them went, and who repeated the same directions, in a manner yet more peremptory. Though it was plain to Xenophon that he was here making himself a sort of instrument to the fraud which Anaxibius had practised upon the army, yet he had no choice but to obey. Accordingly, he as well as the other generals put themselves at the head of the troops, who followed, however reluctantly, and arrived most of them outside of the gates. Eteonikus (a Lacedæmonian officer of consideration, noticed more than once in preceding Grecian history) commanding at the gate, stood close to it in person; in order that when all the Cyreians had gone forth, he might immediately shut it and fasten it with the bar.

Anaxibius knew well what he was doing. He fully anticipated that the communication of the final orders would occasion an outbreak among the Cyreians, and was anxious to defer it until they were outside. But when there remained only the rearmost companies still in the inside and on their march, all the rest having got out — he thought the danger was over, and summoned to him the generals and captains, all of whom were probably near the gates superintending the march through. It seems that Xenophon, having given notice that he intended to depart, did not answer to this summons as one of the generals, but remained outside among the soldiers. "Take what supplies you want (said Anaxibius) from the neighboring Thracian villages, which are well furnished with wheat, barley, and other necessaries. After thus providing yourselves, march forward to the Chersonesus,[1] and there Kyniskus will give you pay."

This was the first distinct intimation given by Anaxibius that he did not intend to perform his promise of finding pay for the soldiers. Who Kyniskus was we do not know, nor was he probably known to the Cyreians; but the march here enjoined was at least 150 miles, and might be much longer. The route was not indicated, and the generals had to inquire from Anaxibius whether they were to go by what was called the Holy Mountain (that is, by

[1] **The Chersonesus** (the peninsula): a peninsula of Southern Thrace, opposite Asia Minor, having numerous Greek cities, and noted for its abundance of grain, much of which was exported to Athens.

the shorter line, skirting the northern coast of the Propontis), or by a more inland and circuitous road through Thrace; — also whether they were to regard the Thracian prince, Seuthês, as a friend or an enemy.

### § 17. Mutiny of the army in leaving Byzantium.

Instead of the pay which had been formally promised to them by Anaxibius if they would cross over from Asia to Byzantium, the Cyreians thus found themselves sent away empty-handed to a long march — through another barbarous country, with chance-supplies to be obtained only by their own efforts, — and at the end of it a lot unknown and uncertain; while, had they remained in Asia, they would have had at any rate the rich satrapy of Pharnabazus within their reach. To perfidy of dealing was now added a brutal ejectment from Byzantium, without even the commonest manifestations of hospitality; contrasting pointedly with the treatment which the army had recently experienced at Trapezus, Sinôpê, and Herakleia; where they had been welcomed not only by compliments on their past achievements, but also by an ample present of flour, meat, and wine. Such behavior could not fail to provoke the most violent indignation in the bosoms of the soldiery; and Anaxibius had therefore delayed giving the order until the last soldiers were marching out, thinking that the army would hear nothing of it until the generals came out of the gates to inform them; so that the gates would be closed, and the walls manned to resist an assault from without. But his calculations were not realized. Either one of the soldiers passing by heard him give the order, or one of the captains forming his audience stole away from the rest, and hastened forward to acquaint his comrades on the outside. The bulk of the army, already irritated by the inhospitable way in which they had been thrust out, needed nothing farther to inflame them into spontaneous mutiny and aggression. While the generals within (who either took the communication more patiently, or at least, looking farther forward, felt that any attempt to resent or resist the ill-usage of the Spartan admiral would only make their position worse) were discussing with Anaxibius the details of the march just enjoined — the soldiers without, bursting into spontaneous movement, with a simultaneous and fiery impulse, made a rush back to get possession of the gate. But Eteonikus, seeing their movement, closed it without a moment's delay, and fastened the bar. The soldiers on reaching the gate and finding it barred, clamored loudly to get it opened, threatened to break it down, and even began to knock violently against it. Some ran down to the sea-coast, and made their way into the city round the line of stones at the base of the city wall, which protected it against the sea; while the rearmost soldiers who had not yet marched out, seeing what was passing, and fearful of being cut off from their comrades, assaulted the gate from the inside, severed the fastenings with axes, and threw it wide open to the army. All the soldiers then rushed up, and were soon again in Byzantium.

Nothing could exceed the terror of the Lacedæmonians as well as of the native Byzantines, when they saw the excited Cyreians again within the walls. The town seemed already taken and on the point of being plundered. Neither Anaxibius nor Eteonikus took the smallest means of resistance, nor stayed to brave the approach of the soldiers, whose wrath they were fully conscious of having deserved. Both fled to the citadel — the former first running to the seashore, and jumping into a fishing-boat to go thither by sea. He even thought the citadel not tenable with its existing garrison, and sent over to Chalkêdon for a reinforcement. Still more terrified were the citizens of the town. Every man in the market-place instantly fled; some to their houses, others to the merchant vessels in the harbor, others to the triremes or ships of war, which they hauled down to the water, and thus put to sea.

To the deception and harshness of the Spartan admiral, there was thus added a want of precaution in the manner of execution, which threatened to prove the utter ruin of Byzantium. For it was but too probable that the Cyreian soldiers, under the keen sense of recent injury, would satiate their revenge, and reimburse themselves for the want of hospitality towards them, without distinguishing the Lacedæmonian garrison from the Byzantine citizens; and that too from mere impulse, not merely without orders, but in spite of prohibitions, from their generals. Such was the aspect of the case, when they became again assembled in a mass within the gates; and such would probably have been the reality, had Xenophon executed his design of retiring earlier, so as to leave the other generals acting without him. Being on the outside along with the soldiers, Xenophon felt at once, as soon as he saw the gates forced open and the army again within the town, the terrific emergency which was impending: first, the sack of Byzantium — next, horror and antipathy, throughout all Greece, towards the Cyreian officers and soldiers indiscriminately — lastly, unsparing retribution inflicted upon all by the power of Sparta. Overwhelmed with these anxieties, he rushed into the town along with the multitude, using every effort to pacify them and bring them into order. They on their parts, delighted to see him along with them, and conscious of their own force, were eager to excite him to the same pitch as themselves, and to prevail on him to second and methodize their present triumph. "Now is your time, Xenophon (they exclaimed), to make yourself a man. You have here a city — you have triremes — you have money — you have plenty of soldiers. Now then, if you choose, you can enrich us; and we in return can make you powerful." — "You speak well (replied he) ; I shall do as you propose ; but if you want to accomplish anything, you must fall into military array forthwith." He knew that this was the first condition of returning to anything like tranquillity ; and by great good fortune, the space called the Thrakion,[1] immediately adjoining the gate inside, was level, open, and clear of houses ; presenting an excellent place of arms or locality for a review. The whole army, — partly from their long military practice, partly under the impression that Xenophon was really about to second their wishes and direct some aggressive operation — threw themselves almost of their own accord into regular array on the Thrakion ; the heavy-armed foot-soldiers eight deep, the light-armed foot-soldiers on each flank. It was in this position that Xenophon addressed them as follows.

### § 18. Xenophon's speech to the soldiers.

"Soldiers, I am not surprised that you are incensed, and that you think yourselves scandalously cheated and ill-used.

[1] **Thrakion**: probably an open space or square near the Thracian Gate of the city.

But if we give way to our wrath — if we punish these Lacedæmonians now before us for their treachery, and plunder this innocent city — reflect what will be the consequence. We shall stand proclaimed forthwith as enemies to the Lacedæmonians and their allies, and what sort of a war that will be, those who have witnessed and who still recollect recent matters of history may easily fancy. We Athenians entered into the war against Sparta with a powerful army and fleet, an abundant revenue, and numerous tributary cities in Asia as well as Europe — among them this very Byzantium in which we now stand. We have been vanquished in the way that all of you know. And what then will be the fate of us soldiers, when we shall have as united enemies, Sparta with all her old allies and Athens besides, — Tissaphernês and the barbaric forces on the coast — and most of all the Great King[1] whom we marched up to dethrone and slay, if we were able? Is any man fool enough to think that we have a chance of making head against so many combined enemies? Let us not plunge madly into dishonor and ruin, nor incur the enmity of our own fathers and friends: who are in the cities which will take arms against us — and will take arms justly, if we, who abstained from seizing any barbaric city, even when we were in force sufficient, shall nevertheless now plunder the first Grecian city into which we have been admitted. As far as I am concerned, may I be buried ten thousand fathoms deep in the earth rather than see you do such things! and I exhort *you* too, as Greeks, to obey the leaders of Greece. Endeavor while thus obedient, to obtain your just rights; but if you should fail in this, rather submit to injustice than cut yourselves off from the

---

[1] **The Great King**: the King of Persia.

Grecian world. Send to inform Anaxibius, that we have entered the city, not with a view to commit any violence, but in the hope, if possible, of obtaining from him the advantages which he promised us. If we fail, we shall at least prove to him that we quit the city not under his fraudulent manœuvres, but under our own sense of the duty of obedience."

This speech completely arrested the impetuous impulse of the army, brought them to a true sense of their situation, and induced them to adopt the proposition of Xenophon. They remained unmoved in their position on the Thrakion, while three of the captains were sent to communicate with Anaxibius. While they were thus waiting, a Theban named Kœratadas approached, who had once commanded in Byzantium under the Lacedæmonians during the previous war. He had now become a sort of professional general looking out for an army to command wherever he could find one, and offering his services to any city which would engage him. He addressed the assembled Cyreians, and offered, if they would accept him for their general, to conduct them against the Delta[1] of Thrace (the space included between the north-west corner of the Propontis[2] and the south-west corner of the Euxine), which he asserted to be a rich territory presenting great opportunity of plunder: he further promised to furnish them with ample subsistence during the march. Presently the envoys returned, bearing the reply of Anaxibius; who received the message favorably, promising that not only the army should have no cause to regret their obedience,

[1] **Delta**: so named because it resembled the Greek capital letter Delta, Δ, corresponding to the English D; hence a triangular-shaped piece of land.
[2] **Propontis** (now, the Sea of Marmora): between Asia and Europe.

but that he would both report their good conduct to the authorities at home, and do everything in his own power to promote their comfort. He said nothing farther about taking them into pay; that delusion having now answered its purpose. The soldiers, on hearing his communication, adopted a resolution to accept Kœratadas as their future commander, and then marched out of the town. As soon as they were on the outside, Anaxibius, not content with closing the gates against them, made public proclamation that if any one of them were found in the town, he should be sold forthwith into slavery.

There are few cases throughout Grecian history in which an able discourse has been the means of averting so much evil, as was averted by this speech of Xenophon to the army in Byzantium. Nor did he ever, throughout the whole period of his command, render to them a more signal service. The miserable consequences, which would have ensued, had the army persisted in their aggressive impulse — first, to the citizens of the town, ultimately to themselves, while Anaxibius, the only guilty person, had the means of escaping by sea, even under the worst circumstances — are stated by Xenophon rather under than above the reality. At the same time no orator ever undertook a more difficult case, or achieved a fuller triumph over unpromising conditions. If we consider the feelings and position of the army at the instant of their breaking into the town, we shall be astonished that any commander could have arrested their movements. Though fresh from all the glory of their retreat, they had been first treacherously entrapped over from Asia, next roughly ejected by Anaxibius; and although it may be said truly that the citizens of Byzantium had no concern either in the one or the other, yet little heed is commonly taken, in military operations, to the distinction between garrison and citizens in an assailed town. Having arms in their hands, with consciousness of force arising out of their exploits in Asia, the Cyreians were at the same time inflamed by the opportunity both of avenging a gross recent injury, and enriching themselves in the process of execution; to which we may add, the excitement of that rush whereby they had obtained re-entry, and the farther fact that, without the gates they had nothing to expect except poor, hard, uninviting service in Thrace. With soldiers already possessed by an overpowering impulse of this nature, what chance was there that a retiring general, on the point of quitting the army, could so work upon their minds as to induce them to renounce the prey before them? Xenophon had nothing to invoke except distant considerations, partly of Hellenic reputation, chiefly of prudence; considerations indeed of unquestionable reality and prodigious magnitude, yet belonging all to a distant future, and therefore of little comparative force, except when set forth in magnified characters by the orator. How powerfully he worked upon the minds of his hearers, so as to draw forth these far-removed dangers from the cloud of present sentiment by which they were overlaid — how skilfully he employed in illustration the example of his own native city — will be seen by all who study his speech. Never did his Athenian accomplishments — his talent for giving words to important thoughts — his promptitude in seizing a present situation and managing the sentiments of an impetuous multitude — appear to greater advantage than when he was thus suddenly called forth to meet a terrible emergency. His pre-established reputation and the habit of obeying his orders, were doubtless essential conditions of success. But none of his colleagues in command would have been able to accomplish the like memorable change on the minds of the soldiers, or to procure obedience for any simple authoritative restraint ; nay, it is probable, that if Xenophon had not been at hand, the other generals would have followed the passionate movement, even though they had been reluctant — from simple inability to repress it. Again — whatever might have been the accomplishments of Xenophon, it is certain that even *he* would not have been able to work upon the minds of these excited soldiers, had they not been Greeks and citizens as well as soldiers, — bred in Hellenic sympathies and accustomed to Hellenic order, with authority operating in part through voice and persuasion, and not through the Persian whip and instruments of torture. The memorable discourse on the Thrakion at Byzantium illustrates the working of that persuasive agency which formed one of the permanent forces and conspicuous charms of Hellenism. It teaches us that if the orator could sometimes accuse innocent defendants and pervert well-disposed assemblies — a part of the case which historians of Greece often present as if it were the whole — he could also, and that in the most trying emergencies, combat the strongest force of present passion, and bring into vivid presence the half-obscured lineaments of long-sighted reason and duty.

§ 19. **The army finally leaves Byzantium; Seuthes offers to hire them.**

After conducting the army out of the city, Xenophon sent, through Kleander, a message to Anaxibius, requesting that he himself might be allowed to come in again singly, in order to take his departure by sea. His request was granted, though not without much difficulty; upon which he took leave of the army under the strongest expressions of affection and gratitude on their part and went into Byzantium along with Kleander; while on the next day Kœratadas came to assume the command according to agreement, bringing with him a prophet, and beasts to be offered in sacrifice. There followed in his train twenty men carrying sacks of barley-meal, twenty more with jars of wine, three bearing olives, and one man with a bundle of garlic and onions. All these provisions being laid down, Kœratadas proceeded to offer sacrifice, as a preliminary to the distribution of them among the soldiers. On the first day, the sacrifices being unfavorable, no distribution took place; on the second day, Kœratadas was standing with the wreath on his head at the altar, and with the victims beside him, about to renew his sacrifice — when Timasion and the other officers interfered, desired him to abstain, and dismissed him from the command. Perhaps the first unfavorable sacrifices may have partly impelled them to this proceeding. But the main reason was, the scanty store, inadequate even to one day's subsistence for the army, brought by Kœratadas — and the obvious insufficiency of his means.

On the departure of Kœratadas, the army marched to take up its quarters in some Thracian villages not far from Byzantium, under its former officers; who however could not agree as to their future order of march. Kleânor and Phryniskus, who had received presents from Seuthês, urged the expediency of accepting the service of that Thracian prince: Neon insisted on going to Chersonese, to be under the Lacedæmonian officers in that peninsula (as Anaxibius had projected); in the idea that he, as a Lacedæmonian, would there obtain the command of the whole army; while Timasion, with the view of re-establishing himself in his native city of Dardanus, proposed returning to the Asiatic side of the strait.

Though this last plan met with decided favor among the army, it could not be executed without vessels. These Timasion had little or no means of procuring; so that considerable delay took place, during which the soldiers, receiving no pay, fell into much distress. Many of them were even compelled to sell their arms in order to get subsistence; while others got permission to settle in some of the neighboring towns, on condition of being disarmed. The whole army was thus gradually melting away, much to the satisfaction of Anaxibius, who was anxious to see the purposes of Pharnabazus accomplished. By degrees, it would probably have been dissolved altogether, had not a change of interest on the part of Anaxibius induced him to promote its reorganization. He sailed from Byzantium to the Asiatic coast, to acquaint Pharnabazus that the Cyreians could no longer cause uneasiness, and to require his own promised reward. It seems moreover that Xenophon himself departed from Byzantium by the same opportunity. When they reached Kyzikus, they met the Lacedæmonian Aristarchus; who was coming out as a newly-appointed governor of Byzantium, to supersede Kleander, and who acquainted Anaxibius that Polus was on the point of arriving to supersede him as admiral. Anxious to meet Pharnabazus and make sure of his bribe, Anaxibius impressed his parting injunction upon Aristarchus to sell for slaves all the Cyreians whom he might find at Byzantium on his arrival, and then pursued his voyage along the southern coast of the Propontis to Parium. But Pharnabazus, having already received intimation of the change of admirals, knew that the friendship of Anaxibius was no longer of any value, and took no farther heed of him; while he at the same time sent to Byzantium to make the like compact with Aristarchus against the Cyreian army.

Anaxibius was stung to the quick at this combination of disappointment and insult on the part of the satrap. To avenge it, he resolved to employ those very soldiers whom he had first corruptly and fraudulently brought across to Europe, cast out from Byzantium, and lastly, ordered to be sold into slavery, so far as any might yet be found in that town. He now resolved to bring them back into Asia for the purpose of acting against Pharnabazus. Accordingly he addressed himself to Xenophon, and ordered him without a moment's delay to rejoin the army, for the purpose of keeping it together, of recalling the soldiers who had departed, and transporting the whole body across into Asia. He provided him with an armed vessel of thirty oars to cross over from Parium to Perinthus, sending over a peremptory order to the Perinthians to furnish him with horses in order that he might reach the army with the greatest speed. Perhaps it would not have been safe for Xenophon to disobey this order, under any circumstances. But the idea of acting with the army in Asia against Pharnabazus, under Lacedæmonian sanction, was probably very acceptable to him. He hastened across to the army, who welcomed his return with joy, and gladly embraced the proposal of crossing to Asia, which was a great improvement upon their forlorn and destitute condition. He accordingly conducted them to Perinthus, and encamped under the walls of the town; refusing, in his way through Selymbria, a second proposition from Seuthês to engage the services of the army.

While Xenophon was exerting himself to procure transports for the passage of the army at Perinthus, Aristarchus, the new governor, arrived there with two triremes from Byzantium. It seems that not only Byzantium, but also both Perinthus and Selymbria, were comprised in his government as governor. On first reaching Byzantium to supersede Kleander, he found there no less than 400 of the Cyreians, chiefly sick and wounded; whom Kleander, in spite of the ill-will of Anaxibius, had not only refused to sell into slavery, but had billeted[1] upon the citizens, and tended with solicitude; so much did his good feeling towards Xenophon and towards the army now come into play. We read with indignation that Aristarchus, immediately on reaching Byzantium to supersede him, was not even contented with sending these 400 men out of the town; but seized them, — Greeks, citizens, and soldiers as they were — and sold them all into slavery. Apprised of the movements of Xenophon with the army, he now came to Perinthus to prevent their transit into Asia; laying an embargo on the transports in the harbor, and presenting himself personally before the assembled army to prohibit the soldiers from crossing. When Xenophon informed him that Anaxibius had given them orders to cross, and had sent him expressly to conduct them — Aristarchus replied, "Anaxibius is no longer in functions as admiral, and I am governor in this town. If I catch any of you at sea, I will sink you." On the next day, he sent to invite the generals

---

[1] **Billeted upon the citizens**: assigned them quarters among the citizens, who were thus bound to provide for them.

and the captains to a conference within the walls. They were just about to enter the gates, when Xenophon, who was among them, received a private warning, that if he went in, Aristarchus would seize him, and either put him to death or send him prisoner to Pharnabazus. Accordingly Xenophon sent forward the others, and remained himself with the army, alleging the obligation of sacrificing. The behavior of Aristarchus — who, when he saw the others without Xenophon, sent them away, and desired that they would all come again in the afternoon — confirmed the justice of his suspicions, as to the imminent danger from which he had been preserved by this accidental warning. It need hardly be added that Xenophon disregarded the second invitation no less than the first; moreover, a third invitation, which Aristarchus afterwards sent, was disregarded by all.

We have here a Lacedæmonian governor, not scrupling to lay a snare of treachery, as flagrant as that which Tissaphernês had practised on the banks of the Zab, to entrap Klearchus and his colleagues — and that too against a Greek, and an officer of the highest station and merit, who had just saved Byzantium from pillage, and was now actually in execution of orders received from the Lacedæmonian admiral Anaxibius. Assuredly, had the accidental warning been withheld, Xenophon would not have escaped falling into this snare; nor could we reasonably have charged him with imprudence — so fully was he entitled to count upon straightforward conduct under the circumstances. But the same cannot be said of Klearchus, who manifested lamentable credulity, nefarious as was the fraud to which he fell a victim.

At the second interview with the other officers, Aristarchus, while he forbade the army to cross the water, directed them to force their way by land through the Thracians who occupied the Holy Mountain, and thus to arrive at the Chersonese; where (he said) they should receive pay. Neon the Lacedæmonian, with about 800 heavy-armed foot-soldiers who adhered to his separate command, advocated this plan as the best. To be set against it, however, there was the proposition of Seuthês to take the army into pay; which Xenophon was inclined to prefer, uneasy at the thoughts of being cooped up in the narrow peninsula of the Chersonese, under the absolute command of the Lacedæmonian governor, with great uncertainty both as to pay and as to provisions. Moreover it was imperiously necessary for these disappointed troops to make some immediate movement: for they had been brought to the gates of Perinthus in hopes of passing immediately on shipboard; it was midwinter — they were encamped in the open field, under the severe cold of Thrace — they had neither assured supplies, nor even money to purchase, if a market had been near. Xenophon, who had brought them to the neighborhood of Perinthus, was now again responsible for extricating them from this untenable situation; and began to offer sacrifices, according to his wont, to ascertain whether the gods would encourage him to recommend a covenant with Seuthês. The sacrifices were so favorable, that he himself, together with a confidential officer from each of the generals, went by night and paid a visit to Seuthês, for the purpose of understanding distinctly his offers and purposes.

Mæsadês, the father of Seuthês, had been apparently a dependent prince under the great monarchy of the Odrysian[1] Thracians; so formidable in the early years of the Peloponnesian war. But political commotions had robbed him of his principality over three Thracian tribes; which it was now the ambition of Seuthês to recover, by the aid of the Cyreian army. He offered to each soldier one stater of Kyzikus (or nearly the same as that which they originally received from Cyrus) as pay per month; twice as much to each captain — four times as much to each of the generals. In case they should incur the enmity of the Lacedæmonians by joining him, he guaranteed to them all the right of settlement and fraternal protection in his territory. To each of the generals, over and above pay, he engaged to assign a fort on the sea-coast, with a lot of land around it, and oxen for cultivation. And to Xenophon in particular, he offered the possession of Bisanthê, his best point on the coast. "I will also (he added, addressing Xenophon) give you my daughter in marriage; and if you have any daughter, I will buy her from you in marriage according to the custom of Thrace." Seuthês farther engaged never on any occasion to lead them more than seven days' journey from the sea, at farthest.

§ 20. The army enters the service of Seuthês.

These offers were as liberal as the army could possibly expect; and Xenophon himself, mistrusting the Lacedæmonians as well as mistrusted by them, seems to have looked forward to the acquisition of a Thracian coast-fortress and territory (such as Miltiadês, Alkibiadês, and other Athenian leaders had obtained before him) as a valuable refuge in case of need. But even if the promise had

[1] **Odrysian:** from Odrysæ, a numerous and powerful people of Thrace.

been less favorable, the Cyreians had no alternative; for they had not even present supplies — still less any means of subsistence throughout the winter; while departure by sea was rendered impossible by the Lacedæmonians. On the next day, Seuthês was introduced by Xenophon and the other generals to the army, who accepted his offers and concluded the bargain.

They remained for two months in his service, engaged in warfare against various Thracian tribes, whom they enabled him to conquer and despoil; so that at the end of that period, he was in possession of an extensive dominion, a large native force, and a considerable tribute. Though the suffering from cold was extreme, during these two months of full winter and amidst the snowy mountains of Thrace, the army were nevertheless enabled by their expeditions along with Seuthês to procure plentiful subsistence; which they could hardly have done in any other manner. But the pay which he had offered was never liquidated; at least, in requital of their two months of service, they received pay only for twenty days and a little more. And Xenophon himself, far from obtaining fulfilment of those splendid promises which Seuthês had made to him personally, seems not even to have received his pay as one of the generals. For him, the result was singularly unhappy; since he forfeited the good-will of Seuthês by importunate demand and complaint for the purpose of obtaining the pay due to the soldiers; while they on their side, imputing to his connivance the non-fulfilment of the promise, became thus in part alienated from him. Much of his mischief was brought about by the treacherous intrigues and calumny of a corrupt Greek from Maroneia, named Heraklcidês; who acted as minister and treasurer to Seuthês.

Want of space compels me to omit the narrative given by Xenophon, both of the relations of the army with Suethês, and of the warfare carried on against the hostile Thracian tribes — interesting as it is from the juxtaposition of Greek and Thracian manners. It seems to have been composed by Xenophon under feelings of acute personal disappointment, and probably in refutation of calumnies against himself as if he had wronged the army. Hence we may trace in it a tone of exaggerated querulousness, and complaint that the soldiers were ungrateful to him. It is true that a portion of the army, under the belief that he had been richly rewarded by Seuthês while they had not obtained their stipulated pay, expressed virulent sentiments and falsehoods against him. Until such suspicions were refuted, it is no wonder that the army were alienated; but they were perfectly willing to hear both sides — and Xenophon triumphantly disproved the accusation. That in the end, their feelings towards him were those of esteem and favor, stands confessed in his own words, proving that the ingratitude of which he complains was the feeling of some indeed, but not of all.

It is hard to say however what would have been the fate of this gallant army, when Seuthês, having obtained from their arms in two months all that he desired, had become only anxious to send them off without pay — had they not been extricated by a change of interest and policy on the part of all-powerful Sparta. The Lacedæmonians had just declared war against Tissaphernês and Pharnabazus; sending Thimbron into Asia to commence military operations. They then became extremely anxious to transport the Cyreians across to Asia, which their governor Aristarchus had hitherto prohibited — and to take them into permanent pay; for which purpose two Lacedæmonians, Charmînus and Polynîkus, were commissioned by Thimbron to offer to the army the same pay as he had promised, though not paid, by Seuthês; and as had been originally paid by Cyrus. Seuthês and Herakleidês, eager to hasten the departure of the soldiers, endeavored to take credit with the Lacedæmonians for assisting their views. Joyfully did the army accept this offer, though complaining loudly of the fraud practised upon them by Seuthês; which Charmînus, at the instance of Xenophon, vainly pressed the Thracian prince to redress. He even sent Xenophon to demand the arrear of pay in the name of the Lacedæmonians, which afforded to the Athenian an opportunity of administering a severe lecture to Seuthês. But the latter was not found so accessible to the workings of eloquence as the Cyreian assembled soldiers. Nor did Xenophon obtain anything beyond a miserable dividend upon the sum due:—together with evil expressions towards himself personally—an invitation to remain in his service with 1000 heavy-armed soldiers instead of going to Asia with the army—and renewed promises, not likely now to find much credit, of a fort and a grant of lands.

§ 21. **Xenophon crosses over with the army to Asia.**

When the army, now reduced by losses and dispersions, to 6000 men, was prepared to cross into Asia, Xenophon was desirous of going back to Athens, but was persuaded to remain with them until the junction with Thimbron. He was at this time so poor, having scarcely enough to pay for his journey home, that he was obliged to sell his horse at Lampsakus, the Asiatic town where the army landed. Here he found Eukleidês, a Phliasian[1] prophet with whom he had been wont to hold intercourse and offer sacrifice at Athens. This man, having asked Xenophon how much he had acquired in the expedition, could not believe him when he affirmed his poverty. But when they proceeded to offer sacrifice together, from some animals sent by the Lampsakenes as a present to Xenophon, Eukleidês had no sooner inspected the entrails of the victims, than he told Xenophon that he fully credited the statement. "I see (he said) that even if money shall be ever on its way to come to you, you yourself will be a hindrance to it, even if there be no other (here Xenophon acquiesced): Zeus (the Gracious[2]) is the real bar. Have you ever sacrificed to him, with entire burnt-offerings, as we used to do together at Athens?" "Never (replied Xenophon), throughout the whole march." "Do so now, then (said Eukleidês), and it will be for your advantage." The next day, on reaching Ophrynium, Xenophon obeyed the injunction; sacrificing little pigs entire to Zeus the Gracious, as was the custom at Athens during the public festival called Diasia.[3] And on the very same day he felt the beneficial effects of the proceeding; for Biton and another envoy came from the Lacedæmonians with an advance of pay to the army, and

[1] Phliasian: from Phliûs, a city of Peloponnesus.

[2] It appears that the epithet (the Gracious) is here applied to Zeus in the same conciliatory sense as the denomination *Eumenides* (Well or Kindly-disposed) to the avenging goddesses. Zeus is conceived as having actually inflicted, or being in a disposition to inflict, evil: the sacrifice to him under this surname represents a sentiment of fear, and is one of atonement, expiation, or purification, destined to avert his displeasure; but the surname itself is to be interpreted so as to designate, not the actual disposition of Zeus (or of other gods), but that disposition which the sacrifice is intended to bring about in him. (Grote.)

[3] Diasia: a Greek festival, celebrated in honor of Zeus (Jupiter) the Gracious.

dispositions so favorable to himself, that they bought back for him his horse, which he had just sold at Lampsakus for fifty darics. This was equivalent to giving him more than one year's pay in hand (the pay which he would have received as general being four darics per month, or four times that of the soldier), at a time when he was known to be on the point of departure, and therefore would not stay to earn it. The shortcomings of Seuthês were now made up with immense interest, so that Xenophon became better off than any man in the army; though he himself slurs over the magnitude of the present, by representing it as a delicate compliment to restore to him a favorite horse.

Thus gratefully and instantaneously did Zeus the Gracious respond to the sacrifice which Xenophon, after a long omission, had been admonished by Eukleidês to offer. And doubtless Xenophon was more than ever confirmed in the belief, which manifests itself throughout all his writings, that sacrifice not only indicates, by the interior aspect of the immolated victims, the tenor of coming events — but also, according as it is rendered to the right god and at the right season, determines his will, and therefore the course of events, for dispensations favorable or unfavorable.

But the favors of Zeus the Gracious, though begun, were not yet ended. Xenophon conducted the army through the Troad,[1] and across Mount Ida, to Antandrus; from thence along the coast of Lydia, through the plain of Thêbê and the town Adramyttium, leaving Atarneus on the right hand, to Pergamus[2] in Mysia; a hill town over-

---

[1] **Troad**: the plain around Troy, the scene of the famous Trojan war, celebrated in Homer's Iliad.

[2] **Pergamus**: a city noted for its library of over 200,000 manuscript rolls,

hanging the river and plain of Kaikus. This district was occupied by the descendants of the Eretrian[1] Gongylus, who, having been banished, for embracing the cause of the Persians when Xerxes invaded Greece, had been rewarded (like the Spartan king Demaratus) with this sort of principality under the Persian empire. His descendant, another Gongylus, now occupied Pergamus, with his wife Hellas and his sons Gorgion and Gongylus. Xenophon was here received with great hospitality. Hellas acquainted him, that a powerful Persian, named Asidatês, was now dwelling, with his wife, family, and property, in a tower not far off on the plain; and that a sudden night march, with 300 men, would suffice for the capture of this valuable booty, to which her own cousin should guide him. Accordingly, having sacrificed and ascertained that the victims were favorable, Xenophon communicated his plan after the evening meal to those captains who had been most attached to him throughout the expedition, wishing to make them partners in the profit. As soon as it became known, many volunteers, to the number of 600, pressed to be allowed to join. But the captains repelled them, declining to take more than 300, in order that the booty might afford an ampler dividend to each partner.

Beginning their march in the evening, Xenophon and his detachment of 300 reached about midnight the tower of Asidatês. It was large, lofty, thickly built, and contained a considerable garrison. It served for protection to his cattle and cultivating slaves around, like a baronial castle in the Middle Ages; but the assailants neglected

which were eventually removed to Alexandria, Egypt. Parchment, a name derived from this place, was invented here.

[1] **Eretrian**: pertaining to Eretria, a city of Ionia, Asia Minor.

this outlying plunder, in order to be more sure of taking the castle itself. Its walls however were found much stronger than was expected; and although a breach was made by force about daybreak, yet so vigorous was the defence of the garrison, that no entrance could be effected. Signals and shouts of every kind were made by Asidatês to procure aid from the Persian forces in the neighborhood; numbers of whom soon began to arrive, so that Xenophon and his company were obliged to retreat. And their retreat was at last only accomplished, after severe suffering and wounds to nearly half of them, through the aid of Gongylus with his forces from Pergamus, and of Proklês (the descendant of Demaratus) from Halisarna, a little farther off seaward.

Though his first enterprise thus miscarried, Xenophon soon laid plans for a second, employing the whole army; and succeeded in bringing Asidatês prisoner to Pergamus, with his wife, children, horses, and all his personal property. Thus (says he, anxious above all things for the credit of sacrificial prophecy) the "previous sacrifices (those which had promised favorably before the first unsuccessful attempt) now came true." The persons of this family were doubtless redeemed by their Persian friends for a large ransom; which, together with the booty brought in, made up a prodigious total to be divided.

In making the division, a general tribute of sympathy and admiration was paid to Xenophon, in which all the army — generals, captains, and soldiers — and the Lacedæmonians besides — unanimously concurred. Like Agamemnon at Troy, he was allowed to select for himself the picked lots of horses, mules, oxen, and other items of booty; insomuch that he became possessor of a share valuable enough to enrich him at once, in addition to the fifty darics which he had before received. "Here then Xenophon (to use his own language) had no reason to complain of the god" (Zeus the Gracious). We may add — what he himself ought to have added, considering the accusations which he had before put forth — that neither had he any reason to complain of the ingratitude of the army.

### § 22. Xenophon takes leave of the army. Conclusion.

As soon as Thimbron arrived with his own forces, and the Cyreians became a part of his army, Xenophon took his leave of them. Having deposited in the temple at Ephesus[1] that portion which had been confided to him as general, of the tenth set apart by the army at Kerasus for the Ephesian Artemis, he seems to have executed his intention of returning to Athens. He must have arrived there, after an absence of about two years and a half, within a few weeks, at farthest, after the death of his friend and preceptor Sokratês,[2] whose trial and condemnation have

---

[1] **Temple of Ephesus**: sacred to the goddess Artemis, or Diana, twin sister of Apollo. This temple ranked among the Seven Wonders of the world. It was held so sacred that it was used as a "safe-deposit" for treasures, which were secure here against robbery or war. See the interesting reference to it in Acts xix. 24-41.

[2] **Sokrates**: the philosopher and moralist, and the friend and instructor of Xenophon, had publicly taught, in the streets of Athens, for thirty years. His method was to convince people how little they really knew, by asking a series of searching questions which eventually led those whom he interrogated to confess their ignorance. "He taught that it is better to suffer wrong than to do wrong; and that the gods wished men to know them, not by beliefs and observances, but by doing good." This teaching, which was misunderstood by many, together with the dislike — not to say hatred — which such a "cross-examining missionary" would inevitably excite, caused his trial for impiety or rejection of the popular deities. He was then over seventy. When asked

been recorded in my last volume. That melancholy event certainly occurred during his absence from Athens; but whether it had come to his knowledge before he reached the city, we do not know. How much grief and indignation it excited in his mind, we may see by his collection of memoranda respecting the life and conversations of Sokratês, known by the name of Memorabilia, and probably put together shortly after his arrival.

That he was again in Asia three years afterwards, on military service under the Lacedæmonian king Agesilaus, is a fact attested by himself; but at what precise moment he quitted Athens for his second visit to Asia, we are left to conjecture. I incline to believe that he did not remain many months at home, but that he went out again in the next spring to rejoin the Cyreians in Asia — became again their commander — and served for two years under the Spartan general Derkyllidas before the arrival of Agesilaus. Such military service would doubtless be very much to his taste; while a residence at Athens, then subject and quiescent, would probably be distasteful to him; both from the habits of command which he had contracted during the previous two years, and from feelings arising out of the death of Sokratês. After a certain interval of repose, he would be disposed to enter again upon the war against his old enemy Tissaphernês; and his service went on when Agesilaus arrived to take the command.

But during the two years after this latter event, Athens

whether he had prepared his defence, he replied "that his whole life had been a preparation, since he had spent it in studying what was right and endeavoring to do it." Condemned by the judges to drink poison, he spent the last hours of his life conversing with his friends on the immortality of the soul. Xenophon has left an entertaining and valuable sketch of his beloved master.

became a party to the war against Sparta, and entered into conjunction with the king of Persia as well as with the Thebans and others; while Xenophon, continuing his service as commander of the Cyreians, and accompanying Agesilaus from Asia back into Greece, became engaged against the Athenian troops and their Bœotian allies at the bloody battle of Korôneia. Under these circumstances, we cannot wonder that the Athenians passed sentence of banishment against him;[1] not because he had originally taken part in aid of Cyrus against Artaxerxês — nor because his political sentiments were unfriendly to democracy, as has been sometimes erroneously affirmed — but because he was now openly in arms, and in conspicuous command, against his own country. Having thus become an exile, Xenophon was allowed by the Lacedæmonians to settle at Skillûs, one of the villages of Triphylia, near Olympia in Peloponnesus, which they had recently emancipated from the Eleians. At one of the ensuing Olympic festivals,[2] Megabyzus, the superintendent of the temple of Artemis at Ephesus, came over as a spectator; bringing with him the money which Xenophon had dedicated therein to the Ephesian Artemis. This money Xenophon invested in the purchase of lands at Skillûs, to be consecrated in permanence to the goddess; having previously consulted her by sacrifice to ascertain her approval of the site contemplated, which site was recommended to him by its resemblance in certain points to that of the Ephesian

[1] **Banished:** Xenophon was banished for attachment to Sparta against his country — Athens. (Grote.)

[2] **Olympic festivals:** the greatest of the religious festivals among the Greeks. It was held at Olympia every four years in honor of Zeus (Olympian Jove), and was celebrated by games and contests lasting several weeks. All Greece sent delegations to attend and take part in the festival.

temple. Thus, there was near each of them a river called by the same name Selinûs, having in it fish and a shelly bottom. Xenophon constructed a chapel, an altar, and a statue of the goddess made of cypress-wood: all exact copies, on a reduced scale, of the temple and golden statue at Ephesus. A column placed near them was inscribed with the following words — "This spot is sacred to Artemis. Whoever possesses the property and gathers its fruits, must sacrifice to her the tenth every year, and keep the chapel in repair out of the remainder. Should any one omit this duty, the goddess herself will take the omission in hand."

Immediately near the chapel was an orchard of every description of fruit-trees, while the estate around comprised an extensive range of meadow, woodland, and mountain — with the still loftier mountain called Pholoê adjoining. There was thus abundant pasture for horses, oxen, sheep, and also excellent hunting-ground near, for deer and other game; advantages not to be found near the Artemision[1] at Ephesus. Residing hard by on his own property, allotted to him by the Lacedæmonians, Xenophon superintended this estate as steward for the goddess; looking perhaps to the sanctity of her name for protection from disturbance by the Eleians, who viewed with a jealous eye the Lacedæmonians at Skillûs, and protested against the peace and convention promoted by Athens after the battle of Leuktra, because it recognized that place, along with the townships of Triphylia, as having the right of self-government. Every year he made a splendid sacrifice, from the tenth of all the fruits of the property; to which solemnity not only all the Skilluntines, but also all the neighboring villages,

[1] **Artemision**: the temple of Artemis or Diana.

were invited. Booths were erected for the visitors, to whom the goddess furnished (this is the language of Xenophon) an ample dinner of barley-meal, wheaten loaves, meat, game, and sweetmeats; the game being provided by a general hunt, which the sons of Xenophon conducted, and in which all the neighbors took part if they chose. The produce of the estate, saving this tithe or tenth and subject to the obligation of keeping the holy building in repair, was enjoyed by Xenophon himself. He had a keen relish for both hunting and horsemanship, and was among the first authors, so far as we know, who ever made these pursuits, with the management of horses and dogs, the subject of rational study and description.

Such was the use to which Xenophon applied the tithe voted by the army at Kerasus to the Ephesian Artemis; the other tithe, voted at the same time to Apollo, he dedicated at Delphi in the treasure-chamber of the Athenians, inscribing upon the offering his own name and that of Proxenus. His residence being only at a distance of a little more than two miles from the great temple of Olympia,[1] he was enabled to enjoy society with every variety of Greeks — and to obtain copious information about Grecian politics, chiefly from philo-Laconian informants, and with the Lacedæmonian point of view predominant in his own mind; while he had also leisure for the composition of his various works. The interesting description which he himself gives of his residence at Skillûs implies a state of things not present and continuing, but past and gone;

[1] **Temple of Olympia:** the magnificent temple of Zeus (Olympian Jove). It contained a colossal statue of the god, seated, and holding the globe and the sceptre as emblems of his power. The work was by the celebrated sculptor Phidias, and was carved in gold and ivory.

other testimonies too, though confused and contradictory, seem to show that the Lacedæmonian settlement at Skillûs lasted no longer than the power of Lacedæmon was adequate to maintain it. During the misfortunes which befell that city after the battle of Leuktra (371 B.C.), Xenophon, with his family and his fellow-settlers, was expelled by the Eleians, and is then said to have found shelter at Corinth. But as Athens soon came to be not only at peace, but in intimate alliance, with Sparta — the sentence of banishment against Xenophon was revoked; so that the latter part of his life was again passed in the enjoyment of his birthright as an Athenian citizen and Knight.[1] Two of his sons, Gryllus and Diodorus, fought among the Athenian horsemen at the cavalry combat which preceded the battle of Mantineia, where the former was slain, after manifesting distinguished bravery; while his grandson Xenophon became in the next generation the subject of a pleading before the Athenian court of justice, composed by the orator Deinarchus.

On bringing this accomplished and eminent leader to the close of that arduous retreat which he had conducted with so much honor, I have thought it necessary to anticipate a little on the future in order to take a glance at his subsequent destiny. To his exile (in this point of view not less useful than that of Thucydidês) we probably owe many of those compositions from which so much of our knowledge of Grecian affairs is derived. But to the contemporary world, the retreat, which Xenophon so successfully conducted, afforded a far more impressive lesson than any of his literary compositions. It taught in the most

---

[1] **Knight**: originally one of an upper class of citizens ranking second in point of wealth and political power.

striking manner the impotence of the Persian land-force, manifested not less in the generals than in the soldiers. It proved that the Persian leaders were unfit for any systematic operations, even under the greatest possible advantages, against a small number of disciplined warriors resolutely bent on resistance; that they were too stupid and reckless even to obstruct the passage of rivers, or destroy roads, or cut off supplies. It more than confirmed the contemptuous language applied to them by Cyrus himself, before the battle of Kunaxa; when he proclaimed that he envied the Greeks their freedom, and that he was ashamed of the worthlessness of his own countrymen. Against such perfect weakness and disorganization, nothing prevented the success of the Greeks along with Cyrus, except his own paroxysm of fraternal antipathy. And we shall perceive hereafter the military and political leaders of Greece — Agesilaus, Jason of Pheræ, and others down to Philip and Alexander[1] — firmly persuaded that with a tolerably numerous and well-appointed Grecian force, combined with exemption from Grecian enemies, they could succeed in overthrowing or dismembering the Persian empire. This conviction, so important in the subsequent history of Greece, takes its date from the retreat of the Ten Thousand. We shall indeed find Persia exercising an important influence, for two generations to come — and at the peace of Antalkidas an influence stronger than ever — over the destinies of Greece. But this will be seen to arise from the treason of Sparta, the chief of the Hellenic world, who abandons the Asiatic Greeks, and even arms herself with the name and the force of Persia, for purposes

[1] Alexander the Great encouraged his soldiers before the battle of Issus by referring to the bravery of the Greeks in the " Retreat of the Ten Thousand."

of aggrandizement and dominion to herself. Persia is strong by being enabled to employ Hellenic strength against the Hellenic cause; by lending money or a fleet to one side or the other of the Grecian parties, and thus becoming artificially strengthened against both. But the Xenophontic Anabasis [1] betrays her real weakness against any vigorous attack; while it at the same time exemplifies the discipline, the endurance, the power of self-action and adaptation, the susceptibility of influence from speech and discussion, the combination of the reflecting obedience of citizens with the mechanical regularity of soldiers — which confer such immortal distinction on the Hellenic character. The importance of this expedition and retreat, as an illustration of the Hellenic qualities and excellence, will justify the large space which has been devoted to it in this History.

[1] **Anabasis** (The March Up-country): the name given by Xenophon to his account of the expedition of Cyrus the younger in his march from the shore of the Mediterranean against the King of Persia at Babylon. The narrative of the "Retreat of the Ten Thousand" forms part of the "Anabasis." Strictly speaking, this portion of the work should be called the Katabasis, or "The March Down"; that is, from Babylonia to the Black Sea.

# SKETCH OF NAPOLEON.

(INTRODUCTORY TO THE RETREAT FROM MOSCOW.)

NAPOLEON BONAPARTE was born at Ajaccio, Corsica (then recently ceded to France), in 1769. He was of Italian descent, and up to the age of ten could speak no French. In 1779 he was sent to the military school of Brienne, in France, and there began his education for the army. As a lieutenant of artillery he did good service in behalf of the French revolutionary government at the siege of Toulon, which had revolted in 1793.

Two years later that government was threatened by the rising of the people of Paris, headed by the National Guard. General Barras gave Napoleon an opportunity of showing his military skill in defence of the authorities, and the young officer, with his well-directed volleys of grape-shot, speedily quelled the insurrection. From that time Napoleon's name became familiar to the French people.

In 1796 he married Madame Josephine Beauharnais, a West Indian lady, whose husband had been guillotined during the Revolution. About the same time Napoleon received the command of the French army of Italy, and with his successful Italian campaign against Austria his reputation as a general began.

From that date until his final abdication in 1815, he was almost constantly engaged in active war, or in preparations for it. During that period of twenty years he fought nearly the whole of Europe; and up to his fatal Russian campaign in 1812, he was victorious in every great battle which he personally directed in the open field. This constant success inspired him with the belief that he was invincible. As one of his friends said, " He appeared like a man walking in a halo of glory " ; and as an eminent statesman declared,

"France gave herself to him, absorbed herself in him, and seemed, at one time, no longer to think, except through him." From a simple artillery officer Napoleon had risen to be the greatest military commander in the world. His adopted country had placed him at the head of the government, and ended by making him Emperor. By his conquests he had enlarged France so that his imperial dominions extended to the Baltic on the north, and beyond Rome on the southeast.

To increase his glory and strengthen his power, he established a circle of dependent thrones and principalities, occupied by his brothers and his favorites, who were bound to obey his will and extend his sway.

Of all the nations of Europe, England alone had been able to withstand him; and in 1812 London, Moscow, and St. Petersburg were the only leading capitals whose streets his triumphant armies had not entered.

It was when he was at the apparent summit of his power that Napoleon divorced his faithful Josephine, in order that he might marry the Princess Maria Louisa, daughter of the emperor of Austria. His object was to found a reigning family allied by blood with one of the oldest and proudest dynasties of Europe. In this, as in all other things, he seemed to accomplish his purpose, for from this union a son was born who, under the title of the "King of Rome," promised to perpetuate his father's name and power.

Having secured an heir to his crown Napoleon now determined to rigorously carry out his "continental policy" of humbling England by shutting out her trade from every port of Europe. If this could be done effectually, as he believed was possible, he might hope to starve his old enemy into submission.

The attempt to accomplish this design was the chief cause of the campaign against Russia, and of Napoleon's ultimate downfall. The Czar, contrary to the provisions of the treaty of Tilsit, made in 1807, was now opposed to continuing the blockade which excluded English commerce from the Baltic. Not only did the

Russian sovereign refuse to yield on this point, but he went so far as to form an alliance with Sweden, in order to resist the French Emperor's demands more effectually.

Napoleon accordingly declared war, and in the spring of 1812 began gathering a force of over 600,000 men for the invasion of Russia. The Grand Army was chiefly French; but the Emperor compelled his allies — Austria, Prussia, Italy, and the German States — to furnish large numbers of troops; and he also received help from Poland. Besides the Imperial Guard, a body of picked men over 50,000 strong, under the command of Marshals Lefebvre, Mortier, and Bessières, there were 13 corps. The French were led by Marshals Davoust, Oudinot, Ney, Murat, King of Naples; the Italians by Prince Eugene; the Poles by Poniatowski; the Austrians by General Schwartzenberg; the Germans and Prussians by St. Cyr, Regnier, Vandamme, Victor, Macdonald, and Augereau.

The Poles fought for Napoleon in the belief that, if successful, he would secure their independence against the power of Russian oppression; the other nations because they dared not refuse.

This enormous force, which was double that of the Czar's, gradually collected on the banks of the Niemen, a river emptying into the Baltic, and forming part of the western boundary of Russia. The army crossed it in three divisions, at a considerable distance from each other.[1] All were to meet at Wilna, a Polish city which Russia had seized in the dismemberment of that country, and which was about fifty miles southeast of the Niemen.

Napoleon himself, at the head of one of the three divisions, with a force of over two hundred thousand, crossed the river at Kowno on the 23d of June, and began his march for Wilna.[2] The weather was intensely hot, and in the course of a few weeks

---

[1] Namely, at Kowno, Pilony, south of Kowno, and Grodno, still further south. At Kowno a monument bears the following inscription in Russian: "In 1812 Russia was invaded by an army numbering 700,000 men. The army recrossed the frontier numbering 70,000."

[2] See map facing p. 1. The upper dotted line represents the advance to Moscow; the lower, the line of retreat from that city.

many thousand men fell out of the ranks through sickness and fatigue, and great numbers of horses died. The French hoped to encounter the Russian forces in a decisive battle before advancing far into the country. But it was the policy of the Czar not to fight, but to keep falling back, destroying all supplies as fast as he retreated, and so compelling the French to depend wholly upon their own resources.

Napoleon himself confessed that the Russians had the advantage. They, he said, would be animated by love of their native land to repel invasion, and all private and public interests would unite them. The French, on the other hand, had nothing to urge them on but the love of conquest and of glory, without even the hope of plunder, for in those desolate regions there was nothing they could seize.

The first real encounter was at Smolensk, a walled city on the Dnieper, about half way between Wilna and the ancient capital of Russia. After a day of hard fighting, the Russians fired the city and abandoned it. The French entered the smoking ruins. They were victors, but such a victory was almost as disheartening as a defeat. From that place a weary seven-days march brought the Grand Army to the village of Borodino, on the banks of the Kologa, a tributary of the Moskwa.[1] Here the Russian general, Kutusoff, had determined to make a stand in defence of that holy city of Moscow, not many leagues distant, for which every peasant stood ready to lay down his life. The result of the battle was in favor of Napoleon, but it cost him the lives of thirty thousand men to gain it; and though the Russians lost double that number, they knew that the time was coming when the elements and the great barren spaces of their country would fight for them. This was the 7th of September. From that date the Russians resumed their old tactics and continued to slowly retreat, burning the villages and the crops as they fell back. At length, at noon of the 14th, the French emperor came in sight of " the city of the Czars."

[1] **Moskwa, Kologa**: these and other Russian geographical names are variously spelled.

## SKETCH OF NAPOLEON.

What followed from that time until Napoleon, baffled and beaten, reached Paris, leaving the wreck of the Grand Army behind him, may best be learned from the ensuing narrative of Count Ségur,[1] who was one of the generals in that army, an officer of the imperial staff, and an eye-witness of what he describes.[2]

His faithful history of that terrible disaster must necessarily be painful. It is in most respects the very opposite of Xenophon's account of the Retreat of the Ten Thousand, which precedes it. But the reader should reflect that the dark and sorrowful scenes of history may have lessons as salutary as the brighter ones; and that the story of a great failure, involving the ruin and death of thousands, may be as instructive and as helpful as the story of a great success. In Xenophon's case, we have the spectacle of a man of more than ordinary ability, stimulated by difficulty and peril until he rises to real greatness of achievement. In Napoleon's career we see a naturally "great mind dragged to ruin by its own faults"; but such a man could not fall alone, and it was inevitable that a multitude should suffer with him and for him.

D. H. M.

[1] Count Ségur was elected a member of the French Academy, and his history of the retreat has not only passed through many editions in France, but it has been translated into all the leading languages of Europe.

[2] The history of Napoleon after the Russian retreat will form the subject of a note at the close of Count Ségur's narrative.

# NAPOLEON'S RETREAT FROM MOSCOW.

### § 1. Description of Moscow; arrival of the Czar.

THE ancient capital of Russia, appropriately denominated by its poets "*Moscow*[1] *with the gilded cupolas*," was a vast and fantastic assemblage of two hundred and ninety-five churches, and fifteen hundred palaces, with their gardens and dependencies. These larger mansions of brick, and their parks, intermixed with neat houses of wood, and even thatched cottages, were spread over several square

[1] **Moscow:** the ancient capital of Russia is situated on the Moskwa river (a tributary of the Oka), from which the city derives its name. It first appears in history in the middle of the twelfth century. It early became the metropolis and seat of government, and continued so until a short time after the founding of St. Petersburg by Peter the Great, in 1703.

For centuries Moscow was both the political and religious centre of the empire. Here the Czars were crowned, here they resided, here they were buried. Here, too, the patriarch, or former head of the Russian church, had his residence, amid cathedrals, monasteries, and shrines, which have always been regarded with peculiar reverence.

To the Russian peasant the city still remains sacred. It is the heart, as it were, of his native land. He cherishes toward it the same feeling which the devout Mohammedan does for Mecca, or the devout Catholic for Rome. He calls it "Our Holy Mother Moscow"; and when he comes in sight of its gilded spires and cupolas he makes the sign of the cross, falls upon his knees, and utters a prayer.

In the centre of Moscow stands the Kremlin, or fortress — for so the Tartar name is usually translated. This famous stronghold marks the original settlement. It covers nearly a hundred acres, and is situated on an eminence on the left bank of the river. It is triangular in shape, and is surrounded by

leagues of irregular ground. They were grouped round the Kremlin, a lofty triangular fortress. The vast double enclosure in which this was situated was about two miles in circuit. It contained, first, several palaces, some churches, and rocky and uncultivated spots, and secondly, a prodigious bazaar,—the town of the merchants and shop-keepers,—where was displayed the collected wealth of the four quarters of the globe.

These palaces, these edifices, nay, the very shops themselves, were all covered with burnished and painted iron. The churches, each surmounted by a balcony and several steeples, terminating in golden balls, then the crescent, and lastly the cross, reminded the spectator of the history of this nation : it was Asia and its religion, at first victori-

a lofty stone wall, considerably more than a mile in extent, which is pierced with five gates and surmounted by eighteen commanding towers.

The Kremlin is almost a city in itself. Besides extensive barracks and an arsenal, with other government buildings, it contains the ancient palace of the Czars, a monastery, and several noted churches, one of which is the oldest and most venerated in Russia.

Formerly the entire fortification was encompassed by a broad, deep moat. This has been filled up, and now forms a spacious boulevard, with pleasure gardens, a library, a museum, and the great bazaar or market, where all kinds of merchandise are offered for sale.

At the time of the French invasion Moscow is supposed to have had a population of at least 325,000; at the present time it has more than double that number.

Napoleon entered the city September 14, 1812. That very night it was set on fire, and the conflagration continued until the whole place, outside the Kremlin, was practically a heap of bricks and ashes.

During the fire Napoleon was obliged to leave his quarters in the fortress and establish them in a suburb of the city, but later he returned to the Kremlin.

He evacuated Moscow on October 19, not quite five weeks after he entered it. He found it a great metropolis. He left it a mass of ruins, where nothing any longer existed to support life.

ous, subsequently vanquished, so that finally the cross of Christ surmounted the crescent of Mohammed.

A ray of sunshine caused this splendid city to glisten with a thousand varied colors. At sight of it the traveller paused, delighted and astonished. It reminded him of the prodigies with which the Eastern poets had amused his childhood. On entering it, a nearer view served but to heighten his astonishment: he recognized the nobles by the manners, the habits, and the different languages of modern Europe, and by the rich and airy elegance of their dress. He beheld, with surprise, the luxury and the Asiatic form of that of the traders, the peculiar costumes of the common people, and their long beards. He was struck by the same variety in the edifices; and all this was tinged with a local and sometimes harsh coloring, such as befitted the country of which Moscow was the ancient capital.

When, lastly, he observed the grandeur and magnificence of the numerous palaces, the wealth which they displayed, the luxury of the equipages, the multitude of slaves and of obsequious menials, the splendor of all these gorgeous spectacles, and heard the noise of those sumptuous festivities, entertainments, and rejoicings which incessantly resounded within its walls, he fancied himself transported to a city of kings — into the midst of an assemblage of princes, who had brought with them their manners, customs, and attendants from every quarter of the world.

These princes were nevertheless but subjects, still opulent and powerful subjects: grandees, vain of their ancient nobility, strong in their collected numbers and in the general ties of blood contracted during the seven centuries which this capital had existed. They were also landed proprietors, proud of their vast possessions; for almost the whole territory of the government of Moscow belonged to them, and they there reigned over a million of serfs.[1] Finally, they were nobles, resting with a patriotic and religious pride upon "the cradle and the tomb of their nobility"; for such is the appellation they give to Moscow.

To this ancient capital necessity brought the Czar[2] Alexander. His first appearance was in the midst of the assembled nobles. There everything was great: the circumstances, the assembly, the speaker, and the resolutions which he inspired. His voice betrayed emotion: no sooner did he cease speaking, than one simultaneous cry burst from all hearts: "Sire, ask what you please! we offer you everything! take our all!"

One of the nobles then proposed the levy of a militia, and for its formation, the gift of one peasant or serf in twenty-five. But a hundred voices interrupted him, exclaiming that "the country required a greater sacrifice; that they should grant one serf in ten, ready armed, equipped, and supplied with provisions for three months." This was offering, for the single government of Moscow, 80,000 men, and a great quantity of warlike stores.

The latter proposition was immediately voted without discussion; some say with enthusiasm; and that it was executed in like manner, so long as the danger was at hand. Others attribute the consent of the assembly to a sentiment of submission alone; which, indeed, in the presence of absolute power, is apt to absorb every other.

[1] **Serfs:** these serfs were slaves in all but name, and were bought and sold like cattle. They were emancipated by law in 1861, the whole number throughout Russia then being over 21,000,000.

[2] **Czar:** the correct Russian spelling of this word is said to be Tsar, which is now gradually coming into use in English. The title was first assumed by Ivan IV. (Ivan the Terrible) in 1533.

They add, that on the breaking up of the meeting, the principal nobles were heard to murmur among themselves against the extravagance of such a measure. "Was the danger, then, so pressing? Did the Russian army, which, as they were told, still numbered 400,000 men, no longer exist? Why deprive them of so many peasants? The service of these men would be, it is said, only temporary; but who could ever hope for their return? and was not even this an event to be dreaded? Would these serfs, habituated to the irregularities of war, bring back their former habits of submission? Undoubtedly not; they would return full of new sentiments and new ideas, with which they would infect the villages; they would there propagate a refractory spirit, which would give infinite trouble to the master by spoiling the slave."

Be this as it may, the resolution of the assembly was generous, and worthy of so great a nation. The details are of little consequence. We well know that it is the same everywhere; that everything in the world loses by being seen too near; and, lastly, that nations should be judged by the general mass and by results.

Alexander then addressed the merchants, but more briefly: he ordered the proclamation to be read to them, in which Napoleon was represented as "a perfidious wretch; a Moloch, who, with treachery in his heart and loyalty on his lips, was striving to blot out Russia from the face of the earth."

It is said that, at these words, his auditors, to whose strongly-marked and flushed faces their long beards imparted a look at once antique, majestic, and wild, were inflamed with rage. Their eyes flashed fire; they were seized with a convulsive fury, of which their stiffened arms, their clenched fists, the gnashing of their teeth, and their subdued execrations, expressed the vehemence. The effect was correspondent. Their chief, whom they elect themselves, proved himself worthy of his station: he put down his name at once for 50,000 rubles.[1] It was two-thirds of his fortune, and he paid it the next day.

These merchants were divided into three classes, and they proceeded to fix the contribution for each; but one of the assembly, who was included in the lowest class, declared that his patriotism would brook no limit, and he immediately subscribed a sum far surpassing the standard proposed: the others all followed his example more or less closely. Advantage was taken of their first emotions. Everything was at hand that was requisite to bind them irrevocably while they were yet together, excited by one another and by the words of their sovereign.

The patriotic donation amounted, it is said, to two millions of rubles. The other governments repeated, like so many echoes, the national cry of Moscow. The emperor accepted all; but all could not be given immediately; and when, in order to complete his work, he claimed the rest of the promised succor, he was obliged to have recourse to constraint, the danger which had alarmed some and inflamed others having by that time ceased to exist.

**§ 2. Alarm in Moscow at the advance of the French army; preparations for destroying the city.**

After the reduction of Smolensk,[2] and when Napoleon reached Viazma, a town about one hundred and seventy

---

[1] **Ruble** (or Rouble): a Russian silver coin worth about seventy-five cents.
[2] **Smolensk**: see Introduction, "Napoleon."

miles from Moscow, consternation reigned in Moscow. The great battle had not yet been lost, and already people began to abandon that capital.

In his proclamation, the governor-general, Count Rostopchin,[1] told the women that "he should not detain them, as the less fear there was, the less danger there would be; but that their brothers and husbands must stay, or they would cover themselves with infamy." He then added encouraging particulars concerning the hostile force, which consisted, according to his statement, of "one hundred and fifty thousand men, who were reduced to the necessity of feeding on horseflesh. The emperor Alexander was about to return to his faithful capital; eighty-three thousand Russians, recruits and militia, with eighty pieces of cannon were marching towards Borodino, to join Kutusoff."[2]

He thus concluded: "If these forces are not sufficient, I will say to you, 'Come, my Muscovite[3] friends, let us march also! We will assemble one hundred thousand men; we will take the image of the Blessed Virgin, and one hundred and fifty pieces of cannon, and put an end to the business at once!'"

It has been remarked, as a purely local singularity, that most of these proclamations were in the scriptural style, and highly poetical in their character.

At the same time, a sort of balloon of prodigious size was constructed by command of Alexander, not far from Moscow, under the direction of a German artificer. The destination of this aerial machine was to hover over the

---

[1] **Rostopchin**: (Ros-top-chen').
[2] **Kutusoff**: commander-in-chief of the Russian army.
[3] **Muscovite**: a native of Muscovy, an old name for Russia.

French army, to single out its chief, and destroy him by a shower of balls and fire. Several attempts were made to raise it, but without success, the springs by which the wings were to be worked always breaking.

Rostopchin, nevertheless, affecting to persevere in the plan, is said to have caused a great quantity of rockets and other combustibles to be prepared. Moscow itself was destined to be the great infernal machine, the sudden nocturnal explosion of which was to destroy the emperor and his army. Should the enemy escape this danger, he would at least no longer have an asylum or resources; and the horror of this tremendous calamity, charged to his account, as had been the disasters of Smolensk, Viazma, and other towns, would not fail to rouse the whole of Russia.[1]

Adverse, therefore, to any treaty, this governor foresaw that in the populous capital, which the Russians themselves style the oracle, the exemplar of the whole empire, Napoleon would have recourse to the weapon of revolution, the only one that would be left him to accomplish his purpose. For this reason he resolved to raise a barrier of fire between that great captain and all weaknesses, from whatever quarter they might proceed, whether from the throne or from his countrymen, either nobles or senators; and more especially between a population of serfs and the soldiers of a free nation; in short, between the latter and that mass of artisans and tradesmen who form in Moscow the commencement of an intermediate class; a class for which the French Revolution was especially brought about.

[1] Rostopchin denied, in a work which he published, that he set fire to the city. He insisted that it was done by the French, together with the rabble of Moscow. It is now thought that the governor began the work of destruction, which was completed partly by the Russians and partly by the French.

All the preparations were made in silence, without the knowledge either of the people, the proprietors of all classes, or perhaps of their emperor. The nation was ignorant that it was sacrificing itself. This is so strictly true, that, when the moment for execution arrived, we heard the inhabitants who had fled to the churches execrating this destruction. Those who beheld it from a distance, the most opulent of the nobles, deceived like their peasants, charged us with it: and, in short, those by whom it was ordered threw the odium of it upon us, having engaged in the work of destruction in order to render us objects of detestation, and caring but little about the maledictions of so many unfortunate creatures, provided they could throw upon us the weight of them.

The silence of Alexander leaves room to doubt whether he approved this dreadful determination or not. What part he took in the catastrophe is still a mystery to the Russians: either they are ignorant on the subject, or they make a secret of the matter: the effect of despotism, which enjoins ignorance or silence.

Some think that no individual in the empire, excepting the sovereign, would have dared to take on himself so heavy a responsibility. His subsequent conduct disavowed without disproving it. Others are of opinion that this was one of the causes of his absence from the army, and that, not wishing to appear either to order or to forbid it, he would not stay to be a witness of the catastrophe.

As to the general abandonment of the houses all the way from Smolensk, it was compulsory, the Russian army defending them till they were carried sword in hand, and describing us everywhere as destructive monsters. The country suffered but little from this emigration. The peasants residing near the high-road escaped through by-ways to other villages belonging to their lords, where they found accommodation.

The forsaking of their huts, made of trunks of trees laid one upon another, which a hatchet suffices for building, and of which a bench, a table, and an image constitute the whole furniture, was scarcely any sacrifice for serfs who had nothing of their own, whose persons did not even belong to themselves, and whose masters were obliged to provide for them, since they were their property and the source of all their income.

These peasants, moreover, in removing their carts, their implements, and their cattle, carried everything with them, most of them being able with their own hands to supply themselves with habitation, clothing, and all other necessaries: for these people are still in but the first stage of civilization, and far from that division of labor which denotes the extension and high improvement of commerce and of society.

But in the towns, and especially in the great capital, how could they be expected to quit so many establishments, to resign so many conveniences and enjoyments, so much wealth, movable and immovable? and yet it cost little or no more to obtain the total abandonment of Moscow than that of the meanest village. There, as at Vienna, Berlin, and Madrid, the principal nobles hesitated not to retire on our approach; for, with them, to remain would seem to be the same as to betray. But here, tradesmen, artisans, day-laborers, all thought it their duty to flee as well as the most powerful of the grandees. There was no occasion to command: these people have not yet ideas sufficient to judge for themselves, to distinguish and to weigh differences; the example of the nobles was sufficient. The few foreigners remaining at Moscow might have enlightened them; some of these were exiled, and terror hindered the rest.

It was, besides, an easy task to excite apprehensions of profanation, pillage, and devastation in the minds of people so cut off from other nations, and in the inhabitants of a city which had been so often plundered and burned by the Tartars. With these examples before their eyes, they could not await an impious and ferocious enemy but for the purpose of fighting him: the rest must necessarily shun his approach with horror, if they would save themselves in this life or in the next. Thus obedience, honor, religion, fear, everything, in short, enjoined them to flee, with all that they could carry with them.

A fortnight before our arrival, the departure of the records, the public chests and treasure, and that of the nobles and of the principal merchants, together with their most valuable effects, indicated to the rest of the inhabitants what course they should pursue. The governor, already impatient to see Moscow evacuated, appointed superintendents to expedite the emigration.

On the 3d of September, a French woman, living in the city, ventured to leave her hiding-place, at the risk of being torn in pieces by the furious Muscovites. She wandered a long time through extensive quarters, the solitude of which astonished her, when a distant and doleful sound thrilled her with terror. It was like the funeral dirge of this vast city: fixed in motionless suspense, she beheld an immense multitude of persons, of both sexes, in deep affliction, carrying their effects and their sacred images, and leading their children along with them. Their priests, laden with the sacred symbols of religion, headed the procession. They were invoking Heaven in hymns of lamentation, in which all of them joined with tears.

On reaching the gates of the city, this crowd of unfortunate creatures passed through them with painful hesitation : turning their eyes once more towards Moscow, they seemed to be bidding a last farewell to their holy city; but, by degrees, their sobs and the doleful tones of their hymns died away in the vast plains by which it is surrounded.

### § 3. Departure of the Russian governor from Moscow.

Thus was this population dispersed in detail or in masses. The roads were covered to the distance of forty leagues by fugitives on foot, and several unbroken files of vehicles of every kind. At the same time, the measures of Rostopchin to prevent dejection and preserve order detained many of these unfortunate people till the very last moment.

To this must be added the appointment of Kutusoff, which had revived their hopes, the false intelligence of a victory at Borodino, and, for those of moderate means, the hesitation natural at the moment of abandoning the only home which they possessed. Lastly, the inadequacy of the means of transport, either because at this time heavy requisitions for the exigencies of the army had reduced the number of vehicles, or because they were too small, as it is customary to make the carriages in this country very light, on account of the sandy soil, and of the roads, which may be said to be rather marked out than constructed.

Kutusoff, although defeated at Borodino, had sent letters to all quarters announcing that he was victorious.

He deceived Moscow, St. Petersburg, and even the commanders of the other Russian armies. Alexander communicated this false intelligence to his allies. In the first transports of his joy he hastened to the altars, loaded the army and the family of his general with honors and money, gave directions for rejoicings, returned thanks to Heaven, and appointed Kutusoff a field-marshal of the empire.

Most of the Russians affirm that their emperor was grossly imposed upon by this report. They are still unacquainted with the motives of such a deception, which at first procured Kutusoff unbounded favors, that were not withdrawn from him, and afterward, it is said, dreadful menaces, that were not put in execution.

If we may credit several of his countrymen, who were perhaps his enemies, it would appear that he had two motives. In the first place, he wished not to shake by disastrous intelligence the little firmness which, in Russia, Alexander was generally, though erroneously, thought to possess. In the second, as his despatch would probably arrive on the very birthday of his sovereign, it is added that his object was to obtain from him the rewards for which this kind of anniversaries affords occasion.

But at Moscow the delusive impression was of short continuance. The rumor of the destruction of half his army was almost immediately propagated in that city, from the singular commotion produced by extraordinary events, which is known frequently to spread almost instantaneously to prodigious distances. Still, however, the language of the chiefs, the only persons who dared to speak, continued haughty and threatening: many of the inhabitants, trusting to it, remained; but they were every day more and more tormented by a painful anxiety. At nearly one and the same moment, they were transported with rage, elevated by hope, and overwhelmed with fear.

During one of these periods of dejection and dismay, while, prostrate before the altars, or in their own houses before the images of their saints, they had abandoned all hope but in Heaven, shouts of joy were suddenly heard: the people instantly thronged the streets and the public places to learn the cause. Intoxicated with delight, their eyes were fixed on the cross of the principal church. A vulture had entangled himself in the chains which supported it, and was held suspended by them. This was a certain presage to minds whose natural superstition was heightened by extraordinary anxiety: it was thus that their God would seize and deliver Napoleon into their power.

Rostopchin took advantage of all these movements, which he excited or checked according as they were favorable to him or otherwise. He caused the most diminutive to be selected from the prisoners taken from the French, and exhibited them to the people, that the latter might derive courage from the sight of their weakness; and yet he emptied Moscow of every kind of supplies, in order to feed the vanquished and to famish the conquerors. This measure was easily carried into effect, as Moscow was provisioned in spring and autumn by water only, and in winter by sledges.

He was still attempting to preserve, with a remnant of hope, the order that was necessary, especially in such a flight, when the effects of the disaster at Borodino were fully manifested. The long train of wounded, their groans, their garments and linen dyed with blood; their most powerful nobles struck and overthrown like the rest: all this was a novel and alarming sight to a city which had for such a length of time been exempt from the horrors of war. The police redoubled their activity; but the terror which they excited could not long make head against a still greater terror.

Rostopchin once more addressed the people. He declared that "he would defend Moscow to the last extremity; that the courts were already closed, but that was of no consequence; that there was no occasion for tribunals to try the guilty": he added that "in two days he would give the signal." He recommended to the people to "arm themselves with hatchets, and especially with three-pronged forks, as the French were not heavier than a sheaf of wheat." As for the wounded, he said he should cause "masses to be said, and the water to be blessed, in order to their speedy recovery. The next day," he added, "he should repair to Kutusoff, to take final measures for exterminating the enemy."

The Russian army, in their position in front of Moscow, numbered ninety-one thousand men, six thousand of whom were Cossacks,[1] sixty-five thousand veteran troops (the remnant of one hundred and twenty-one thousand engaged at the Moskwa),[2] and twenty thousand recruits, armed half with muskets and half with pikes.

The French army, one hundred and thirty thousand strong the day before the great battle, had lost about forty

[1] **Cossacks:** a race of people inhabiting the south of Russia. On account of their great skill in horsemanship they are largely employed in the Russian army as cavalry.

[2] **Moskwa:** the French often spoke of the battle of Borodino as the Battle of the Moskwa, though it is not on that river, but on the Kologa, a tributary of it. The accounts of the number killed differ.

thousand men at Borodino, and still consisted of ninety thousand. Some regiments on the march, and the divisions of Laborde and Pino, had just joined it: so that, on its arrival before Moscow, it still amounted to nearly one hundred thousand men. Its march was retarded by six hundred and seven pieces of cannon, two thousand five hundred artillery carriages, and five thousand baggage-wagons: it had no more ammunition than would suffice for one engagement. Kutusoff perhaps calculated the disproportion between his effective force and ours. On this point, however, nothing but conjecture can be advanced, for he assigned purely military motives for his retreat.

Thus much is certain, that Kutusoff deceived Rostopchin to the very last moment. He even swore to him "by his gray hair that he would perish with him before Moscow," when all at once the governor was informed that, in a council of war held at night in the camp, it had been determined to abandon the capital without a battle.

Rostopchin was incensed at this intelligence, but his resolution remained unshaken. There was now no time to be lost; no farther pains were taken to conceal from Moscow the fate that was destined for it; indeed it was not worth while to dissemble for the sake of the few inhabitants who were left; and, besides, it was necessary to induce them to seek their safety in flight.

At night, therefore, emissaries went round, knocking at every door and announcing the conflagration. Fuses were introduced at every favorable aperture, especially into the shops covered with iron, in the tradesmen's quarter, and the fire-engines were carried off. The desolation had now attained its highest pitch, and each individual, according to his disposition, was either overwhelmed with despair or urged to a decision. Most of those who were left formed groups in the public places; they crowded together, questioned each other, and asked each other's advice; while many wandered about at random, some depressed by terror, others in a frightful state of exasperation. At length the army, their last hope, deserted them: the troops began to traverse the city, and in their retreat they hurried along with them the still considerable remnant of its population.

They departed by the Kolomna gate,[1] surrounded by a multitude of women, children, and aged persons, in the deepest affliction. The fields were covered with them. They fled in all directions, by every path, across the country, without provisions, and laden with such of their effects as, in their agitation, they had first laid their hands on. Some, for want of horses, had harnessed themselves to carts, and in this manner dragged along their infant children, a sick wife, or an infirm father; in short, whatever they held most dear. The woods afforded them shelter, and they subsisted on the charity of their countrymen.

On that day a terrific scene terminated this melancholy drama. This, the last day of Moscow, having arrived, Rostopchin collected together all whom he had been able to retain and arm. The prisons were thrown open. A squalid and disgusting crew tumultuously issued from them. These wretches rushed into the streets with ferocious joy. Two men, a Russian and a Frenchman, the one accused of treason, the other of political indiscretion, were selected from among this horde, and dragged before Rostopchin, who fiercely reproached the Russian with his

[1] **Kolomna gate**: a gate leading to Kolomna, a town on the Moskwa River.

crime. He was the son of a tradesman, and had been apprehended while exciting the people to insurrection. A circumstance which occasioned alarm was the discovery that he belonged to a sect of German religious and political fanatics. His audacity had never failed him in prison. It was imagined, for a moment, that the spirit of equality had penetrated into Russia. He did not, however, disclose any accomplices.

At this crisis his father arrived. It was expected that he would intercede for his son; but, on the contrary, he insisted on his death. The governor granted him a few moments, that he might once more speak to and bless him. "What, I! I bless a traitor!" exclaimed the enraged Russian, and, turning to his son, with a horrid voice and gesture he pronounced a curse upon him.

This was the signal for his execution. The poor wretch was struck down by an ill-directed blow of a sabre. He fell, but wounded only, and perhaps the arrival of the French might have saved him, had not the people perceived that he was yet alive. They forced the barrier, fell upon him, and tore him to pieces.

The Frenchman, during this scene, was petrified with terror. "As for thee," said Rostopchin, turning towards him, "being a Frenchman, thou canst not but wish for the arrival of the French army: be free, then, and go and tell thy countrymen that Russia had but one traitor, and that he has been punished." Then, addressing himself to the wretches who surrounded him, he called them sons of Russia, and exhorted them to make atonement for their crimes by serving their country. He was the last to quit the doomed city, and he then rejoined the Russian army.

From that moment the mighty Moscow belonged neither

to the Russians nor to the French, but to that guilty horde whose fury was directed by a few officers and soldiers of the police. They were organized, and each had his post allotted to him, in order that pillage, fire, and devastation might commence everywhere at once.

### § 4. Napoleon's first view of Moscow; the French enter the city.

That very day (September the 14th), Napoleon, being at length satisfied that Kutusoff had not thrown himself on his right flank, rejoined his advanced guard. He mounted his horse a few leagues from Moscow. He marched slowly and cautiously, sending scouts before him to examine the woods and the ravines, and to ascend all the eminences to look out for the enemy's army. A battle was expected, and the ground favored the opinion: works also had been begun, but they had all been abandoned, and we experienced not the slightest resistance.

At length the last eminence only remained to be passed: it is contiguous to Moscow, which it commands. It is called *The Hill of Salvation*, because on its summit the inhabitants, at sight of their holy city, cross and prostrate themselves. Our scouts soon gained the top of this hill. It was two o'clock: the sun caused this great city to glisten with a thousand colors. Struck with astonishment at the sight, they paused, exclaiming, " Moscow! Moscow!" Every one quickened his pace; the troops hurried on in disorder; and the whole army, clapping their hands, repeated with transport, " Moscow! Moscow!" just as sailors shout "Land! land!" at the conclusion of a long and toilsome voyage.

At the sight of this gilded city, of this splendid capital,

uniting Europe and Asia, of this magnificent emporium of the luxury and arts of the two fairest divisions of the globe, we stood still, in proud contemplation. What a glorious day had now arrived! It would furnish the grandest, the most brilliant recollection of our whole lives. We felt at this moment that all our actions would engage the attention of the astonished world, and that every movement we made, however trivial, would be recorded by history.

At that moment dangers and sufferings were all forgotten: was it possible to purchase too dearly the proud felicity of being able to say during the rest of life, "I belonged to the army of Moscow!"

Napoleon himself hastened up. He paused in transport: an exclamation of delight escaped his lips. Ever since the great battle, the discontented marshals had shunned him; but at the sight of captive Moscow, at the intelligence of the arrival of a flag of truce, struck with so important a result, and intoxicated with all the enthusiasm of glory, they forgot their grievances. They pressed around the emperor, paying homage to his good fortune, and already tempted to attribute to the foresight of his genius the little pains he had taken on the 7th to complete his victory.

But in Napoleon, first emotions were of short duration. He had too much to think of to indulge his sensations for any length of time. His first exclamation was, "There at last is that famous city!" and the second, "It was high time!"

His eyes fixed on this capital, already expressed nothing but impatience: in it he beheld in imagination the whole Russian empire. Its walls enclosed all his hopes, peace, the expenses of the war, immortal glory: his eager looks, therefore, intently watched all its outlets. When would its gates at length open? When should he see that deputation come forth, which would place its wealth, its population, its senate, and the principal of the Russian nobility at his disposal? Henceforth that enterprise in which he had so rashly engaged, brought to a successful termination by dint of boldness, would pass for the result of a deep combination; his imprudence for greatness: henceforth his victory at the Moskwa, incomplete as it was, would be deemed his greatest achievement. Thus all that might have turned to his ruin would begin to decide whether he was the greatest man in the world, or the most rash; in short, whether he had raised himself an altar or dug for himself a grave.

Anxiety, however, soon began to take possession of his mind. On his left and right he beheld Prince Eugene and Poniatowski approaching the hostile city; Murat, with his scouts, had already reached the entrance of the suburbs, and yet no deputation appeared: an officer sent by Miloradovitch[1] merely came to declare that his general would set fire to the city if his rear was not allowed time to evacuate it.

Napoleon granted every demand. The troops of the two armies were for a short time intermingled. Murat was recognized by the Cossacks, who, with the familiarity of the wandering tribes, and curious and ardent as the people of the south, thronged around him: then by their gestures and exclamations they extolled his valor and intoxicated him with their admiration. Murat took the watches of his officers, and distributed them among these barbarous warriors. One of them called him his chief.

[1] **Miloradovitch**: a Russian general.

Murat was tempted to believe that among them he should find a new Mazeppa,[1] or that he himself might become one: he imagined that he had completely gained them over. This momentary armistice, under the actual circumstances, sustained the hopes of Napoleon, such need had he of self-delusion. He was amused in this way for two hours.

Meanwhile the day was declining, and Moscow continued dull, silent, and seemingly inanimate. The anxiety of the emperor increased, and the impatience of the soldiers could scarcely be repressed. Some officers ventured within the walls of the city. Moscow was deserted!

At this intelligence, which he angrily refused to credit, Napoleon ascended the Hill of Salvation, and approached the Moskwa and the Dorogomilow gate.[2] He paused once more, but in vain, at the entrance of that barrier. Murat pressed him to permit his soldiers to occupy the city. "Well!" he replied, "let them enter, then, since they wish it!" He recommended the strictest discipline: he still indulged hopes. "Perhaps these inhabitants," he said, "do not even know how to surrender, for here everything is new; they to us, and we to them."

Reports now began rapidly to succeed each other: they all agreed. Some Frenchmen, residents of Moscow, ventured to quit the hiding-places which for some days had concealed them from the fury of the populace, and

---

[1] Mazeppa: a Pole, who having been detected in a crime was bound to the back of a wild horse and carried by the animal to the country of the Cossacks. There he became head of the Cossack forces, and when Peter the Great attempted to seize that country, Mazeppa formed an alliance with Charles XII. of Sweden for the independence of the Cossacks.

[2] Dorogomilow: the name of a quarter of the city.

confirmed the fatal tidings. The emperor called Daru.[1] "Moscow deserted!" he exclaimed: "what an improbable story! We must know the truth of it. Go and bring me the boyars."[2] He imagined that those men, stiff with pride or paralyzed by terror, remained motionless in their houses; and he, who had hitherto been always met by the submission of the vanquished, would encourage their confidence and anticipate their prayers.

How, indeed, was it possible for him to persuade himself that so many magnificent palaces, so many splendid temples, so many rich mercantile establishments, had been forsaken by their owners, like the paltry hamlets through which he had recently passed? Daru's mission, however, was fruitless. Not a Muscovite was to be seen; not a particle of smoke arose from a single chimney; not the slightest noise issued from this vast and populous city: its three hundred thousand inhabitants seemed to be struck dumb and motionless by enchantment: it was the silence of the desert!

But such was the incredulity of Napoleon that he was not yet convinced, and waited for further information. At length an officer, wishing to gratify him, or persuaded that whatever he willed must necessarily be accomplished, entered the city, seized five or six vagabonds, drove them before his horse to the emperor, and presented them to him as a deputation. From the first words they uttered, however, Napoleon detected the imposture, and perceived that they were only poor laborers.

It was not till then that he ceased to doubt the entire evacuation of Moscow, and gave up all the hopes that he had built upon it. He shrugged his shoulders, and with

[1] **Daru**: a distinguished French author and statesman who accompanied Napoleon in his Russian campaign. [2] **Boyars**: nobles, or men of rank.

that contemptuous look with which he met everything that crossed his wishes, he exclaimed, "Ah! the Russians do not know yet the effect which the taking of their capital will produce upon them!"

It was now an hour since Murat and the long and close column of his cavalry had entered Moscow: they penetrated to the centre of that gigantic body, as yet untouched, but inanimate. Struck with profound astonishment at finding a soltitude so complete, they replied to the stillness of this modern Thebes by a silence equally solemn. These warriors listened, with a secret shuddering, to the sound of their horses' steps among these deserted palaces. They were amazed to hear nothing but the noise they themselves made amid such numerous habitations. No one thought of stopping or of plundering, either from prudence, or because highly civilized nations respect themselves in enemies' capitals.

Meanwhile they were silently observing this mighty city, which would have been truly remarkable had they met with it in a flourishing and populous country, but which was here in these deserts still more astonishing. It was like a rich and beautiful oasis. They had at first been struck by the sudden view of so many magnificent palaces, but they now perceived that they were intermingled with mean cottages: a circumstance which indicated the want of gradation among the classes, and that luxury had not been generated there, as in other countries, by industry, but had preceded it; whereas, in the natural order, it ought to be more or less its proper consequence.

Amid these reflections, which were favored by the slowness of our march, the report of firearms was all at once heard: the column halted. Its last horses were still crossing the fields; its centre was in one of the longest streets of the city; its head had reached the Kremlin. The gates of that citadel appeared to be closed; ferocious cries issued from within it; men and women, of savage and disgusting aspect, appeared fully armed upon its walls. In a state of drunken fury, they uttered the most horrible imprecations. Murat sent them amicable proposals, but to no purpose. It was found necessary to employ cannon to break open the gate.

We penetrated, partly without opposition, partly by force, among these wretches. One of them rushed close to Murat and endeavored to kill one of his officers. It was thought sufficient to disarm him; but he again fell upon his victim, threw him to the ground, and attempted to suffocate him; and even after his arms were seized and held, he strove to tear him with his teeth. These were the only Muscovites who had waited our coming! and who seemed to have been left behind as a savage and frightful emblem of the national hatred.

It was easy to perceive, however, that there was no unison in this patriotic fury. Five hundred recruits, who had been forgotten in the Kremlin, took no part in this scene: at the first summons they dispersed; and farther on we overtook a convoy of provisions, the escort of which immediately threw down its arms. Several thousand stragglers and deserters from the enemy voluntarily remained in the power of our advance guard. The latter left to the corps which followed the task of picking them up; these, again, to others, and so on; and thus they remained at liberty in the midst of us, till the conflagration and pillage of the city reminding them of their duty, and rallying in them one general feeling of antipathy, they went and rejoined Kutusoff.

Murat, who had been stopped but a few moments by the Kremlin, dispersed this despicable crew. Ardent and indefatigable as in Italy and Egypt, after a march of twenty-seven hundred miles, and sixty battles fought to reach Moscow, he traversed that proud city without deigning to halt in it, and pursuing the Russian rear guard, he boldly and without hesitation took the road for Vladimir and Asia.

Several thousand Cossacks, with four pieces of cannon, were retreating in that direction: the armistice was at an end; and Murat, tired of this peace of half a day, immediately ordered it to be broken by a discharge of carbines. But our cavalry considered the war as finished; Moscow appeared to them to be the goal of it; and the advanced posts of the two empires seemed unwilling to renew hostilities. A fresh order arrived, but the same hesitation prevailed. At length Murat, incensed at this disobedience, gave his commands in person; and the firing, with which he seemed to threaten Asia, but which was not destined to cease till we had retreated to the banks of the Seine, was renewed.

### § 5. Napoleon takes up his quarters in the Kremlin; the city discovered to be on fire.

Napoleon did not enter Moscow till after dark. He stopped in one of the first houses of the Dorogomilow suburb. There he appointed Marshal Mortier governor of that capital. "Above all," he said to him, "no pillage. For this you shall be answerable to me with your life. Defend Moscow against all, whether friend or foe."

That was a gloomy night: sinister reports rapidly followed each other. Some Frenchmen, resident in the country, and even a Russian officer of police, came to give intelligence respecting the conflagration. He related all the particulars of the preparations that had been made for it. The emperor, alarmed by these accounts, strove in vain to compose himself to rest. He called every moment, and fatal tidings were repeated to him. Still he persisted in his incredulity till about two in the morning, when news was brought to him that the fire had actually broken out.

It was at the Exchange, in the centre of the city, in its richest quarter. Instantly he issued orders upon orders. As soon as it was light, he himself hastened to the spot and threatened the Young Guard and Mortier. The marshal pointed out to him some houses covered with iron; they were closely shut up, still untouched and uninjured without, and yet a black smoke was already issuing from them. Napoleon dejectedly entered the Kremlin.

At the sight of this half-Gothic, half-modern palace of the Ruricks and the Romanoffs, of their throne still standing, of the cross of the great Ivan, and of the finest part of the city, which is overlooked by the Kremlin, and which the flames, as yet confined to the bazaar, seemed disposed to spare, his former hopes revived. His ambition was flattered by this great conquest. "At length, then," he exclaimed, "I am in Moscow, in the ancient palace of the Czars, in the Kremlin!" He examined every part of it with pride, curiosity, and gratification.

He required a statement of the resources of the city; and, in this brief moment given to hope, sent proposals of peace to the Emperor Alexander. A superior officer of the enemy had just been found in the great hospital: he was charged with the delivery of this letter. It was by the baleful light of the flames of the bazaar that Napoleon finished it, and the Russian departed. He was to be the bearer of the news of the disaster to his sovereign, whose only answer was the conflagration of his capital.

Daylight favored the efforts of the Duke of Treviso to subdue the flames. The incendiaries kept themselves concealed. Doubts even were entertained of their existence. At length, strict injunctions being issued, order restored, and alarm for a moment suspended, each took possession of a commodious house or sumptuous palace, under the idea of finding comforts that had been dearly purchased by long and excessive privations.

Two officers had taken up their quarters in one of the buildings of the Kremlin. The view from thence embraced the north and west of the city. About midnight they were awakened by an extraordinary light. They looked out and beheld palaces filled with flames, which at first merely illuminated, but ere long totally consumed these superb and noble structures. They observed that the north wind drove these flames directly towards the Kremlin, and they became alarmed for the safety of that fortress, in which the flower of their army and its commander reposed. They were apprehensive also for the surrounding houses, where our soldiers, attendants, and horses, weary and exhausted, were doubtless buried in profound sleep. Sparks and burning fragments were already flying over the roofs of the Kremlin, when the wind, shifting from north to west, blew them in another direction.

One of these officers, relieved from apprehension respecting his own corps, then composed himself again to sleep, exclaiming, " Let others look to it; 'tis no affair of ours"; for such was the unconcern produced by the multiplicity of events and misfortunes, such the selfishness arising from excessive suffering and fatigue, that they left to each only just strength and feeling sufficient for his personal service and preservation.

But it was not long before fresh and more vivid lights again awoke them. They beheld other flames rising in the direction which the wind had again taken towards the Kremlin, and they cursed French imprudence and want of discipline, to which they imputed this disaster. Three times did the wind thus change from west to north, and three times did these hostile fires, as if obstinately bent on the destruction of the imperial quarters, appear eager to follow its course.

At this sight a strong suspicion seized their minds. Could the Muscovites, aware of our rash and thoughtless negligence, have conceived the hope of burning, with Moscow, our soldiers, heavy with wine, fatigue, and sleep; or, rather, had they dared to imagine that they should involve Napoleon in this catastrophe, believing that the loss of such a man would be a full equivalent for that of their capital; that it was a result of sufficient importance to justify the sacrifice of all Moscow to obtain it; that Heaven, perhaps, in order to grant them so signal a triumph, had decreed so great a sacrifice?

Whether this was actually their plan we cannot tell; but nothing less than the emperor's good fortune was required to prevent its being realized. In fact, not only did the Kremlin contain, unknown to us, a magazine of powder, but that very night, the guards, asleep and carelessly posted, suffered a whole park of artillery to enter and draw up under the windows of Napoleon.

It was at this moment that the flames were driven from

all quarters, with the greatest violence, towards the Kremlin; for the wind, drawn towards this vast conflagration, increased every moment in strength. The flower of the army and the emperor himself would have been destroyed, if but one of the brands that flew over our heads had alighted on one of the powder-wagons. Thus upon a single spark out of the multitudes that were for several hours floating in the air, depended the fate of the whole army.

At length the day, a dismal day it was, appeared; it came only to add to the horrors of the scene, and to take from it all its brilliancy. Many of the officers sought refuge in the halls of the palace. The chiefs, and Mortier himself, who had been contending for thirty-six hours against the fire, there dropped down from fatigue, and in despair.

They said nothing, and we accused ourselves. Most of us supposed that want of discipline on the part of our troops and drunkenness had begun the disaster, and that the high wind had completed it. We viewed ourselves with feelings of disgust. The cry of horror which all Europe would not fail to set up, terrified us. Filled with consternation at so tremendous a catastrophe, we accosted each other with downcast looks. We were roused only by our eagerness to obtain intelligence; and every account now began to accuse the Russians alone of the disaster.

In fact, officers arrived from all quarters, and they all agreed on this point. The very first night, that of the 14th, a fire-balloon had settled on the palace of Prince Trubetskoi, and consumed it: this had been the signal. Fire was now immediately set to the Exchange; and Russian police soldiers had been seen stirring it up with tarred lances. In some places, shells, perfidiously placed in the stoves of the houses, had exploded and wounded the military who crowded around them. Retiring to other quarters still standing, they sought there for fresh retreats; but when on the point of entering houses that were closely shut up and uninhabited, they had heard faint explosions within; these were succeeded by a light smoke, which immediately became thick and black, then reddish, lastly fire was seen, and presently the whole edifice was involved in flames.

All had seen hideous-looking men, covered with rags, and women resembling furies, wandering among these flames. These wretches, intoxicated with wine and with the success of their crimes, no longer took any pains to conceal themselves: they proceeded in triumph through the blazing streets; they were caught, armed with torches, striving to spread the conflagration; and it was necessary to strike down their hands with sabres to oblige them to loose their hold. It was said that these banditti had been let loose from the prisons by the Russian generals for the express purpose of burning the city; and that, in fact, a resolution so extreme could only have been conceived by patriotism, and executed by guilt.

Orders were immediately issued to shoot all the incendiaries on the spot. The army was on foot. The Old Guard, which exclusively occupied one part of the Kremlin, was under arms: the baggage, and the horses ready loaded, filled the courts; we were struck dumb with astonishment, surprise, and disappointment at witnessing the destruction of such admirable quarters. Though masters of Moscow, we were forced to go and bivouac,[1] without provisions, outside its gates.

[1] **Bivouac** (biv-wak'): to encamp without tents or shelter.

While our troops were yet struggling with the conflagration, and disputing their prey with the flames, Napoleon, whose sleep none had dared to disturb during the night, was awakened by the twofold light of day and of the burning city. His first feeling was that of irritation, and he would have stayed the devouring element by the breath of his command; but he soon paused, and yielded to impossibility. Surprised that when he had struck at the heart of an empire he should find there any other sentiment than that of abject submission, he felt himself vanquished, and surpassed in heroic determination.

This conquest, for which he had sacrificed everything, was like a phantom which he had eagerly pursued, and, at the moment when he imagined he had grasped it, he saw it vanish from him in a mingled mass of smoke and flame. He was then seized with extreme agitation: he seemed, as it were, consumed by the fires which were around him. He rose every moment from his seat, paced to and fro, and again sat abruptly down. He traversed his apartments with hurried steps: his sudden and vehement gestures betrayed a painful uneasiness; he quitted, resumed, and again as suddenly abandoned an urgent occupation, to hasten to the windows and watch the progress of the flames. Short and incoherent exclamations burst from his laboring bosom! "What a tremendous spectacle! It is their own work! So many palaces! What extraordinary resolution! What men! These are indeed Scythians!"[1]

Between the fire and his quarters there was an extensive vacant space, then the Moskwa and its two quays;

[1] **Scythians**: a race of fierce barbarians, formerly inhabiting the country north and east of the Black Sea. Napoleon intimates that these men are their descendants.

and yet the panes of the windows against which he leaned felt already burning to the touch, and the constant exertions of sweepers, placed on the iron roofs of the palace, were not sufficient to keep them clear of the numerous flakes of fire which were continually lighting upon them.

At this moment a rumor was spread that the Kremlin had been mined; and the fact, it was said, was confirmed later by the declarations of the Russians, and by written documents. Some of his attendants were beside themselves with fear, while the military awaited unmoved what the orders of the emperor and fate should decree; but he replied to their alarm only with a smile of incredulity.

Still, he continued to walk about in the utmost agitation: he stopped at every window, to gaze on the terrible, the victorious element that was furiously consuming his brilliant conquest; seizing on all the bridges, on all the avenues to his fortress, enclosing, and, as it were, besieging him in it; spreading every moment wider and wider; constantly reducing him within narrower limits, and confining him at length to the site of the Kremlin alone.

We breathed already nothing but smoke and ashes: night approached, and was about to add darkness to our other dangers; while the equinoctial gales, as if in alliance with the Russians, increased in violence. Then Murat and Prince Eugene hastened to the emperor's quarters: in company with the Prince of Neufchâtel they made their way to him, and urged him by their entreaties, and on their knees, to remove from this scene of desolation. All was in vain.

Master, after so many sacrifices, of the palace of the Czars, he was bent on not yielding that conquest even to the conflagration, when all at once the shout of "the

Kremlin is on fire!" passed from mouth to mouth, and roused us from the contemplative stupor into which we had been plunged. The emperor went out to ascertain the danger. Twice had the fire communicated to the building in which he was and twice had it been extinguished; but the tower of the arsenal was still burning. A soldier of the police had been found in it. He was brought in, and Napoleon caused him to be interrogated in his presence. This man was the incendiary; he had executed his commission at the signal given by his chief. It was now evident that everything was devoted to destruction, the ancient and sacred Kremlin not excepted.

The gestures of the emperor bespoke disdain and vexation: the wretch was hurried into the first court, and there the enraged soldiers despatched him with their bayonets.

### § 6. The fire compels Napoleon to leave the city.

This occurrence decided Napoleon. He hastily descended the northern staircase, famous for the massacre of the Strelitzes,[1] and requested to be conducted out of the city, to the distance of a league on the road to St. Petersburg, towards the imperial palace of Petrowski.

But we were besieged by an ocean of fire, which blocked up all the gates of the citadel, and frustrated our first attempts to escape. After some search, we discovered a postern-gate[2] leading between the rocks to the Moskwa. It was by this narrow pass that Napoleon, his officers and guard, made their way from the Kremlin. But what had they gained by this movement? They had approached

---

[1] **Strelitzes**: a body of military guards that revolted under Peter the Great.
[2] **Postern-gate**: a small rear or side gate.

nearer to the fire, and could neither retreat nor remain where they were; and how were they to advance? how force a passage through the billows of this sea of flame? Those who had traversed the city, stunned by the tempest and blinded by the ashes, could no longer find their way, since the streets themselves were not distinguishable amid smoke and ruins.

There was no time to be lost. The roaring of the flames around us became every moment more terrific. A single narrow winding street, completely enveloped in fire on either side, appeared rather the entrance than the outlet of this hell. The emperor, however, on foot, and without hesitation, rushed into this frightful passage. He advanced amid the crackling of the flames, the crash of floors, and the fall of burning timbers, and of fragments of red-hot iron roofs which tumbled around him. These ruins impeded his progress. The flames, while with impetuous roar they consumed the edifices between which we were proceeding, spreading beyond the walls, were blown out by the wind, and formed an arch over our heads. We walked on a ground of fire, beneath a fiery canopy and between two walls of fire. The intense heat burned our eyes, which we were nevertheless obliged to keep open and fixed on the danger. A consuming atmosphere parched our throats, and rendered our respiration short and difficult; and we were already almost suffocated by the smoke. Our hands were burned, either in endeavoring to protect our faces from the insupportable heat, or in brushing off the sparks which every moment fell upon our garments. In this inexpressible distress, and when a rapid advance seemed to be our only means of safety, our guide stopped in uncertainty and agitation. Here probably would have terminated our adventurous career, had not some pillagers of the first corps recognized the emperor amid the whirling flames: they ran up and guided him towards the smoking ruins of a quarter which had been reduced to ashes in the morning.

It was there that we met the Prince of Echmühl. This marshal, who had been wounded at the Moskwa, had desired to be carried back among the flames to rescue Napoleon, or to perish with him. He threw himself into his arms with transport; the emperor received him kindly, but with that composure which in danger he never lost for a moment.

To escape from this vast region of desolation, it was farther necessary to pass a long convoy of powder which was defiling amid the fire. This was not the least of his dangers, but it was the last, and by nightfall he arrived at Petrowski.

The next morning, the 17th of September, Napoleon cast his first look towards Moscow, hoping to see that the conflagration had subsided. But he beheld it again raging with the utmost violence: the city appeared like one vast column of fire, rising in whirling eddies to the sky, which it deeply colored. Absorbed by this melancholy contemplation, he maintained a long and gloomy silence, which he broke only by the exclamation, "This forebodes to us great misfortunes!"

The effort which he had made to reach Moscow had expended all his means of warfare. Moscow had been the limit of his projects, the aim of all his hopes, and Moscow was no more! What was now to be done? Here this decisive genius was forced to hesitate. He who in 1805 had ordered the sudden and total abandonment of the expedition prepared at an immense expense, for the invasion of England; and determined at Boulogne on the surprise and annihilation of the Austrian army, in short, on all the operations of the campaign between Ulm and Munich exactly as they were executed; this same man, who in the following year dictated at Paris with like infallibility all the movements of his army as far as Berlin, the day of his entrance into that capital, and the appointment of the governor whom he destined for it; he it was who, astonished in his turn, was now in perplexity what course to pursue. Never had he communicated his most daring projects to the most confidential of his ministers but in order for their execution; he was now, however, constrained to consult and put to the proof those who were around him.

But, in doing this, he still preserved the same show of confidence and of determination. He declared that he would march for St. Petersburg. This conquest was already marked out on his maps, hitherto so prophetic: orders were even issued to the different corps to hold themselves in readiness. But this was all only a feint: it was but a better face that he strove to assume, or an expedient for diverting his grief at the loss of Moscow; so that Berthier, and more especially Bessières, soon convinced him that he had neither time, provisions, roads, nor a single requisite for so distant an expedition.

At this moment he was apprised that Kutusoff, after having fled towards the east, had suddenly turned to the south, and thrown himself between Moscow and Kaluga. This was an additional circumstance against the expedition to St. Petersburg. There was a threefold reason for marching upon the beaten army, and endeavoring to extinguish it : to secure his right flank and his line of operation ; to possess himself of Kaluga and of Tula, the one the granary, the other the arsenal of Russia ; and, lastly, to open safe, short, new, and untouched retreat to Smolensk and Lithuania.[1]

Some one proposed to return upon Wittgenstein and Witepsk.[2] Napoleon, however, remained undecided between these different plans. That for the conquest of St. Petersburg alone flattered him : the others appeared but as ways of retreat, as acknowledgments of error; and whether from pride, or policy which would not admit itself to be in the wrong, he rejected them.

Besides, where was he to halt in case of a retreat ? He had so fully calculated on concluding a peace at Moscow, that he had no winter-quarters provided in Lithuania. Kaluga had no temptations for him. Wherefore lay waste fresh provinces ? It would be wiser only to threaten them, and thus leave the Russians something to lose, in order to induce them to conclude a peace by which they might be preserved. Would it be possible to march to another battle, to fresh conquests, without exposing a line of operation covered with sick, stragglers, wounded, and convoys of all sorts ? Moscow was the general rallying point : how could it be changed ? What other name would have any attraction ?

Lastly, and above all, how could he relinquish a hope to which he had made so many sacrifices, when he knew that his letter to Alexander had just passed the Russian ad-

---

[1] **Lithuania**: a province of Russia bordering on the Niemen and hence near supplies.

[2] **Witepsk**: a point passed on the march to Moscow, about midway from the Niemen ; here the Russian general, Wittgenstein, appears to have been stationed.

vanced posts; when eight days would be sufficient for receiving an answer, so ardently desired; when he required that time to rally and reorganize his army, to collect the relics of Moscow, the conflagration of which had but too strongly sanctioned pillage, and to draw his soldiers away from that vast infirmary.

Meanwhile, scarcely a third of that army and of that capital now existed. But himself and the Kremlin were still standing: his renown was still entire, and he persuaded himself that those two great names, Napoleon and Moscow, combined, would be sufficient to accomplish everything. He determined, therefore, to return to the Kremlin, which a battalion of his guard had unfortunately preserved.

### § 7. Napoleon returns to the Kremlin; plunder of the city.

The camps which he traversed on his way thither presented an extraordinary sight. In the fields, in the midst of the mud, were large fires, kept up with mahogany furniture, windows and gilded doors. Around these fires, on litters of damp straw, imperfectly sheltered by a few boards, were seen the soldiers and their officers, splashed all over with mud, and blackened with smoke, seated in arm-chairs or reclining on silken couches. At their feet were spread, or heaped together, Cashmere shawls, the rarest furs of Siberia, the gold stuffs of Persia, and silver dishes, off which they had nothing to eat but black dough baked in the ashes, and half broiled and bloody horseflesh. Strange combination of abundance and want, of riches and filth, of luxury and wretchedness!

Between the camp and the city were met troops of soldiers dragging along their booty, or driving before them, like beasts of burden, Muscovites bending under the weight of the pillage of their capital : for the fire brought to light nearly twenty thousand inhabitants, previously concealed in that immense city. Some of these, of both sexes, were well dressed : they were tradespeople. They came with the wreck of their property, to seek refuge at our fires. They lived pell-mell with our soldiers, protected by some, and tolerated, or, rather, scarcely remarked by others.

About ten thousand of the enemy's troops were in the same predicament. For several days they wandered about among us, free, and some of them even still armed. Our soldiers met these vanquished Russians without the slightest animosity, and without thinking of making them prisoners ; either that they considered the war at an end, or from thoughtlessness or pity, or because, when not in battle, the French delight in having no enemies. They suffered them to share their fires ; nay, more, they allowed them to pillage in their company. But when some degree of order was restored, or, rather, when the officers had organized this marauding as a regular system of forage, the great number of these Russian stragglers attracted notice, and orders were given to secure them; but seven or eight thousand had already escaped. It was not long before we had to fight them.

On entering the city the emperor was struck by a sight still more extraordinary: a few houses scattered here and there among the ruins were all that was left of the mighty Moscow. The smell issuing from this vast city, overthrown, burned, and calcined, was horrible. Heaps of ashes, and, at intervals, fragments of walls or half-demolished pillars, were now the only vestiges that marked the sites of streets.

In the suburbs were found a few Russians of both sexes, covered with garments scorched and blackened by the fire. They flitted like spectres among the ruins; some of them were scratching up the earth in gardens in quest of vegetables, while others were disputing with the crows for the relics of the dead animals which their army had left behind. Farther on, others again were seen plunging into the Moskwa to bring out some of the grain which had been thrown into it by command of Rostopchin, and which they devoured without preparation, soured and spoiled as it was.

Meanwhile the sight of the booty in the camps, where everything was yet wanting, inflamed the soldiers, whom a sense of duty or stricter officers had hitherto kept with their colors. They murmured. "Why were they to be kept back? Why were they to perish by famine and want, when everything was within their reach? Was it right to allow the enemy's fires to destroy what might be saved? Why was such respect to be paid to the conflagration?" They added, that "as the inhabitants of Moscow had not only abandoned, but even endeavored utterly to destroy it, all that they could save would be fairly gained; that the remains of that city, like the arms of the conquered, belonged by right to the victors, as the Muscovites had turned their capital into a vast machine of war for the purpose of annihilating us."

The best principled, and the best disciplined were those who argued thus, and it was impossible to reply satisfactorily to them. Exaggerated scruples, however, at first preventing the issuing of orders for pillage, it was permitted, unrestrained by regulations. Then it was, urged by the most imperious wants, that all hurried to share the spoil, soldiers of the highest class, and even officers. Their chiefs were obliged to shut their eyes: only such guards as were absolutely indispensable remained with the colors and the piled arms.

The emperor saw his whole army dispersed over the city. His progress was obstructed by long files of marauders going in quest of booty or returning with it; by tumultuous assemblages of soldiers grouped around the entrances of cellars, or the doors of palaces, shops, and churches, which the fire had nearly reached, and which they were endeavoring to break into.

His steps were impeded by the fragments of furniture of every kind which had been thrown out of. the windows to save them from the flames, or by rich pillage which had been abandoned from caprice for other booty, for such is the way with soldiers; they are incessantly beginning their fortunes afresh, taking everything indiscriminately, loading themselves beyond measure, as if they could carry all that they find; then, after they have gone a few steps, compelled by fatigue to throw away successively the greatest part of their burden.

The roads were obstructed by these accumulations; and the open places, like the camp, were turned into markets, whither every one repaired to exchange superfluities for necessaries. There the rarest articles, the value of which was not known to their possessors, were sold for the merest pittance; while others of little worth, but more showy appearance, were purchased at the most exorbitant prices. Gold, from being most portable, was bought at an immense loss with silver that the knapsacks were incapable of holding. Everywhere soldiers were seen seated on bales of merchandise, on heaps of sugar and coffee, amid wines and the most exquisite liquors, all of which they were offering in exchange for a morsel of bread. Many, in a state of intoxication aggravated by hunger, had fallen near the flames, which, reaching them, put a miserable end to their lives.

The houses and palaces which had escaped the fire served as quarters for the officers, who respected whatever was found in them. They beheld with pain this vast destruction, and the pillage which was its necessary consequence. Some of our best men were reproached with being too greedy in collecting whatever they could rescue from the flames; but their number was so small that they were all mentioned by name. In these ardent men war was a passion which presupposed the existence of many others. It was not covetousness, for they did not hoard; they spent lavishly what they had thus picked up, taking in order to give, believing that one hand washed the other, and that they paid for everything with the danger they encountered in acquiring it.

It was amid this confusion that Napoleon again entered Moscow. He had allowed the pillage, hoping that his army, scattered over the ruins, would find much that was valuable; but when he learned that the disorder increased; that the Old Guard[1] itself had yielded to the temptation; that the Russian peasants, who were at length allured thither with provisions, for which he caused them to be liberally paid, that they might induce others to come, were robbed of what they brought to us by our famished soldiers; when he was informed that the different corps, destitute of everything, were ready to fight each other for the

[1] **Old Guard**: the emperor's body-guard, composed of a large force of veterans.

relics of Moscow; that, finally, all our existing resources were wasted by this lawless freebooting, he then issued severe orders, and forbade his guard to leave their quarters. The churches in which our cavalry had sheltered themselves, were evacuated, and restored to their religious uses.[1] The business of plunder was ordered to be taken in turn by the different corps, like any other duty, and directions were at length given for securing the Russian stragglers.

But it was too late. These soldiers had fled; the affrighted peasants returned no more; and great quantities of provisions were wasted. The French army have sometimes fallen into these faults, but on the present occasion the fire must plead their excuse; no time was to be lost in anticipating the flames. It is, however, a remarkable fact, that at the first command of the emperor perfect order was restored.

Most of our men behaved generously, considering the small number of inhabitants who remained, and the great number of enemies they met with. But if, in the first moments of pillage, some excesses were perpetrated, ought this to appear surprising in an army exasperated by such urgent wants, such severe sufferings, and composed of so many different nations?

Misfortunes having since overwhelmed these warriors, reproaches, as in such circumstances is ever the case, have been raised against them. Who can be ignorant that similar disorders have always been the bad side of great wars,

---

[1] "Napoleon also took measures for relieving the unfortunate of all classes. He ordered lists to be made of all the citizens whom the conflagration had deprived of the means of subsistence, opened houses of refuge for them, and supplied them with food."

or, so to speak, the inglorious part of glory; that the renown of conquerors casts its shadow like everything else in this world? Does there exist a creature however diminutive, on every side of which the sun can shine at once? It is a law of nature, therefore, that great bodies shall cast great shadows.

### § 8. Rostopchin sets fire to his country-seat; anxiety of Napoleon at not hearing from the Czar.

Meanwhile Kutusoff, on leaving Moscow, had drawn Murat towards Kolomna, the point where the Moskwa intersects the road. Here, under favor of the night, he suddenly turned to the south, proceeding by the way of Podol, to throw himself between Moscow and Kaluga. This night march of the Russians around Moscow, the ashes and flames of which were wafted to them by the violence of the wind, was gloomy in the extreme. They were lighted on their march by the baleful conflagration which was consuming the centre of their commerce, the sanctuary of their religion, the cradle of their empire! Filled with horror and indignation, they kept a sullen silence, which was unbroken save by the dull and monotonous sound of their footsteps, the roaring of the flames, and the howling of the blast. The dismal light was frequently varied by livid and sudden flashes. The brows of these warriors might then be seen contracted by intense and unutterable grief, and the fire of their sombre and threatening looks answered to these flames, which they regarded as our work; they already betrayed the ferocious revenge which was rankling in their hearts, which spread throughout the empire, and of which so many Frenchmen were the victims.

At that solemn moment, Kutusoff, in a firm and impressive tone, addressed his sovereign, and informed him of the loss of his capital. He stated that, "in order to save the fertile provinces of the south, and to keep up his communications with Tormasoff and Tchitchakoff, he had been obliged to abandon Moscow, but emptied of its inhabitants, who were its life; and," said he, "as the people are the soul of every country, so where the Russian people are, there will be Moscow and the empire of Russia."

It is said that on receiving this intelligence Alexander was thunderstruck. Napoleon, it was known, built hopes on the weakness of his rival, and the Russians themselves dreaded the effects of that weakness. But the Czar disappointed as well these hopes as fears. In his addresses to his subjects he exhibited himself no less great than his misfortune: "No pusillanimous dejection!" he exclaimed; "let us vow redoubled courage and perseverance! The enemy is in deserted Moscow as in a tomb, without means of domination or even of existence. He entered Russia with three hundred thousand men of all countries, without union or any national or religious bond: he has already lost half of them by the sword, by famine, and by desertion: he has but the wreck of this army in Moscow: he is in the heart of Russia, and not a single Russian is at his feet.

"Meanwhile our forces are increasing and closing around him. He is in the midst of a mighty population, encompassed by armies which are waiting his movements and keeping him in check. To escape from famine, he will soon be obliged to direct his flight through the ranks of our brave soldiers. Shall we then recede, when all Europe is looking on and encouraging us? Let us, on the contrary, set it an example, and kiss the hand which has thus led us forth to be the first among the nations to vindicate the cause of independence and virtue." He concluded with an invocation to the Almighty.

This circuitous march of Kutusoff, whether made from indecision or as a stratagem, was much in his favor. Murat lost all traces of him for three days. The Russian general employed all this interval in studying the ground and in intrenching himself. His advanced guard had nearly reached Woronowo, one of the finest domains belonging to Count Rostopchin, when that nobleman proceeded on before it. The Russians supposed that he had gone to take a last look at this splendid mansion, when all at once it was wrapped from their sight by clouds of smoke.

They hurried on to extinguish the fire, but Rostopchin himself repelled their aid. They beheld him, amid the flames which he was encouraging, smiling at the demolition of this magnificent edifice, and then with a firm hand penning these words, which the French, shuddering with astonishment, afterwards read on the iron gate of a church which was left standing: "For eight years I have been embellishing this country-seat, where I have lived happily in the bosom of my family. The inhabitants of this estate, to the number of 1720, leave it on your approach, while I have set fire to my house, that it may not be polluted by your presence. Frenchmen, I have relinquished to you my two houses at Moscow, with their furniture, worth half a million of rubles. Here you will find nothing but ashes!"

It was near this place that Murat came up with Kutusoff. On the 29th of September there was a smart engagement of cavalry and another on the 4th of October. Murat fought till nightfall, and repulsed the Russian force.

Meanwhile, the conflagration at Moscow, which commenced in the night of the 14th of September, suspended through our exertions during the day of the 15th, revived the following night, and, raging with the utmost violence on the 16th, 17th, and 18th, abated on the 19th: it ceased altogether on the 20th, and on that day Napoleon returned to the Kremlin. To this point he attracted the looks of all Europe. There he awaited his convoys, his re-enforcements, and the stragglers of his army; certain that his soldiers would all be rallied by his victory, by the allurements of a rich booty, by the imposing sight of captive Moscow, and, above all, by his own glory, which, from the summit of this immense pile of ruins, still shone attractive like a beacon upon a rock.

Twice, however, on the 22d and 28th of September, letters from Murat had wellnigh drawn him from this fatal abode. They announced a battle; and twice the orders for departure were written, and then burned. It seemed as though the war was finished for the emperor, and that he was only waiting for an answer from St. Petersburg. He nourished his hopes with the recollections of Tilsit and Erfurt.[1] Was it possible that at Moscow he should have less ascendancy over Alexander? Then, as is common with men who have long been the favorites of fortune, what he ardently wished he confidently expected.

His genius possessed, besides, the extraordinary faculty of being able to throw aside the most important occupation

---

[1] **Tilsit and Erfurt**: at these places Napoleon had negotiated treaties, greatly in favor of the French, with the Czar of Russia.

whenever he pleased, either for the sake of variety or for rest; for in him the power of will surpassed that of imagination. In this respect he reigned over himself no less despotically than he did over others.

Thus Paris diverted his attention from Petersburg. His accumulating affairs and the couriers, which in the first days succeeded each other without intermission, served to engage him. But the rapidity with which he transacted business soon left him again with nothing to do. His expresses,[1] which at first came from France in a fortnight, now ceased to arrive. A few military posts, placed in four towns reduced to ashes, and in wooden houses rudely palisaded, were wholly insufficient to guard a road of nearly two hundred and eighty miles; for we had been able to fix only these few steps, and at so great a distance apart, on so long a ladder. This too lengthened line of operation was consequently broken at every point where it was touched by the enemy: a few peasants, or a handful of Cossacks, were quite sufficient for the purpose.

Still no answer was received from Alexander. The uneasiness of Napoleon increased, while his means of diverting his attention from it diminished. The activity of his genius, accustomed to the government of all Europe, had nothing with which to occupy itself but the management of one hundred thousand men; and then, the organization of his army was so perfect, that this was scarcely any occupation to him. Here everything was fixed: he held all the wires in his hand: he was surrounded by ministers who could tell him immediately, at any hour of the day, the position of each man in the morning or at night, whether with his colors, in the hospital, on leave of ab-

[1] **Expresses**: messengers.

sence, or wherever else he might be, and that, from Moscow to Paris: to such a degree of perfection had the science of a concentrated administration been then brought, so experienced and well chosen were the officers, and so much was required by their commander.

But eleven days had already elapsed: still Alexander was silent, and still did Napoleon hope to overcome his rival by obstinacy: thus losing the time which he ought to have gained, and which might have been made so serviceable against attack.

From this period all his actions indicated to the Russians, still more strongly than at Witepsk, that their mighty foe was resolved to fix himself in the heart of their empire. Moscow, though in ashes, received a governor and municipal officers: orders also were issued to provision it for the winter: and a theatre was formed amid its ruins. The first actors of Paris, it is said, were sent for. An Italian singer strove to reproduce in the Kremlin the evening entertainments of the Tuileries. By such means Napoleon expected to dupe a government which the habit of reigning over ignorance and error had rendered an adept in all these delusions.

He was himself sensible of the inadequacy of these means, and yet September was past, and October had begun. Alexander had not deigned to reply! it was an affront! he was exasperated. On the 3d of October, after a night of restlessness and irritation, he summoned his marshals. "Come in," said he, as soon as he perceived them; "hear the new plan which I have conceived: Prince Eugene, read it." They listened. "We must burn the remains of Moscow, and march by Twer to St. Petersburg, where we shall be joined by Macdonald. Murat and Davoust will form the rear guard." The emperor, all animation, fixed his sparkling eyes on his generals, whose rigid and silent countenances expressed nothing but astonishment.

Then exalting himself in order to rouse them, "What!" said he, "and are *you* not inflamed by this idea? Was there ever so great a military achievement? Henceforth this conquest is the only one that is worthy of us! With what glory shall we be covered, and what will the whole world say when it learns that in three months we have conquered the two great capitals of the North!"

But Davoust, as well as Daru, objected to him "the season, the want of supplies, a sterile desert, and artificial road, that from Twer to St. Petersburg runs for a hundred leagues through morasses, and which three hundred peasants might in a single day render impassable. Why keep proceeding north? Why go to meet, to provoke, and to defy the winter? it was already too near; and what was to become of the six thousand wounded still in Moscow? Were they then to be left to the mercy of Kutusoff? That general would not fail to follow close at our heels. We should have at once to attack and to defend, thus marching to a conquest as though we were in flight."

These officers have declared that they themselves then proposed various plans: a useless trouble with a prince whose genius outstripped all other imaginations, and whom their objections would not have stopped, had he been fully determined to march on St. Petersburg. But that idea was in him only a sally of anger, an inspiration of despair, on finding himself obliged in the face of Europe to give way, to relinquish his conquest and to fall back.

It was more especially a threat to frighten his officers

as well as the enemy, and to bring about and to promote a negotiation which Caulaincourt was to open. That officer had made himself agreeable to Alexander; he was the only one of the grandees of Napoleon's court who had acquired any influence over his rival; but for some months past Napoleon had kept him at a distance, because he had not been able to induce him to approve of his expedition.

It was nevertheless to this very man that he was now obliged to have recourse, and to disclose his anxiety. He sent for him; but, when alone with him, he hesitated. Taking him by the arm, he walked to and fro for a long time in great agitation, his pride preventing him from breaking so painful a silence: at length he yielded, but in a threatening manner. Caulaincourt, who had formerly been minister to Russia, was to persuade the enemy to solicit peace of him, as if it were by his condescension that it was to be granted.

After a few words, which were scarcely articulate, he said that "he was about to march to St. Petersburg. He knew that the destruction of that city would give pain to General Caulaincourt. Russia would then rise against the Emperor Alexander; there would at once be a conspiracy against that monarch; he would be assassinated, which would be a most unfortunate circumstance. He esteemed that prince, and should regret him, both for his own sake and that of France. His disposition," he added, "was suited to our interests: no prince could replace him with so much advantage to us. He had thought, therefore, of sending General Caulaincourt to him, to prevent such a catastrophe."

General Caulaincourt, however, more obstinate than disposed to flattery, did not alter his tone. He maintained that "these overtures would be useless; that, unless the Russian territory was entirely evacuated, Alexander would listen to no proposals; that Russia was sensible of all her advantage at this season of the year; nay, more, that this step would be detrimental to himself, inasmuch as it would demonstrate the need which he had of peace, and betray all the embarrassment of our situation."

He added, "that the more particular he was in the selection of his negotiator, the more clearly would he show his anxiety; that, therefore, he (Caulaincourt) would be more likely to fail than any other, especially as he would go with the certainty of failing." The emperor abruptly terminated the conversation by these words: "Well, then, I will send Lauriston."

The latter asserts that he added fresh objections to the preceding, and that, being urged by the emperor, he recommended to him to begin his retreat that very day, by way of Kaluga. Napoleon, irritated at this, sharply replied, "that he liked simple plans, less circuitous routes, high roads, the road by which he had come, yet he would not retrace it but with peace." Then showing to him, as he had done to General Caulaincourt, the letter which he had written to Alexander, he ordered him to go and obtain of Kutusoff a safe conduct to St. Petersburg. The last words of the emperor to Lauriston were, "I want peace, I must have peace, I absolutely will have peace only save my honor."

The general set out, and reached the advanced posts of the Russians on the 5th of October. Hostilities were instantly suspended, and an interview granted, at which Wolkonsky, aid-de-camp to Alexander, and Beningsen were present, without Kutusoff. Wilson asserts that the Russian generals and officers, suspicious of their commander, and accusing him of weakness, had raised a cry of treason, and that the latter had not dared to leave his camp.

As Lauriston's instructions purported that he was to address himself to no one but Kutusoff, he peremptorily rejected any intermediate communication; and seizing, as he said, this occasion for breaking off a negotiation which he disapproved, he retired, in spite of all the solicitations of Wolkonsky, with the intention of returning to Moscow. Had he carried this into effect, no doubt Napoleon, exasperated, would have fallen upon Kutusoff, overthrown him and destroyed his army, as yet very incomplete, and forced him into a peace. In case of less decisive success, he would at least have been able to retire without loss upon his reinforcements.

Unfortunately, Beningsen desired an interview with Murat. Lauriston waited. The chief of the Russian staff, an abler negotiator than soldier, strove to charm this monarch of yesterday by demonstrations of respect; to seduce him by praises; to deceive him with smooth words, breathing nothing but a weariness of war and the hope of peace; and Murat, tired of battles, anxious respecting their result, and, as it is said, regretting his throne, now that he had no hope of a better, suffered himself to be charmed, seduced, and deceived.

It was soon demonstrated that the chief point in which they were all agreed was to deceive Murat and the emperor; and in this they succeeded. These details transported Napoleon with joy. Credulous from hope, perhaps from despair, he was for some moments dazzled by these appearances: eager to escape from the inward feeling which oppressed him, he seemed desirous to deaden it by resigning himself to an expansive joy. He therefore summoned all his generals, and triumphantly announced to them a speedy peace. "They had but to wait another fortnight. None but himself was acquainted with the Russian character. On the receipt of his letter St. Petersburg would be illuminated." But the armistice [1] proposed by Kutusoff was so unsatisfactory to him, that he ordered Murat to break it instantly; it nevertheless continued to be observed, the cause of which is not known.

This armistice was a very singular one. If either party wished to break it, three hours' notice was to be sufficient. It was confined to the fronts of the two camps, but did not extend to their flanks: such, at least, was the interpretation put upon it by the Russians. Thus, we could not bring up a convoy, or send out a foraging party, without fighting; so that the war continued everywhere excepting where it could be favorable to us.

As for the emperor, who was not so easily deceived, he had but a few moments of factitious joy. He soon complained "that an annoying warfare of partisans [2] hovered around him; that, notwithstanding all these pacific demonstrations, bodies of Cossacks were prowling on his flanks and in his rear. Had not one hundred and fifty dragoons of his Old Guard been surprised and routed by a number of these barbarians? And this two days after the armistice, on the road to Mojaisk, on his line of operation, that by which the army communicated with its magazines, its reinforcements, and he himself with Europe?"

Our soldiers, and especially our cavalry, were obliged every morning to go to a great distance in quest of pro-

[1] **Armistice**: a temporary suspension of hostilities.
[2] **Partisans**: soldiers detached to intercept convoys of provisions and the like.

visions for the evening and for the next day; and as the environs of Moscow and Winkowo became gradually more and more drained, they were daily compelled to extend their excursions. Both men and horses returned worn out with fatigue, that is to say, such of them as returned at all; for we had to fight for every bushel of rye and for every truss of forage. It was a series of incessant surprises and skirmishes, and of continual losses. The peasantry took part in it. They punished with death such of their number as the prospect of gain had allured to our camp with provisions. Others set fire to their own villages to drive our foragers out of them, and to give them up to the Cossacks, whom they had previously summoned, and who kept us there in a state of siege.

Thus the war was everywhere: in our front, on our flanks, and in our rear. Our army was constantly weakening, and the enemy becoming daily more enterprising. This conquest seemed destined to fare like many others, which are won in the mass, and lost piece-meal.

Murat himself at length grew uneasy. In these daily skirmishes he had seen half the remnant of his cavalry melted away. At the advanced posts, the Russian officers, on meeting with ours, either from weariness, vanity, or military frankness carried to indiscretion, exaggerated the disasters which threatened us. Showing us those wild-looking horses, scarcely at all broken in, whose long manes swept the dust of the plain, they said, "Did not this tell us that a numerous cavalry was joining them from all quarters, while ours was gradually perishing? Did not the continual discharges of firearms within their line apprise us that a multitude of recruits were then training under favor of the armistice?"

And, in fact, notwithstanding the long journeys which they had to make, all these recruits joined the army. There was no occasion to defer calling them together, as in other years, till deep snows, obstructing all the roads excepting the high road, rendered their desertion impossible. Not one failed to obey the national appeal; all Russia rose: mothers, it was said, wept for joy on learning that their sons had been selected for soldiers: they hastened to acquaint them with the glorious intelligence, and even accompanied them to see them marked with the sign of the Crusaders, to hear them cry, '*Tis the will of God!*

The Russian officers added "that they were particularly astonished at our security on the approach of their frightful winter, which was their natural and most formidable ally, and which they expected every moment: they pitied us and urged us to fly. In a fortnight," said they, "your nails will drop off, and your muskets will fall from your benumbed and half-dead fingers."

The language of some of the Cossack chiefs was also remarkable. They asked our officers "if they had not, in their own country, corn enough, air enough, and graves enough: in short, room enough to live and die? Why, then, did they come so far from home to throw away their lives, and to fatten a foreign soil with their blood?" They added that "this was a robbery of their native land, which while living it is our duty to cultivate, to defend, and to embellish; and to which, after our death, we owe our bodies, which we received from it, which it has fed, and which, in their turn, ought to feed it."

The emperor was not ignorant of these warnings, but he would not suffer his resolution to be shaken by them.

The uneasiness which had again seized him betrayed itself in angry orders. It was then that he caused the churches of the Kremlin to be stripped of everything that could serve for a trophy to the Grand Army. These objects, devoted to destruction by the Russians themselves, belonged, he said, to the conquerors, by the double right conferred by victory and by the conflagration.

It required long efforts to remove the gigantic cross from the steeple of Ivan the Great, to the possession of which the Russians attached the salvation of their empire. The emperor determined that it should adorn the dome of the Invalides[1] at Paris. During the work it was remarked that a great number of ravens kept flying round this cross, and that Napoleon, weary of their hoarse croaking, exclaimed that "it seemed as if these flocks of ill-omened birds meant to defend it." We cannot pretend to tell all that he thought in this critical situation, but it is well known that he was accessible to every kind of presentiment.

His nights, in particular, became irksome to him. He passed part of them with Count Daru. It was then only that he admitted the danger of his situation. "From Wilna to Moscow, what submission, what point of support, of rest, or of retreat, marked his power? It was a vast, bare, and desert field of battle, in which his diminished army was imperceptible, insulated, and, as it were, lost in the horrors of an immense void. In this country of foreign manners and religion he had not conquered a single individual: he was, in fact, master only of the ground on which he stood. That which he had just quitted and left

[1] **Invalides**: one of the great public buildings at Paris; a soldiers' home and hospital. Napoleon is buried here.

behind him was no more his than that which he had not reached. Insufficient for these vast deserts, he was lost, as it were, in their immense space."

He then reviewed the different resolutions of which he still had the choice. "People imagined," he said, "that he had nothing to do but march, without considering that it would take a month to refit his army and to evacuate his hospitals; that if he relinquished his wounded, the Cossacks would daily be seen triumphing over his sick and his stragglers. He would appear to fly. All Europe would resound with the report! Europe, which envied him, which was seeking a rival under whom to rally, and would imagine that it had found such a rival in Alexander."

The letter of which Lauriston was the bearer to the Czar had been despatched on the 6th of October, and the answer to it could scarcely arrive before the 20th: still, in spite of so many threatening demonstrations, the pride, the policy, and perhaps the health of Napoleon induced him to pursue the worst of all courses, that of waiting for this answer, and of trusting to time, which was destroying him. Daru, as well as his other officers, was astonished to find in him no longer that prompt decision, variable and rapid as the occurrences which called it forth: they asserted that his genius could no longer accommodate itself to circumstances; and they placed it to the account of his natural persistence, which had led to his elevation, and which seemed destined to cause his downfall.

### § 9. Napoleon determines to leave Moscow.

Napoleon, however, was completely aware of his situation. To him everything seemed lost if he receded in the face of astonished Europe, and everything saved if he could surpass Alexander in determination. He appreciated but too well the means that were left him to shake the constancy of his rival; he knew that the diminishing number of his effective troops, that his situation, the season, in short, everything, would become daily more and more unfavorable to him; but he reckoned upon that magic force which his renown gave him. Hitherto that had lent to him a real and never failing strength: he endeavored, therefore, to keep up, by specious arguments, the confidence of his army, and perhaps, also, the faint hope that was still left to himself.

Moscow, empty of inhabitants, no longer furnished him with anything to lay hold of. "It is no doubt a misfortune," he said, "but this misfortune is not without its advantage. Had it been otherwise, he would not have been able to keep order in so large a city, to overawe a population of three hundred thousand souls, and to sleep in the Kremlin but at the hazard of assassination. They have left us nothing but ruins, but at least we are quiet among them. Millions have no doubt slipped through our hands, but how many thousand millions is Russia losing! Her commerce is ruined for a century to come. The nation is thrown back fifty years, which of itself is an important result; and when the first moment of enthusiasm is passed, this reflection will fill them with consternation." The conclusion which he drew was, "that so violent a shock would convulse the throne of Alexander, and force that prince to sue for peace."

In reviewing his different corps, their reduced battalions now presented so narrow a front that he was but a moment in traversing it, and this palpable diminution of their numbers evidently vexed him; either, therefore, to deceive his enemies or his own soldiers, he declared that the practice hitherto pursued of ranging the men three deep was wrong, and that two were sufficient; and he ordered his infantry in future to be drawn up in two ranks only.

Nay, more: he even insisted that the inflexibility of the regimental returns should give way to this illusion. He disputed their results; and the obstinacy of Count Lobau could not overcome his. He was desirous, no doubt, of making his aid-de-camp[1] understand what he wished others to believe, and that nothing could shake his resolution.

Meanwhile the attitude of his army seconded his wishes. Most of the officers persevered in their confidence. The common soldiers, who saw their whole lives in the present, and expected but little from the future, were for the most part unconcerned about it, and still retained their thoughtlessness, the most valuable of their qualities. The rewards, however, which the emperor bestowed profusely upon them in the daily reviews, were received at best with a sedate joy, mingled with some degree of dejection. The vacant places about to be filled up were yet freshly dyed with blood: these favors were menacing.

On the other hand, when leaving Wilna, many of them had thrown away their winter garments, that they might load themselves with provisions. Their shoes were worn out by the length of the march, and the rest of their apparel by the successive actions in which they had been engaged; but, in spite of all, their attitude was still lofty. They carefully concealed their wretched plight from the notice of the emperor, and appeared before him with their

[1] **Aid-de-camp**: an officer who carries orders and directs movements for a general.

arms bright and in the best order. In this first court of the palace of the Czars, full sixteen hundred miles from their resources, and after so many battles and bivouacs, they were anxious to appear still clean, alert, and prompt, for herein consists the pride of the soldier; and here they piqued themselves upon it the more, on account of the difficulty, in order to astonish, and because man prides himself on whatever requires extraordinary effort.

The emperor complaisantly affected to know no better, catching at everything to keep up his hopes; when all at once the first snows fell. With them fell all the illusions with which he had endeavored to surround himself. From that moment he thought of nothing but retreat, without, however, pronouncing the word, and yet no positive order for it could be obtained from him. He merely said that in twenty days the army must be in winter quarters, and he urged the departure of his wounded. On this as on other occasions, he would not consent to the voluntary relinquishment of anything, however trifling: there was a deficiency of horses for his artillery, now too numerous for an army so reduced; but it did not signify, and he flew into a passion at the proposal to leave part of it behind. "No; the enemy would make a trophy of it;" and he insisted that everything should go along with him.

In this desert country he gave orders for the purchase of 20,000 horses, and he expected forage for two months to be provided on a tract where the most distant and dangerous excursions were not sufficient for the supply of the passing day. Some of his officers were astonished to hear orders which it was so impossible to execute; but we have already seen that he sometimes issued such orders to deceive his enemies, and more frequently to indicate to his own troops the extent of their necessities, and the exertions they were called on to make in order to supply them.

His distress manifested itself only in paroxysms of ill-humor, and this most frequently in the morning, at his levee. There, amid his assembled chiefs, in whose anxious looks he imagined he could read disapprobation, he seemed desirous to awe them by the severity of his manner, by his sharp tone, and his abrupt language. From the paleness of his face, however, it was evident that Truth, whose best time for obtaining a hearing is in the stillness of night, had annoyed him grievously by her presence, and oppressed him with her unwelcome light. Sometimes, on these occasions, his bursting heart would overflow, and pour forth its sorrows without any restraint. His agitation was manifested at such times by movements of extreme impatience; but, so far from lightening his griefs, he only aggravated them by those acts of injustice for which he reproached himself, and which he was afterwards anxious to repair.

It was only to Count Daru that he unbosomed himself frankly, but without any weakness. He said "he should march upon Kutusoff, crush or drive him back, and then turn suddenly towards Smolensk." Daru, who had before approved this course, replied that "it was now too late; that the Russian army was re-enforced, his own weakened, and his victory forgotten; that, the moment his troops turned their faces towards home, they would slip away from him by degrees; that each soldier, laden with booty, would try to get the start of the army, for the purpose of disposing of it in France." "What, then, is to be done?" exclaimed the emperor. "Remain here," replied Daru; "make one vast intrenched camp of Moscow, and pass the winter in it. He would answer for it that there would be no want of bread and salt : the rest foraging on a large scale would supply. Such of the horses as they could not procure food for might be salted down. As to lodgings, if there were not houses enough, the cellars might make up the deficiency. Here we might stay till the return of spring, when our re-enforcements and all Lithuania in arms would come to relieve, to join us, and to complete the conquest."

After listening to this proposal the emperor was for some time silent and thoughtful : he then replied, "This is a lion's counsel! But what would Paris say? What would they do there? What have they been doing there for the last three weeks that they have not heard from me? Who knows what would be the effect of a suspension of communication for six months? No : France would not accustom itself to my absence, and Prussia and Austria would take advantage of it."

Still Napoleon could not make up his mind either to stay or to depart. Though overcome in this struggle of pertinacity, he deferred from day to day the avowal of his defeat. Amid the threatening storm of men and elements which was gathering around him, his ministers and aids-de-camp saw him pass whole days in discussing the merits of some new verses which he had received, or the regulations for one of the French theatres at Paris, which he took three evenings to finish. As they were acquainted with his deep anxiety, they could not but admire the strength of his genius, and the facility with which he could take off the whole force of his attention from, or fix it on, whatever subject he pleased.

It was merely remarked that he prolonged his meals, which had hitherto been so simple and so short. He seemed desirous of stifling thought by repletion. He would then pass whole hours half reclined, and as if torpid, awaiting with a novel in his hand the catastrophe of his terrible history. In contemplating this obstinate and inflexible character thus struggling with impossibility, his officers would observe to each other that, having arrived at the summit of his glory, he no doubt foresaw that from his first retrograde step would date its decline; that for this reason he continued immovable, clinging to, and lingering a few moments longer on, his proud elevation.

Kutusoff, meanwhile, was gaining the time which we were losing. His letters to Alexander described "his army as being in the midst of plenty; his recruits arriving from all quarters, and being rapidly trained; his wounded recovering in the bosom of their families; the whole of the peasantry on foot, some in arms, some on the look-out from the tops of steeples or in our camp, while others were stealing into our habitations, and even into the Kremlin. Rostopchin received a daily report of what was passing at Moscow as regularly as before its capture. If they undertook to be our guides, it was for the purpose of delivering us into his hands. His partisans were every day bringing in some hundreds of prisoners. Everything concurred to destroy the enemy's army and to strengthen his own; to serve him and to betray us; in a word, the campaign, which was over for us, was but just about to begin for them."

Kutusoff neglected no advantage. He made his camp ring with the news of the victory of Salamanca. "The French," said he, "are expelled from Madrid. The hand of the Most High presses heavily upon Napoleon. Moscow will be his prison, his grave, and that of the whole of his Grand Army. We shall soon subdue France in Russia!"

It was in such language that the Russian general addressed his troops and his emperor; and still he kept up appearances with Murat. At once bold and crafty, he contrived gradually to prepare a sudden and impetuous warfare, and to cover his plans for our destruction with demonstrations of kindness and honeyed words.

But at length, after so many days of illusion, the charm was all at once dispelled. A single Cossack dissolved it. This barbarian fired at Murat, at the moment when that prince came as usual to show himself at the advanced posts. Highly exasperated, the king immediately declared to Miloradovitch that an armistice which had been incessantly violated was now at an end, and that thenceforward each party must look only to itself.

At the same time he apprised the emperor that the woody country on his left might favor the enemy's attempts against his flank and rear; that his first line, being backed against a ravine, might be precipitated into it; that, in short, the position which he then occupied, in advance of a defile, was dangerous, and rendered a retrograde movement absolutely necessary. But Napoleon would not consent to this step, though he had at first pointed out Woronowo as a more secure position. In this war, still in his view rather political than military, he dreaded above all things the appearance of receding. He preferred risking everything rather than acknowledge to his enemies the slightest irresolution.

Amid these preparations, and at the moment when Napoleon was reviewing Ney's divisions in the first court of the Kremlin, a report was all at once circulated that the sound of cannon was heard towards Vinkowo. It was some time before any one dared to apprise him of the circumstance; some from incredulity or uncertainty, and dreading the first movement of his impatience; others from weakness, hesitating to provoke a terrible explosion or apprehensive of being sent to verify the assertion, and exposed to a fatiguing excursion.

Duroc at length took courage to inform him. The emperor was at first agitated; but, quickly recovering himself, he continued the review. An aid-de-camp, young Béranger, arrived shortly after with intelligence that Murat's first line had been surprised and overthrown, his left turned by favor of the woods, his flank attacked, and his retreat cut off: that twelve pieces of cannon, twenty ammunition wagons, and thirty wagons belonging to the train were taken, two generals killed, three or four thousand men lost, as well as the baggage; and, lastly, that the king himself was wounded. He had not been able to rescue the relics of his advanced guard from the enemy but by repeatedly charging their numerous troops, which already occupied the high road in his rear, his only retreat.

Our honor, however, had been saved. The attack in front, directed by Kutusoff, was feeble; Poniatowski, at some leagues' distance on the right, made a glorious resistance; Murat and his resolute men, by almost superhuman exertions, checked Bagawout, who was ready to penetrate our left flank, and restored the fortunes of the day; while Claparède and Latour-Maubourg cleared the defile of Spaskapli, two leagues in the rear of our line, which was already occupied by Platoff. Two Russian generals were killed, and others wounded: the loss of the enemy was considerable, but the advantage of the attack, our cannon, our position, the victory, in short, was theirs.

As for Murat, he had no longer an advanced guard.

The armistice had destroyed half the remnant of his cavalry. This engagement had finished it; the survivors, emaciated with hunger, were so few as scarcely to furnish a charge. Thus had the war in earnest recommenced; and it was now the 18th of October.

At these tidings Napoleon recovered the fire of his youth. A thousand orders, general and particular, all differing, yet all in unison and all necessary, burst at once from his impetuous genius. Night had not yet arrived, and the whole army was already in motion. The emperor himself quitted Moscow before daylight on the 19th of October. "Let us march upon Kaluga," said he, "and woe be to those whom I meet with by the way!"

§ 10. Departure from Moscow; the first battle.

On the southern side of Moscow, near one of its gates, is an extensive suburb, divided by two high roads; both run to Kaluga: that on the right is the more ancient, the other is quite new. It was on the first that Kutusoff had just beaten Murat. By the same road Napoleon left Moscow on the 19th of October, announcing to his officers his intention to return to the frontiers of Poland. One of them, Rapp, observed that "it was late, and that winter might overtake them by the way." The emperor replied "that he had been obliged to allow time to the soldiers to recruit themselves, and to the wounded collected at Moscow, and at other places, to move off towards Smolensk." Then, pointing to a still serene sky, he asked "if in that brilliant sun they did not recognize his star." But this appeal to his fortune, and the sinister expression of his looks, belied the security which he affected.

Napoleon entered Moscow with ninety thousand fighting men, and twenty thousand sick and wounded, and quitted it with more than a hundred thousand combatants. He left there with only twelve hundred sick. His stay, therefore, notwithstanding daily losses, had served to rest his infantry, to complete his stores, to augment his force by ten thousand men, and to protect the recovery or the retreat of a great part of his wounded. But on this very first day he could perceive that his cavalry and artillery might be said rather to crawl than to march.

A melancholy spectacle added to the gloomy presentiments of our chief. The army had, ever since the preceding day, been pouring out of Moscow without intermission. In this column of one hundred and forty thousand men and about fifty thousand horses of all kinds, the hundred thousand combatants marching at its head with their knapsacks and their arms, upward of five hundred and fifty pieces of cannon, and two thousand artillery wagons, still exhibited a formidable appearance, worthy of soldiers who had conquered the world. But the rest, whose numbers were in an alarming proportion, resembled a horde of Tartars after a successful invasion. They formed three or four files of almost infinite length, in which there was a confused mixture of chaises, ammunition wagons, handsome carriages, and, in short, vehicles of every kind. Here trophies of Russian, Turkish, and Persian colors, and the gigantic cross of Ivan the Great; there, long-bearded Russian peasants carrying or driving along our booty, of which they constituted a part; and some dragging even wheelbarrows filled with whatever they could remove. The fools were not likely to proceed in this manner till the conclusion of the first day, and yet their senseless avidity made them think nothing of battles and a march of two hundred leagues.

Among these followers of the army were particularly remarked a multitude of men of all nations, without uniform and without arms, and servants swearing in every language, and urging by dint of shouts and blows the progress of elegant carriages, drawn by pigmy horses harnessed with ropes. These were filled with provisions, or with booty saved from the flames. They carried, also, many French women with their children. Formerly these females had been happy inhabitants of Moscow; but they now fled from the hatred of the Muscovites, which the invasion had drawn upon their heads, and the army was their only asylum.

A few Russian girls, voluntary captives, also followed. It looked like a caravan, a wandering nation, or, rather, one of those armies of antiquity returning loaded with slaves and with spoils after a great devastation. It was inconceivable how the head of this column could draw and protect such a prodigious mass of equipages in so long a route.

Notwithstanding the width of the road and the shouts of his escort, Napoleon had great difficulty in obtaining a passage through this immense throng. No doubt the obstruction of a defile, a few forced marches, or a handful of Cossacks would have been sufficient to rid us all of this encumbrance; but fortune or the enemy had alone a right to lighten us in this manner. As for the emperor, he was fully sensible that he could neither deprive his soldiers of this fruit of so many toils, nor reproach them for securing it. Besides, provisions concealed the booty; and was it for him, who could not give his troops the subsistence he should have done, to forbid their carrying it along with them? Lastly, in case of the failure of military conveyances, these vehicles would be the only means of preservation for the sick and wounded.

Napoleon therefore extricated himself in silence from the immense train which he drew after him, and advanced on the old road leading to Kaluga. He pushed on in this direction for some hours, declaring that he would go and beat Kutusoff on the very field of his victory. But all at once, about midday, opposite to the castle of Krasnopachra, where he halted, he suddenly turned to the right with his army, and in three marches across the country gained the new road to Kaluga.

The rain, which overtook him in the midst of this manœuvre, spoiled the cross-roads, and obliged him to halt in them. This was a most unfortunate circumstance. It was with difficulty that our cannon were drawn out of the sloughs.

At any rate, the emperor had masked his movement by Ney's corps and the remnants of Murat's cavalry, which had remained behind the Motscha and at Woronowo. Kutusoff, deceived by this feint, was still waiting for the Grand Army on the old road, while, on the 23d of October, the whole of it had been transferred to the new one, and had but one march to make in order to pass quietly by him, and to get between him and Kaluga.

On the first day of this flanking march, a letter was sent from Berthier to Kutusoff, as a last attempt at peace, or perhaps merely as a ruse. No satisfactory answer was returned to it.

On the 23d the imperial quarters were at Borowsk. That night was an agreeable one for the emperor: he was informed that, at six in the evening, Delzons with his division, who was four leagues in advance of him, had found the town of Malo-jaroslavetz and the woods which command it unoccupied: this was a strong position within reach of Kutusoff, and the only point where he could cut us off from the new road to Kaluga.

The emperor wished at first to secure that advantage by his presence: the order to march was even given, but shortly after withdrawn, we know not why. He passed the whole of that evening on horseback, not far from Borowsk, on the left of the road, the side on which he supposed Kutusoff to be. He reconnoitered the ground in the midst of a heavy rain, as if he anticipated that it might become a field of battle. Next day, the 24th, he learned that the Russians had disputed the possession of the town with Delzons. Either from confidence or uncertainty in his plans, this intelligence appeared to give him very little concern.

He quitted Borowsk, therefore, late and leisurely, when the noise of a very smart engagement reached where he was; he then became uneasy, hastened to an eminence and listened. "Had the Russians anticipated him? Was his manœuvre thwarted? Had he not used sufficient expedition in that march, the object of which was to pass the left flank of Kutusoff?"

The emperor was still listening: the noise increased. "Is it then a battle?" he exclaimed. Every discharge agitated him, for the chief point with him was no longer to conquer, but to preserve, and he urged on with all possible speed, Davoust accompanying him; but he and that marshal did not reach the field of battle till dark, when the firing was already subsiding, and the whole was over.

The emperor saw the close of the battle, but without

being able to assist the viceroy.[1] A band of Cossacks from Twer had nearly captured one of his officers, who was only a very short distance from him.

At this time an officer, sent by Prince Eugene, came to him and explained the whole affair. "The troops had," he said, "in the first place, been obliged to cross the Louja at the foot of the town, at the bottom of an elbow which the river makes in its course, and then to climb a steep hill. It is on this precipitous declivity, broken by pointed crags, that the town is built. Beyond is an elevated plain, surrounded with woods, from which run three roads, one in front coming from Kaluga, and two on the left, from Lectazowo, the seat of the intrenched camp of Kutusoff."

After crossing the Louja by a narrow bridge, the high road from Kaluga runs along the bottom of a ravine which ascends to the town, and then enters it. The enemy in mass occupied this hollow way; Delzons and his Frenchmen rushed upon them pell-mell; the Russians were broken and overthrown; they gave way, and presently our bayonets glistened on the heights.

Delzons, conceiving himself sure of the victory, announced it as won. He had nothing but a pile of buildings to storm; but his soldiers hesitated. He himself advanced, and was encouraging them by his words, actions, and example, when a ball struck him in the forehead, and extended him on the ground. His brother threw himself upon him, covered him with his body, clasped him in his arms, and was striving to bear him out of the fire and the fray, when a second ball hit him also, and both expired together.

This loss left a great void, which required to be filled.

[1] **The viceroy:** Prince Eugene.

Guilleminot succeeded Delzons, and the first thing he did was to throw a hundred men into a church and the yard around it, in the walls of which they made loopholes. This church stood on the left of the high road, which it commanded, and to its possession we owed the victory. Five times during the day was this post passed by the Russian columns as they were pursuing ours, and five times did its fire, seasonably poured upon their flank and rear, harass them and retard their progress: afterward, when we resumed the offensive, this position placed them between two fires, and ensured the success of our attacks.

Scarcely had that general made this disposition when he was assailed by a host of the enemy: he was driven back towards the bridge, where the viceroy had stationed himself in order to judge how to act and to prepare his reserves. At first the re-enforcements which he sent came up but slowly one after another; and, as is almost always the case where there is this tardy movement, being singly inadequate to any great effort, each was successively destroyed without result.

At length the whole of the 14th division was engaged; and the combat was carried for the third time to the heights. But when the French had passed the houses, advanced beyond the central point from which they had set out, and reached the plain where they were exposed, and where the circle expanded, they could advance no farther; overwhelmed by the fire of a whole Russian army, they were daunted and shaken; fresh columns incessantly came up: our thinned ranks gave way and were broken; the obstacles of the ground increased their confusion; and at length they retired precipitately, and abandoned everything.

Meanwhile, the shells having set fire to the wooden town behind them, in their retreat they were stopped by the conflagration : one fire drove them back upon another; the Russian recruits, wrought up to a pitch of fanatic fury, closely pursued them ; our soldiers became enraged ; they fought man to man ; some were seen seizing each other with one hand and striking with the other, until both rolled down the precipices into the flames without quitting their hold. There the wounded expired, either suffocated by the smoke or consumed by the flames.

The 15th division was still left. The viceroy summoned it : as it advanced, it threw a brigade into the suburb on the left, and another into the town on the right. It consisted of Italians, recruits, who had never before been in action. They ascended, shouting enthusiastically, ignorant of the danger or despising it, from that singular disposition which renders life less dear in its flower than in its decline, either because while young we fear death less from the feeling of its distance, or because at that age, rich in years and lavish of everything, we are prodigal of life as the wealthy are of their fortune.

The shock was terrible: everything was reconquered for the fourth time, and speedily lost again in like manner. More eager to begin than their seniors, these young troops were sooner disheartened, and returned flying to the old battalions, which supported them, and were obliged to lead them back to danger.

The Russians, imboldened by their constantly increasing numbers and by success, descended by their right to gain possession of the bridge and to cut off our retreat. Prince Eugene had nothing left but his last reserve : he and his guard, therefore, now took part in the combat. At this sight, and in obedience to his call, the remains of the 13th, 14th, and 15th divisions resumed their courage: they made a last and desperate effort, and for the fifth time the combat was transferred to the heights.

At the same time, Colonel Peraldi and the Italian troops overthrew with their bayonets the Russians who were already approaching the left of the bridge: infuriated by the smoke and the fire through which they had passed, and encouraged by their success and the havoc which they made, they pushed forward without stopping on the elevated plain, and endeavored to make themselves masters of the enemy's cannon; but one of those deep clefts with which the soil of Russia is intersected stopped them in the midst of a destructive fire, their ranks opened, the enemy's cavalry attacked them, and they were driven back to the very gardens of the suburb. There they paused and rallied: all, both French and Italians, obstinately defended the upper avenues of the town, and the Russians, being at length repulsed, drew back and concentrated themselves on the road to Kaluga, between the woods and Malo-jaroslavetz.

In this manner did 18,000 Italians and French, crowded together at the bottom of a ravine, defeat 50,000 Russians, posted over their heads, and seconded by all the obstacles that a town built on a steep declivity is capable of presenting.

The army, however, surveyed with sorrow this field of battle, where seven generals and 4000 French and Italians had been killed or wounded. The sight of the enemy's loss afforded no consolation; it was not twice the amount of ours, and their wounded would be saved. It was moreover recollected, that in a similar situation, Peter I., in sacrificing ten Russians for one Swede, thought that he was not sustaining merely an equal loss, but that he was gaining even by so terrible a bargain. But what caused the greatest pain was the reflection that this sanguinary conflict might have been spared.[1]

### § 11. Napoleon holds a council of war and decides to retreat northward.

Do you recollect, comrades, that fatal field? Can you still figure to yourselves the blood-stained ruins of that town, those deep ravines, and the woods which surround that elevated plain, and mark it, as it were, for a field of combat? On the one side were the French, quitting the north, from which they sought to fly; on the other, at the entrance of the wood, were the Russians, guarding the south, and striving to drive us back upon their all-subduing winter. In the midst of this plain, between the two armies, was Napoleon, his steps and his eyes wandering from south to west, along the roads to Kaluga and Medyn, both which were closed against him. On that to Kaluga were Kutusoff and one hundred and twenty thousand men, ready to dispute with him sixty miles of defiles; towards Medyn he beheld a numerous cavalry: it was Platoff and those same hordes which had just penetrated the flank of the army, traversed it through and through, and burst forth, laden with booty, to form again on his right flank, where reenforcements and artillery were waiting for them. It was

[1] The indecisive battle of Malo-jaroslavetz, a town about fifty miles southwest of Moscow, compelled Napoleon to give up his original plan of retreat, which would have taken him through an unexhausted country to the southward, and forced him to go back to the north, retracing his steps by the route he came.

on that side that the eyes of the emperor were fixed the longest; it was principally in regard to it that he listened to reports of his officers, and consulted his maps: until, oppressed with regret and gloomy forebodings, he slowly returned to his headquarters.

Murat, Prince Eugene, Berthier, Davoust and Bessières followed him. This miserable habitation of an obscure artisan contained within it an emperor, two kings, and three generals. Here they were about to decide the fate of Europe, and of the army which had conquered it. Smolensk was the goal. Should they march thither by Kaluga, Medyn, or Mojaisk? Napoleon was seated at a table, his head supported by his hands, which concealed his features, as well as the anguish which they no doubt expressed.

A silence fraught with such imminent perils was for some time respected, until Murat, whose actions were always the result of impetuous feeling, became weary of this hesitation.

"Give him but the remnant of his cavalry and that of the Guard," he said, "and he would force his way into Russian forests and the Russian battalions, overthrow all before him, and open anew to the army the road to Kaluga."

Here Napoleon, raising his head, extinguished all his fire by saying that "we had exhibited temerity enough already; that we had done but too much for glory, and it was now high time to give up thinking of anything but how to save the rest of the army."

Bessières, either because his pride revolted at the idea of being put under the command of the King of Naples, or from a desire to preserve uninjured the cavalry of the Guard, which he had formed, for which he was answerable to Napoleon, and which he exclusively commanded, finding himself supported, then ventured to add, that "neither the army nor even the Guard had sufficient spirit left for such efforts." The marshal concluded by giving his opinion in favor of retreat, which the emperor approved by his silence.

The Prince of Eckmühl then immediately said that, "as a retreat seemed decided upon, he proposed that it should be by Medyn and Smolensk." But Murat here interrupted him; and, whether from enmity, or from that discouragement which usually succeeds the rejection of a rash measure, he declared himself astonished "that any one should dare propose so imprudent a step to the emperor. Had Davoust sworn the destruction of the army? Would he have so long and heavy a column trail along in utter uncertainty, without guides, and on an unknown track, within reach of Kutusoff, presenting its flank to all the attacks of the enemy? Would he, Davoust, defend it? When in our rear Borowsk and Vereïa would lead us without danger to Mojaisk, why reject that safe route? There provisions must have been already collected, there everything was known to us, and we could not be misled by any traitor."

At these words, Davoust, burning with a rage which he could scarcely repress, replied that "he proposed a retreat through a fertile country, by an untouched, plentiful, and well supplied route, where the villages were still standing, and by the shortest road, that the enemy might not be able to cut us off, as on the route by Mojaisk to Smolensk, recommended by Murat. And what a route! a desert of sand and ashes, where convoys of wounded would increase our embarrassment, where we should meet with nothing but ruins, traces of blood, skeletons, and famine!

"Moreover, though he deemed it his duty to give his opinion when it was asked, he was ready to obey orders contrary to it with the same zeal as if they were consonant with his suggestions; but that the emperor alone had a right to impose silence on him, and not Murat, who was not his sovereign, and never should be!"

The quarrel growing warm, Bessières and Berthier interposed. As for the emperor, still absorbed and in the same attitude, he appeared insensible to what was passing. At length he broke up the council with the words, "Well, gentlemen, I will decide."

He decided on retreat, and by that road which would carry him most speedily to a distance from the enemy; but it required another desperate effort before he could bring himself to give an order of march so new to him. So painful, indeed, was this effort, that in the inward struggle which it produced he lost the use of his senses.

It is a remarkable fact, that he issued orders for this retreat northward at the very moment that Kutusoff and his Russians, dismayed at their defeat at Malo-jaroslavetz, were retiring towards the south.

From that moment Napoleon had nothing in his view but Paris, just as on leaving Paris he saw nothing but Moscow. It was on the 26th of October that the fatal movement of our retreat commenced. Davoust, with twenty-five thousand men, remained as a rear-guard. While by advancing a few paces, without being aware of it, he was spreading consternation among the Russians, the Grand Army, in astonishment, was turning its back on them. It marched with downcast eyes, as if ashamed and humbled. In the midst of it, its commander, gloomy and silent, seemed to be anxiously measuring his line of communication with the fortresses on the Vistula.

For the space of more than two hundred and fifty leagues it offered but two points where he could halt and rest, the first Smolensk, the second Minsk. He had made those towns his two great depôts, where immense magazines were established.

Napoleon, however, reckoned upon the Duke of Belluno and his thirty-six thousand fresh troops. That corps had been at Smolensk ever since the beginning of September. He relied also upon detachments being sent from his depôts, on the sick and wounded who had recovered, and on the stragglers, who would be rallied and formed at Wilna into marching battalions. All these would successively come into line, and fill up the chasms made in his ranks by the sword, famine, and disease. He should therefore have time to regain that position on the Dwina and the Borysthenes, where he wished it to be believed that his presence, added to that of Victor, Saint-Cyr, and Macdonald, would overawe Wittgenstein,[1] check Kutusoff, and threaten the Czar Alexander even in his second capital.

He accordingly announced that he was going to take post on the Dwina. But it was not in truth, upon that river and the Borysthenes that his thoughts rested: he was sensible that it was not with a harassed and reduced army that he could guard the interval between those two rivers and their courses, which the ice would speedily seal.

It was therefore a hundred leagues beyond Smolensk, in a more compact position, behind the morasses of the Berezina — to Minsk, that it was necessary to repair in search of winter quarters, from which he was then forty marches distant.

[1] **Wittgenstein**: commander of one division of the Russian forces, held a position on the Dwina River and later on the Berezina, a tributary of the Dnieper.

### § 12. Napoleon's attempt to destroy the Kremlin: view of the battle-field of Borodino.

Napoleon had arrived quite pensive at Vereïa,[1] when Mortier presented himself before him. But I here discover, that, hurried along in the relation just as we then were in reality, by the rapid succession of violent scenes and memorable events, my attention has been diverted from occurrences worthy of notice. On the 23d of October, at half past one in the morning, the air was shaken by a tremendous explosion, which for a moment startled both armies, though amid such mighty anticipations scarcely anything then much excited their astonishment.

Mortier had obeyed his orders: the Kremlin was no more.[2] Barrels of powder had been placed in all the halls of the palaces of the Czars, and one hundred and eighty-three thousand pounds under the vaults which supported them. The marshal, with eight thousand men, had remained on this volcano, which a single Russian shell might have exploded. Here he covered the march of the army upon Kaluga, and the retreat of our different convoys towards Mojaisk.

Among these eight thousand men there were scarcely two thousand on whom Mortier could rely; the others were dismounted cavalry, men of different countries and regiments, under new officers, with dissimilar habits, with no common recollections, in short, without any bond of union, forming a rabble rather than an organized body, and who could scarcely fail in a short time to disperse.

[1] **Vereïa:** a village about twenty-five miles northwest of Malo-jaroslavetz.
[2] **Kremlin:** it was afterward found that the fortress was but slightly injured.

This marshal, therefore, was looked upon as a doomed man. The other chiefs, his old companions in glory, had left him with tears in their eyes, as well as the emperor himself, who said to him "that he relied on his good fortune; but still, in war, we must sometimes make part of a sacrifice." Mortier resigned himself without hesitation to his fate. His orders were to defend the Kremlin, and on retreating to blow it up, and to burn what still remained of the city. It was on the 21st of October, that Napoleon sent him his last commands. After executing them, the marshal was to march upon Vereïa, and to form the rear guard of the army.

In this letter Napoleon particularly recommended to him "to put the men still remaining in the hospitals into the carriages belonging to the young rear guard, those of the dismounted cavalry, and any others that he might find. The Romans," he added, "awarded a civic crown to him who had saved a citizen: so many soldiers as he should save, so many crowns would the Duke of Treviso deserve."

At length, after four days' resistance, the French bade a final adieu to that fatal city. They carried with them four hundred wounded, and, on retiring, deposited in a safe and secret place a firework, skilfully prepared, which was already slowly consuming: the rate of its burning had been minutely calculated, so that it was known precisely at what hour the fire would reach the immense collection of powder buried among the foundations of these devoted palaces.

Mortier hastened his flight; but as he was retiring, some greedy Cossacks and miserable-looking Muscovites, allured probably by the prospect of pillage, approached: they listened, and, imboldened by the apparent quiet which pervaded the fortress, they ventured to penetrate into it: they ascended; and their greedy hands were already stretched forth to lay hold on their plunder, when in an instant they were all hurled into the air with the buildings they had come to pillage, and with thirty thousand stand of arms that had been left in them; and soon their mangled limbs, mingled with fragments of walls and shattered weapons, thrown to a great distance, descended in a horrible shower.

The earth shook under the feet of Mortier: at Fominskoé, thirty miles off, the emperor heard the explosion; and in that indignant tone in which he sometimes addressed Europe, he published the following day a bulletin, at Borowsk, announcing that "the Kremlin, the arsenal, the magazines, were all destroyed; that that ancient citadel, which dated from the origin of the monarchy, and was the first palace of the Czars, no longer existed; that Moscow was now but a heap of ruins, without importance either political or military. He had abandoned it to Russian beggars and plunderers, in order to march against Kutusoff, to throw himself on the left wing of that general, to drive him back, and then to proceed quietly to the banks of the Dwina, where he should take up his winter quarters." Then, apprehensive lest he should appear to be retreating, he added that "there he should be within eighty leagues of Wilna and of St. Petersburg, a double advantage; that is to say, twenty marches nearer to his resources and his object." By this remark he hoped to give to his retreat the air of an offensive movement.

It was on this occasion he declared that "he had refused to give orders for the entire destruction of the country which he was quitting: he felt a repugnance to aggravate the miseries of its inhabitants. To punish the Russian incendiary, and a few wretches who made war like Tartars, he would not ruin nine thousand proprietors, and leave two hundred thousand serfs, innocent of all these barbarities, absolutely destitute of resources."

On the 28th of October we again beheld Mojaisk.[1] That town was still full of wounded: some were carried away, and the rest collected together and abandoned, as at Moscow, to the generosity of the Russians. Napoleon had proceeded but a short distance from that place when the winter began. Thus, after an obstinate combat, and ten days' marching and countermarching, the army, which had brought from Moscow only fifteen rations of flour per man, had advanced but three days' march on its retreat. It was in want of provisions, and now overtaken by the winter.

Some leagues from Mojaisk we had to cross the Kologa. It was but a large rivulet: two trees, the same number of props, and a few planks were sufficient to ensure the passage; but such was the confusion and inattention that the emperor was detained there. Several pieces of cannon, which it was attempted to get across by fording, were lost. It seemed as if each corps was marching separately, as if there were no staff, no general order, no common tie, nothing, in short, that bound them together. In fact, the elevation of the chiefs rendered them too independent of each other. The emperor himself had become so exceedingly great, that he was at an immeasurable distance from the details of his army; while Berthier, holding an intermediate place between him and officers, all of whom were kings, princes, or marshals, was obliged to act with a great deal of caution. He was, besides, incompetent to his situation.

---

[1] **Mojaisk:** about ten miles northwest of Vereïa and seventy west of Moscow.

The emperor, stopped by the frivolous obstacle of a broken bridge, confined himself to a gesture expressive of dissatisfaction and contempt, to which Berthier replied only by a look of resignation. On this particular point he had received no orders from the emperor: he therefore conceived that he was not to blame; for Berthier was a faithful echo, a mirror, and nothing more. Always ready, clear, and distinct, he, so to speak, exactly repeated the emperor, reflected him, but added nothing of his own; and what Napoleon forgot was never supplied.

After passing the Kologa we marched on, absorbed in thought, when some of us, raising our eyes, uttered a cry of horror. Each one instantly looked about him, and there lay stretched before us a plain trampled, bare, and devastated, all the trees cut down within a few feet from the surface, and farther off craggy hills, the highest of which appeared misshapen, and bore a striking resemblance to an extinguished volcano. The ground around us was everywhere covered with fragments of helmets and cuirasses, with broken drums, gun-stocks, tatters of uniforms, and standards dyed with blood.

On this desolate spot [1] lay thirty thousand half-devoured corpses; while a pile of skeletons on the summit of one of the hills overlooked the whole. It seemed as though Death had here fixed his throne. Presently the cry was heard, "It is the field of the great battle!" forming a long and doleful murmur. The emperor passed quickly by. No one stopped. Cold, hunger, and the enemy were urging us on: we merely turned our faces as we marched along to take a last melancholy look at the vast grave of so many

[1] The battle-field of Borodino, which Napoleon had fought on his march to Moscow. See Introduction.

companions in arms, uselessly sacrificed, and whose remains we were obliged to leave behind, unheeded and uninterred.

### § 13. Napoleon reaches Viazma.  Battle near that place.

At length the emperor reached Viazma.[1] He here halted to wait for Prince Eugene and Davoust, and to reconnoitre the road to Medyn and Yucknow, which at this place unites with the high road to Smolensk. It was this cross-road which might possibly bring the Russian army from Malo-jaroslavetz on his passage. But on the first of November, after waiting thirty-six hours and seeing no indications of that army, he again set out, wavering between the hope that Kutusoff had fallen asleep, and the fear lest he might have left Viazma on his right, and proceeded two marches farther to cut off his retreat. He left Ney, however, at Viazma to collect the first and fourth corps, and to relieve, by forming the rear guard, Davoust, whom he judged to be fatigued.

He complained of the tardiness of the latter, and wrote to reproach him with being still five marches behind, when he ought to have been no more than three: the genius of that marshal he considered too methodical to direct, in a suitable manner, so irregular a march.

But this delay was accounted for by the fact that Davoust had found a marsh without a bridge, and completely encumbered with wagons. He had dragged them out of the slough in sight of the enemy, and so near them that their fires lighted his labors, and the sound of their drums mingled with that of his own voice. For the marshal and his generals could not yet resolve on abandoning

---

[1] **Viazma:** about fifty miles west of Borodino.

to the enemy so many trophies; nor did they make up their minds to it until after fruitless exertions, and in the last extremity.

The road they were traversing was crossed at short intervals by marshy hollows. A slope, slippery as glass with the ice, hurried the carriages into them, and there they stuck fast: to draw them out it was necessary to climb on the opposite side a similar slope, where the horses, whose shoes were worn entirely smooth, could obtain no footing, and where every moment they and their drivers dropped down exhausted together. The famished soldiers immediately fell upon these luckless animals and tore them to pieces; then at fires, kindled with the remains of their carriages, they broiled the yet bleeding flesh, and devoured it.

Meanwhile the artillerymen, a chosen corps, and their officers, all brought up in the first military school in the world, kept off these unfortunate wretches whenever they could, and took the horses from their own carriages and wagons, which they abandoned to save the guns. To these they harnessed their horses, nay, even themselves; while the Cossacks, observing their disasters from a distance, though they dared not attack, with their light pieces mounted on sledges, threw their balls among these disorderly groups, and increased the confusion.

On the 3d of November, Prince Eugene was advancing towards Viazma, preceded by his equipages and his artillery, when the first light of day all at once discovered to him his retreat threatened by an army on his left, behind him his rear guard cut off, and on his left the plain covered with stragglers and scattered vehicles, fleeing before the lances of the enemy. At the same time, towards Viazma he heard Marshal Ney, who should have assisted him, fighting for his own preservation.

At the same time, Compans, one of Davoust's generals, joined the Italian rear guard with his division. These cleared a passage for themselves, and while, united with the viceroy, they were warmly engaged, Davoust with his column passed rapidly behind them, along the left side of the high road, then crossing it, as soon as he had got beyond them, he claimed his place in the order of battle, took the right wing, and found himself between Viazma and the Russians. Prince Eugene gave up to him the ground which he had been defending, and crossed to the other side of the road. The enemy then began to extend himself in front of them, and endeavored to outflank their wings.

Miloradovitch, the Russian general, left to himself, now tried to break the French line of battle; but he could penetrate it by his fire alone, which made dreadful havoc in our ranks. Eugene and Davoust were growing weak; and, as they heard another action in the rear of their right, they imagined that the rest of the Russian army was approaching Viazma by the Yuknof road, the outlet of which Ney was defending.

It was only, however, an advanced guard: but they were alarmed at the noise of this engagement in the rear of their own, threatening their retreat. The action had now continued ever since seven in the morning, and night was approaching: the baggage must by this time have got away, and the French generals began to retire.

This retrograde movement increased the ardor of the enemy, and but for a memorable effort of the 25th, 57th, and 85th regiments, and the protection of a ravine,

Davoust's corps would have been broken, turned by its right, and destroyed. Prince Eugene, who was not so briskly attacked, was able to effect his retreat more rapidly through Viazma; but the Russians followed him thither, and had penetrated into the town at the very time when Davoust, pursued by 20,000 men, and overwhelmed by eighty pieces of cannon, in his turn attempted to pass.

Morand's division first entered the place: it was marching on with confidence, under the idea that the action was over, when the Russians, who were concealed by the windings of the streets, suddenly fell upon it. The surprise was complete, and the confusion great: Morand nevertheless rallied and encouraged his men, retrieved matters, and fought his way through.

It was Compans who put an end to the affair. He closed the march with his division. Finding himself too closely pressed by the bravest troops of Miloradovitch, he turned about, dashed in person at the most eager, overthrew them, and having thus made them fear him, he finished his retreat without farther molestation. This conflict, glorious to each, was in its result disastrous to all. It was, unhappily, without unity or order. There were troops enough to conquer had there not been too many commanders. It was not till near two o'clock that the latter met to concert their manœuvres, and these were even then executed without harmony.

When at length the river, the town of Viazma, night, mutual fatigue, and Marshal Ney had established a barrier between them and the enemy, the danger being adjourned and the bivouacs established, the numbers were counted. Several pieces of cannon which had been broken, the baggage, and four thousand killed or wounded were found missing. Many of the soldiers, too, had dispersed. Their honor had been saved, but there were immense gaps in their ranks. It was necessary to close them up, to bring everything within a narrower compass, to form what remained into a more compact whole. Each regiment scarcely composed a battalion, each battalion scarcely a platoon. The soldiers remaining had no longer their accustomed places, comrades, or officers.

This sad reorganization took place by the light of the conflagration of Viazma, and during the successive discharges of the cannon of Ney and Miloradovitch, the thunders of which were prolonged amid the double gloom of the night and of the forests. Several times the remnants of these brave battalions, conceiving they were attacked, crawled to their arms. The next morning, when they again fell into their ranks, they were astonished at the smallness of their numbers.

### § 14. Dreadful snow-storm on the 6th of November; its effects upon the troops.

The spirits of the troops were nevertheless still supported by the example of their leaders, by the hopes of finding all their wants supplied at Smolensk, and still more by the aspect of a yet brilliant sun, that universal source of hope and life, which seemed to contradict and deny the spectacles of despair and death that already encompassed us.

But on the 6th of November the heavens changed. Their azure disappeared. The army marched enveloped in a chilling mist. This mist became thicker, and presently a blinding storm of snow descended upon it. It seemed as if the sky itself were falling, and uniting with the earth and our enemies to complete our destruction. All objects rapidly changed their appearance, becoming utterly confounded, and not to be recognized any more: we proceeded without knowing where we were, without perceiving the point to which we were bound; everything was converted into an obstacle to stop our progress. While we were struggling with the tempest of wind and snow, the latter, driven by the storm, lodged and accumulated in every hollow, concealing unknown abysses, which perfidiously opened beneath our feet. There the soldiers were ingulfed, and the weakest, resigning themselves to their fate, found their grave in these treacherous pits.

Those who followed turned aside; but the tempest, driving into their faces the snow that was descending from the sky and that which it raised from the earth, seemed resolved to arrest their farther progress. The Russian winter, in this new form, attacked them at every point: it penetrated through their light garments, and their rent and worn-out shoes. Their wet clothes froze to their bodies: an icy envelope encased them, and stiffened all their limbs. A piercing and violent wind almost prevented respiration; and, seizing their breath the moment it was exhaled, converted it into icicles, which hung from their beards all about their mouths.

The miserable creatures still crawled shivering along, till the snow, gathering in balls on the soles of their shoes, or a fragment of some broken article, a branch of a tree, or the body of one of their comrades, encountered in the way, caused them to stumble and fall. There their groans were unheeded; the snow soon covered them; slight hillocks marked the spots where they lay: there was their only grave. The road, like a cemetery, was thickly studded with these elevations; the most intrepid and the most indifferent were affected; they passed quickly on with averted looks. But before them and around them there was nothing but snow; this immense and dismal uniformity extended farther than the eye could reach; the imagination was astounded: it seemed a vast winding-sheet which Nature had thrown over the army. The only objects not enveloped by it were some gloomy pines, trees of the tombs, with their funereal verdure and their gigantic and motionless trunks completing the solemnity of a general mourning, and of an army dying amid nature already dead.

Everything, even to their very arms, still offensive at Malo-jaroslavetz, but since defensive only, now turned against our men. They seemed to their frozen limbs an insupportable weight. In the falls they experienced, they dropped almost unperceived from their hands, and were broken or buried in the snow. If they rose again it was without them: they had not thrown them away, but hunger and cold had wrested them from their grasp. The fingers of others were frozen to the muskets they still held, depriving them of the motion necessary to keep up some degree of warmth and of life.

We soon met with numbers of men belonging to all the different corps, sometimes singly, sometimes in troops. They had not basely deserted their colors: it was cold and exhaustion which had separated them from them. In this mortal struggle, at once general and individual, they had parted from each other, and there they were, disarmed, vanquished, defenceless, without leaders, obeying nothing but the most urgent instinct of self-preservation.

Most of them, attracted by the sight of by-paths, dispersed themselves over the country in hopes of finding bread and shelter for the coming night; but on their first passage all had been laid waste to the extent of seven or eight leagues: they met only with Cossacks and an armed population, which gathered around them, wounded and stripped them naked, and then left them, with bursts of savage laughter, to perish in the snow. These people, who had risen at the call of Alexander and Kutusoff, and who had not then learned, as they since have, to avenge nobly a country which they had been unable to defend, hovered on both flanks of the army under favor of the woods. Those whom they did not despatch with their pikes and hatchets, they drove back to the fatal and all-devouring high road.

Night then came on: a night of sixteen hours! But on that snow, which covered everything, where were they to halt, where sit, where lie down, where find even a root to satisfy their hunger, or dry wood to kindle a fire? Fatigue, darkness, and repeated orders nevertheless stopped those whom their moral and physical strength and the efforts of their officers had still kept together. They strove to establish themselves; but the tempest, not yet subsided, dispersed the first preparations for bivouacs. The pines, laden with frost, obstinately resisted ignition; while the snow, which still continued to fall from the sky, and that on the ground, which melted with the effect of the first heat, extinguished their kindling fires, and, with them, the strength and spirits of the men.

When at length the flames gained the ascendancy, the officers and soldiers around them commenced preparing their wretched repast: it consisted of lean and ragged pieces of flesh torn from the horses that had given out, and at most a few spoonfuls of rye flour mixed with snow-water. The next morning circular ranges of soldiers extended lifeless marked the sites of the bivouacs, and the ground about them was strewed with the bodies of several thousand horses.

From that day we began to place less reliance on one another. In that vivacious army, susceptible of all impressions, and taught to reason by an advanced civilization, despondency and neglect of discipline rapidly spread, the imagination knowing no bounds in evil any more than in good. Henceforward, at every bivouac, at every difficult passage, nay, every moment, some portion separated from the yet organized lines and fell into disorder. There were some, however, who were proof against this widespread contagion of insubordination and despair. These were officers, non-commissioned officers, and the firmest among the soldiers. They were extraordinary men; they encouraged one another by repeating the name of Smolensk, which town they knew they were approaching, and where they had been promised that all their wants should be supplied.

It was thus, after this deluge of snow, and the increase of cold which it foreboded, that each one, whether officer or soldier, either preserved or lost his fortitude, according to his disposition, age, or constitution; while he who of all our leaders had hitherto been the most strict in enforcing discipline, now paid but little attention to it. Thrown out of his established ideas of regularity, order, and method, he was seized with despair at the sight of such universal confusion: and conceiving, before the rest, that all was lost, he felt himself ready to abandon all.

From this point for some distance, nothing remarkable

occurred in the imperial column except that it was found necessary to throw the spoils of Moscow into the Lake of Semlewo; cannon, Gothic armor, the ornaments of the Kremlin, and the cross of Ivan the Great, were all buried in its waters. Trophies, glory, those acquisitions to which we had sacrificed everything, all now became a burden to us: our object was no longer to embellish life, but to preserve it. In this vast wreck, the army, which might be compared to a mighty ship tossed by the most tremendous of tempests, threw without hesitation into that sea of ice and snow everything that could burden or impede its progress.

The attitude of Napoleon was the same that he retained throughout the whole of this dismal retreat. It was grave, silent, and resigned: suffering much less in body than others, but far more in mind, and brooding with speechless agony over his misfortunes. At that moment General Charpentier sent him from Smolensk a convoy of provisions. Bessières wished to take possession of them; but the emperor instantly ordered them to be forwarded to the Prince of Moskwa, saying that "those who were fighting must eat before the rest." At the same time, he sent word to Ney "to defend himself long enough to allow him some stay at Smolensk, where the army should eat, rest, and be reorganized."

The Russians, however, advanced under favor of a wood and of our forsaken carriages, whence they kept up a fire of musketry on Ney's troops. Half of the latter, whose icy arms froze their stiffened fingers, became discouraged; they gave way, excusing themselves by their want of firmness on the preceding day, and fleeing because they had before fled, which but for this, they would have considered as impossible. But Ney, rushing in among them, seized one of their muskets, and led them back to action, which he was himself the first to renew; exposing his life like a private soldier, with a firelock in his hand, the same as though he had been neither possessed of wealth, nor power, nor consideration; in short, as if he had still everything to gain, when in fact he had everything to lose. But, though he had again turned soldier, he ceased not to be general: he took advantage of the ground, supported himself against a height, and covered his approach by occupying a palisaded house. His generals and colonels, among whom he particularly remarked Fezenzac, strenuously seconded him; and the enemy, who had expected to pursue, was obliged to retreat.

By this action Ney afforded the army a respite of twenty-four hours; and it profited by it to proceed towards Smolensk. The next day, and every succeeding day, he displayed the same heroism. Between Viazma and Smolensk he fought ten whole days.

### § 15. Defeat and entire dissolution of Prince Eugene's corps at the passage of the Wop.

On the 13th of November Ney was approaching that city, which he was not to enter till the ensuing day, and had faced about to beat off the enemy, when all at once the hills upon which he intended to support his left were seen covered with a multitude of fugitives. In their terror, these unfortunate wretches fell, and rolled down to where he was upon the frozen snow, which they stained with their blood. A band of Cossacks, which was soon perceived in the midst of them, sufficiently accounted for this disorder. The astonished marshal, having caused this horde of enemies to be dispersed, discovered behind it the army of Italy, returning completely stripped, without baggage and without cannon.

Platoff had kept it besieged, as it were, all the way from Dorogobouje.[1] Near that town Prince Eugene had quitted the high road, and, in order to proceed towards Witepsk, had taken that which, two months before, had brought him from Smolensk; but the Wop, which, when he had crossed it before, was a mere brook, and had scarcely been noticed, he now found swollen into a river. It ran over a muddy bed, and was bounded by two steep banks. It was found necessary to cut a passage in these precipitous and frozen banks, and to give orders for the demolition of the neighboring houses during the night, for the purpose of building a bridge with the materials. But those who had taken shelter in them opposed their being destroyed; and, as the viceroy was more beloved than feared, his instructions were not obeyed. The bridge-builders became disheartened, and when daylight, with the Cossacks, appeared, the bridge, after being twice broken down, was at last abandoned.

Five or six thousand soldiers still in order, twice the number of disbanded men, the sick and wounded, upward of a hundred pieces of cannon, ammunition-wagons, and a multitude of vehicles of every kind, lined the bank and covered a league of ground. An attempt was made to ford the river through the floating ice which was carried along by its current. The first guns that were attempted to be got over reached the opposite bank; but the water kept rising every moment, while at the same time the bed

---

[1] **Dorogobouje:** a town about fifty miles west of Viazma and nearly two hundred west of Moscow. It is situated on the river Wop, a branch of the Dnieper.

of the stream at the place of passage was continually deepened by the wheels and by the efforts of the horses. One carriage stuck fast, others did the same, and at length the stoppage became general.

Meanwhile the day was advancing; the men were exhausting themselves in vain efforts : hunger, cold, and the Cossacks became pressing, and the viceroy finally found himself compelled to order his artillery and all his baggage to be left behind. A distressing spectacle ensued. The owners were allowed scarcely a moment to part from their effects : while they were selecting from them such articles as they most needed, and loading their horses with them, a multitude of soldiers came rushing up : they fell in preference upon the vehicles of luxury ; these they broke in pieces and rummaged every part, avenging their poverty on the wealth, and their privations on the superfluities they here found, and snatching them from the Cossacks, who were in the meantime looking on at a distance.

But it was provisions of which most of them were in quest. They threw aside embroidered clothes, pictures, ornaments of every kind, and gilt bronzes for a few handfuls of flour. In the evening it was a strange sight to behold the mingled riches of Paris and of Moscow, the luxuries of two of the largest cities in the world, lying scattered and despised on the snow of the desert.

At the same time, most of the artillery-men spiked their guns in despair, and scattered their powder about. Others laid a train with it as far as some ammunition-wagons, which had been left at a considerable distance behind our baggage. They waited till the most eager of the Cossacks had come up to them, and when a great number, greedy of plunder, had collected about them, they threw a brand from a bivouac upon the train. The fire ran, and in a moment reached its destination; the wagons were blown up, the shells exploded, and such of the Cossacks as were not killed on the spot dispersed in dismay.

The army of Italy, thus completely dismantled, soaked in the waters of the Wop, without food, without shelter, passed the night on the snow near a village where its officers expected to find lodgings for themselves. Their soldiers, however, beset its wooden houses. They rushed like madmen, and in swarms, on every habitation, profiting by the darkness, which prevented them from recognizing their officers or being known by them. They tore down everything, doors, windows, and even the woodwork of the roofs, feeling but little compunction in compelling others, be they who they might, to bivouac like themselves.

Their generals attempted in vain to drive them off: they took their blows without a murmur or the least opposition, but without desisting — even the men of the royal and imperial guards; for, throughout the whole army, such were the scenes that occurred every night. The unfortunate fellows kept silently but actively at work on the wooden walls, which they pulled in pieces on every side at once, and which, after vain efforts, their officers were obliged to relinquish to them, for fear they would fall upon their own heads. It was an extraordinary mixture of perseverance in their design and of respect for the anger of their superiors.

Having kindled good fires, they spent the night in drying themselves, amid the shouts, imprecations, and groans of those who were still crossing the torrent, or who, slipping from its banks, were precipitated into it and drowned.

## § 16. The Grand Army reaches Smolensk.

At length the army once more came in sight of Smolensk: it had reached the goal so often announced to it of all its sufferings. The soldiers exultingly pointed it out to each other. There was that land of promise where their hunger was to find abundance, their fatigue rest; where bivouacs in a cold of nineteen degrees would be forgotten in houses warmed by good fires. There they would enjoy refreshing sleep; there they might repair their apparel; there they would be furnished with new shoes, and clothing adapted to the climate.

At this sight, the corps of picked men, the veteran regiments, and a few other soldiers alone kept their ranks; the rest ran forward with all possible speed. Thousands of men, chiefly unarmed, covered the two steep banks of the Borysthenes: they crowded in masses around the lofty walls and gates of the city; but this disorderly multitude, with their haggard faces begrimed with dirt and smoke, their tattered uniforms, and the grotesque habiliments which they had substituted in place of them: in short, with their strange, hideous looks, and their impetuous ardor, excited alarm. It was believed, that if the irruption of this crowd, maddened with hunger, were not repelled, that a general pillage would be the consequence, and the gates were closed against it.

It was also hoped that by exercising this rigor these men would be forced again to rally about their standards. A horrible struggle between order and disorder now commenced in the remnant of this unfortunate army. In vain did they entreat, weep, threaten, strive to burst open the gates, and even drop down dead at the feet of their comrades placed to repel them; they found the latter inexorable, and were forced to wait the arrival of the first troops that were still officered and in order.

These were the Old and the Young Guard; and it was not till after them that the disbanded men were allowed to enter: the latter, and the other corps which arrived in succession, from the 8th to the 14th, believed that their admission had been delayed merely to give more rest and more provisions to this favored guard. Their sufferings rendered them unjust: they execrated it. "Were they, then, to be forever sacrificed to this privileged class; fellows kept for mere parade, who were never foremost but at reviews, festivals, and distributions? Was the army to put up with their leavings, always to wait till they had glutted themselves?" It was useless to tell them in reply, that to attempt to save all was the way to lose all; that it was necessary to keep at least one corps entire, and to give the preference to that which in the last extremity would be capable of making the most powerful effort.

At length these poor creatures were admitted into that Smolensk for which they had so long ardently wished, while the banks of the Borysthenes were strewed with their expiring companions, the weakest of whom impatience and several hours' waiting had brought to that state. Others, again, were left on the icy steep, which they had to climb to reach the upper town. The rest ran to the magazines, where many fell exhausted while they beset the doors; for here also they were repulsed. "Who were they?" it was asked. "To what corps did they belong? What had they to prove it? The persons appointed to distribute the provisions were responsible for them: they had orders to deliver them only to authorized officers bringing receipts, for which alone they could exchange the rations committed to their care." These poor famished creatures had no officers, nor could they tell where their regiments were: two-thirds of the army were in this predicament.

These miserable men then dispersed themselves through the streets, having no longer any hope but in pillage. But horses dissected to the very bones everywhere denoted a famine; the doors and windows of the houses had been all broken and torn away to feed the fires of the bivouacs; they found no shelter in them, no winter quarters prepared, no wood. The sick and wounded were left in the streets, in the carts which had brought them. It was again, it was always the same fatal high road, passing through a town which was but an empty name: it was a new bivouac among deceitful ruins, colder even than the forests they had just quitted.

Then only did these disorganized troops seek their colors: they rejoined them for a moment in order to obtain food; but all the bread that could be baked had been distributed; and there was no biscuit, no butcher's meat. Rye flour, dry vegetables, and spirits were dealt out to them. It required the most strenuous efforts to prevent the detachments of the different corps from murdering each other at the doors of the magazines; and when, after long formalities, their wretched fare was at last delivered to them, the soldiers refused to carry it to their regiments; they fell upon their sacks, snatched out of them a few pounds of flour, and ran to secrete themselves till they had devoured it. The same was the case with the spirits; and the next day the houses were found full of the bodies of these miserable creatures.

In short, that Smolensk, which the army had looked forward to, as the term of their sufferings, marked, as it were, only their commencement. Inexpressible hardships still awaited us: we had yet to march forty days under that yoke of iron. Some, already borne down by present miseries, sank under the frightful prospect of those which were before them. Others sternly resolved to battle with their destiny; and, finding they had nothing to rely on but themselves, they determined to live at all hazards.

Thenceforward, according as they found themselves the stronger or the weaker, by violence or stealth they plundered their companions of their subsistence, of their garments, and of the gold with which they had filled their knapsacks instead of provisions. These wretches, whom despair had thus made robbers, then threw away their arms to save their infamous booty, profiting by the general confusion, an obscure name, a uniform no longer distinguishable, and night: in short, by every kind of concealment favorable to cowardice and guilt. If works already published had not exaggerated these horrors, I should have passed over in silence such terrible details; for atrocities so extreme were, after all, comparatively rare, and justice was dealt to the most criminal.

On the 9th of November the emperor arrived amid this scene of desolation. He shut himself up in one of the houses in the new square, and never quitted it till the 14th to resume his retreat. He had calculated upon fifteen days' provisions and forage for an army of one hundred thousand men; but there was not more than half this quantity of flour, rice, and spirits, and no meat at all. Cries of rage were now directed against the principal individual appointed to provide these supplies; and the commissary saved his life only by prostrating himself on his knees at the feet of Napoleon, and remaining in that posture for a long time. But the reasons which he assigned for his failure did more for him than his supplications.

Many of these reasons were well founded. A chain of other magazines had been formed from Smolensk to Minsk and Wilna. These two towns were, in a still greater degree than Smolensk, centres of provisioning, of which the fortresses of the Vistula formed the first line. The total quantity of provisions, indeed, distributed over this space was incalculable; the efforts for transporting them thither had been gigantic; while the result was little better than nothing. Scattered over such a vast extent, immense as they were, they were found wholly insufficient.

Thus great expeditions are crushed by their own weight. Human limits had been surpassed: the genius of Napoleon, in attempting to soar above time, climate, and distance, had, as it were, lost itself in space; great as was its measure, it had gone beyond it.

Napoleon had been at Smolensk for five days. It was known that Ney had received orders to arrive there as late as possible, and Eugene to halt for two days at a point near Smolensk. Then it was not the necessity of waiting for the army of Italy which detained him! To what, then, must we attribute this delay, in the midst of famine, disease, and when the winter and three hostile armies were gradually surrounding us?

The emperor no doubt fancied that by dating his despatches for five days from that city, he would give to his disorderly flight the appearance of a slow and glorious retreat. In the same spirit, no doubt, he had ordered the destruction of the towers which surrounded Smolensk, from the wish, as he expressed it, of not being again stopped short by its walls! as if there were any idea of our returning to a place which we were not even sure that we should ever get out of.

The emperor, however, made an effort that was not altogether fruitless. This was to rally under one commander all that remained of the cavalry; when it was found that of this force, thirty-seven thousand strong at the passage of the Niemen, there now remained only eight hundred men on horseback. He gave the command of these to Latour-Maubourg; and, whether from the esteem felt for him, or from the general indifference, no one objected to it.

This army, which left Moscow one hundred thousand strong, in five-and-twenty days had been reduced to thirty-six thousand men, while the artillery had lost three hundred and fifty of their cannon; and yet these feeble remains continued as before to be divided into eight armies, which were encumbered with sixty thousand unarmed stragglers, and a long train of cannon and baggage.

Whether it was the encumbrance of so many men and carriages, or a mistaken sense of security, which led the emperor to order a day's interval between the departure of each marshal, is uncertain; but most probably it was the latter. Be that, however, as it may, he, Eugene, Davoust, and Ney, quitted Smolensk in succession; and Ney was not to leave it till the 16th or 17th. He had orders to make the artillery dismount the cannon left behind, and bury them; to destroy the ammunition, to drive all the stragglers before him, and to blow up the towers which surrounded the city.

Kutusoff, meanwhile, was waiting for us at some leagues' distance, prepared to cut in pieces, one after the other, those remnants of corps thus extended and parcelled out.

### § 17. Napoleon leaves Smolensk; battle of Krasnoë.

It was on the 14th of November, about five in the morning, that the imperial column at last quitted Smolensk. Its march was still firm, but gloomy and silent as night, like the mute and sombre aspect of the country through which it was advancing.

This stillness was only interrupted by the cracking of the whips applied to the horses, and by short and violent imprecations when they met with ravines, and when down these icy declivities, men, horses, and artillery were rolling in the darkness one over the other. The first day they advanced five leagues, and the artillery of the guard took twenty-two hours to get over that distance.

Kutusoff, at the same time, with the bulk of his army, moved forward, and took a position in the rear of these advanced corps, within reach of them all, felicitating himself on the success of his manœuvres, which, after all, would inevitably have failed, owing to his tardiness, had it not been for our want of foresight; for this was a contest of errors, in which, ours being the greatest, we narrowly escaped total destruction. Having made these dispositions, the Russian commander must have believed that the French army was entirely in his power; but this belief saved us. Kutusoff was wanting to himself at the moment of action; his old age executed only half, and that badly, the plans which it had wisely combined.

During the time that all these masses were arranging

themselves round Napoleon, he remained perfectly tranquil in a miserable hut, the only one left standing in Korythnia, apparently quite unconscious of all these movements of infantry, artillery, and cavalry, which were surrounding him in all directions; at least he sent no orders to the three corps which had halted at Smolensk, to expedite their march, and he himself waited for daylight to proceed.

His column was advancing without precaution, preceded by a crowd of stragglers, all eager to reach Krasnoë, when, at two leagues from that place, a line of Cossacks, extending from the heights on our left across the great road, appeared before them. Seized with astonishment, these stragglers instantly halted: they had looked for nothing of the kind, and with their first impressions were led to believe that relentless fate had traced upon the snow between them and Europe that long, black, and motionless line as the fatal term assigned to their hopes.

Suddenly a Russian battery began firing. Their balls crossed the road. The German corps became confused and made no attempt to meet this attack. But a wounded officer who chanced to be there assumed the command of the Germans, and the men obeyed him as if he had been their rightful leader. On seeing this advanced column of Germans march forward in such good order, the enemy confined himself to attacking it with his artillery, which it disregarded and soon left behind. When it came to the turn of the Old Guard to pass through this fire, they closed their ranks around Napoleon like a movable fortress, proud of the honor of protecting him. Their band of music expressed their satisfaction. When the danger was greatest, it played the well-known air, "*Where can one be happier than in the bosom of his family?"* But the emperor, whom nothing escaped, stopped them with the exclamation, " Rather play, '*Let us watch for the safety of the empire!*'" words much better suited to the feelings which then occupied him, and to the general condition of affairs.

At the same time, the enemy's fire becoming troublesome, he gave orders to silence it, and in two hours he reached Krasnoë.

On the 17th, before daylight, Napoleon issued his orders, armed himself, and going out on foot at the head of his Old Guard, began his march. But it was not towards Poland, his ally, that he directed it, nor towards France, where he would still be received as the head of a new dynasty, and the Emperor of the West. His words on grasping his sword on this occasion were, "I have sufficiently acted the emperor; it is time I should become the general." He turned back upon eighty thousand of the enemy, plunging into the thickest of them, in order to draw all their efforts against himself, to make a diversion in favor of Davoust and Ney, and to rescue them from a country, the gates of which were closed against them.

Daylight at last appeared, exhibiting on the one part the Russian battalions and batteries, which on three sides, in front, on our right, and in our rear, bounded the horizon, and on the other Napoleon, with his six thousand guards, advancing with a firm step, and proceeding to take his place in the centre of that terrible circle. At the same time, Mortier, a few yards in front of the emperor, deployed,[1] in the face of the whole Russian army, with the five thousand men still remaining to him.

---

[1] **Deployed**: formed a more extended front or line.

Here, then, it was made evident that renown is something more than a vain shadow, that it is real strength, and doubly powerful from the inflexible pride which it imparts to its favorites, and the timid precautions it imposes on those who venture to attack it. The enemy had only to march forward without manœuvring, or even firing; their mass alone was sufficient to crush Napoleon with all his feeble battalions; still they did not dare come to close quarters with him. They were awed at the presence of the conqueror of Egypt and of Europe. The Pyramids, Marengo, Austerlitz, Friedland, a host of victories seemed to rise between him and the astounded Russians. Might we not also fancy that, in the eyes of that passive and superstitious people, a renown so extraordinary appeared like something supernatural? that they regarded it as wholly beyond their power, or, at least, believed that they could safely assail it only from a distance? and, in short, that against that Old Guard, that living fortress, that column of granite, as it had been called by its leader, human efforts were impotent, or that cannon alone could demolish it?

But every moment strengthened the enemy and weakened Napoleon. The noise of artillery, as well as Claparède, apprised him that in the rear of Krasnoë and his army Beningsen was proceeding to take possession of the road to Liady, and entirely cut off his retreat. The east, the west, and the south were flashing with the enemy's fires; one side alone remained open, that of the north and the Dnieper, towards an eminence, at the foot of which were the high road and the emperor. We fancied we saw the enemy already covering this eminence with his cannon. In that situation they would have been just over Napoleon's head, and might have crushed him at a few yards' distance. He was apprised of his danger, cast his eyes for an instant towards the height, and uttered merely these words, "Very well, let one of my battalions take possession of it." Immediately afterward, without giving farther heed to it, his whole attention was directed to the perilous situation of Mortier.

Fortunately, some troops which Davoust had rallied and the appearance of another troop of his stragglers, attracted the enemy's attention. Mortier availed himself of it. He gave orders to the three thousand men he had still remaining to retreat slowly in the face of their fifty thousand enemies. "Do you hear, soldiers?" cried General Laborde, "the marshal orders ordinary time! Ordinary time, soldiers!" And this brave and unfortunate troop, dragging with them some of their wounded, under a shower of balls and grape-shot, retired as deliberately from this field of carnage as they would have done from a field of manœuvre.

### § 18. Napoleon reaches Dombrowna and Orcha; he holds a council.

As soon as Mortier had succeeded in placing Krasnoë between him and Beningsen, he was in safety.

The next day the march was resumed, though with reluctance. The impatient stragglers took the lead, and all of them got the start of Napoleon: he was on foot with a stick in his hand, walking slowly and hesitatingly, and halting every quarter of an hour, as if unwilling to tear himself away from that old Russia, whose frontier he was then passing, and in which he had left his unfortunate companions in arms.

In the evening he reached Dombrowna,[1] a wooden town, and inhabited as well as Liady: a novel sight for an army, which had for three months seen nothing but ruins. At last, then, we had emerged from Russia proper, and her deserts of snow and ashes, and were entering into a friendly and inhabited country, whose language we understood. The weather just then became milder, a thaw began, and we received some provisions.

Thus the winter, the enemy, solitude, and, with some, famine and bivouacs, all ceased at once; but it was too late. The emperor saw that his army was destroyed: every moment the name of Ney escaped from his lips, with expressions of the deepest grief. That night he was heard groaning and exclaiming "that the misery of his poor soldiers cut him to the heart, and yet that he could not succor them without establishing himself in some place: but where was it possible for him to stop without ammunition, provisions, or artillery? He was no longer strong enough to halt: he must reach Minsk as quickly as possible."

He had scarcely spoken the words, when a Polish officer arrived with the news that Minsk itself, his magazine, his retreat, his only hope, had just fallen into the hands of the Russians, Tchitchakoff having entered it on the 16th. Napoleon at first was mute, and completely overpowered by this last blow; but immediately afterward, elevating himself in proportion to his danger, he coolly replied, "Very well! we have now nothing to do but to clear ourselves a passage with our bayonets."

Napoleon then turned to his Old Guard, and, stopping in

[1] **Dombrowna:** a town about fifty miles west of Smolensk and two hundred from Moscow.

front of each battalion, "Grenadiers!"[1] said he, to them, "we are retreating without being conquered by the enemy; let us not be vanquished by ourselves! Set an example to the army. Several of you have already deserted your colors, and even thrown away your arms. I have no wish to have recourse to military laws to put a stop to this disorder, but appeal entirely to your sense of duty. Do justice to yourselves. To your own honor I commit the maintenance of your discipline!"

The other troops he addressed in a similar style. These few words were quite sufficient to the old grenadiers, who probably had no occasion for them. The others received them with acclamations; but an hour afterward, when the march was resumed, they were entirely forgotten. As to his rear guard, throwing the blame of this wild alarm mostly upon it, he sent an angry message to Davoust on the subject.

At Orcha we found rather an abundant supply of provisions, a bridge equipage of sixty boats, with all its appurtenances, which we burned, and thirty-six pieces of cannon, with their horses, which were distributed between Davoust, Eugene, and Latour-Maubourg.

Napoleon entered Orcha with six thousand guards, the remains of thirty-five thousand! Eugene, with eighteen hundred soldiers, the remains of forty-two thousand! and Davoust, with four thousand, the remains of seventy thousand!

This marshal had lost everything, was actually without linen, and emaciated with hunger. He seized upon a loaf,

[1] **Grenadiers**: these were men of long service and acknowledged bravery. Originally these soldiers threw hand grenades or small explosive shells. When these grenades went out of use the name grenadiers was still retained.

which was offered him by one of his comrades, and voraciously devoured it. A handkerchief was given him to wipe his face, which was white with frost. He exclaimed "that none but men with constitutions of iron could support such trials; that it was physically impossible to resist them; that there were limits to human strength, the utmost of which had been exceeded."

The emperor made fruitless efforts to check this general despondency. When alone, he was heard compassionating the sufferings of his soldiers; but in their presence, even upon that point, he wished to appear inflexible. He issued a proclamation, "ordering all who had deserted their ranks to return to them: if they did not, he would strip the officers of their commissions, and the soldiers should be shot."

A threat like this produced no impression whatever upon men who had become insensible, or were reduced to despair, fleeing not from danger, but from suffering, and caring as little for the death with which they were menaced as for the life that was offered them.

But Napoleon's confidence increased with his perils: in his eyes, this handful of men, in these deserts of snow and ice, was still the Grand Army! and himself the conqueror of Europe! nor was there any affectation in this firmness: we were certain of it, when in this very town, we saw him burn, with his own hands, everything belonging to him that might serve as a trophy to the enemy, in the event of his fall.

But everything was now changed: two hostile armies were opposing his retreat; and the question to be decided was, through which of them he should cut his way. As he knew nothing of the Lithuanian forests into which he was about penetrating, he summoned such of his officers as had been through them, in order to obtain information.

The emperor began by remarking that "too great familiarity with victory was often the precursor of great disasters, but that recrimination was now out of the question." He then mentioned the capture of Minsk, and, admitting the skilfulness of Kutusoff's persevering manœuvres on the right flank, he said that "it was his intention to abandon his line of operations on Minsk, unite with the Dukes of Belluno and Reggio, cut his way through Wittgenstein's army, and regain Wilna by turning the sources of the Berezina." Jomini combated this plan.

Finally Napoleon decided upon Borizoff.[1] But he said, "that it was cruel to retreat without fighting, to present the appearance of flight. Had he only a magazine, some point of support which would allow him to halt, he would prove to Europe that he still knew how to fight and how to conquer."

All these were mere illusions. At Smolensk, where he arrived first, and from which he was the first to depart, he had rather been informed of his disasters than witnessed them himself. At Krasnoë, where our miseries had been more fully unfolded before him, the peril by which we were surrounded had diverted his attention from them; but at Orcha he could contemplate, at one view and leisurely, the whole extent of his misfortunes.

At Smolensk, thirty-six thousand combatants, one hundred and fifty cannon, the army-chest, and the hope of life, and of breathing at liberty on the other side of the Bere-

---

[1] **Borizoff**: a town on the Berezina River, about 320 miles southwest of Moscow, and about 75 west of Orcha.

zina, still remained; here there were scarcely ten thousand soldiers, almost without clothing or shoes, entangled amid a crowd of dying men, with but a few cannon, and a plundered army-chest.

### § 19. Arrival of Marshal Ney.

Being at length, on the 20th of November, compelled to quit Orcha, he left there Eugene, Mortier, and Davoust, and halted after a march of six miles from that place, still inquiring for Marshal Ney, who was advancing by a different route, and still expecting him. The same feeling of grief pervaded the portion of the army remaining at Orcha. As soon as the most pressing wants allowed a moment's rest, the thoughts and looks of every one were directed towards the Russian bank. They listened for any warlike sounds which might announce the arrival of Ney, or, rather, his last desperate struggle with the foe; but nothing was to be seen but parties of the enemy, who were already menacing the bridges of the Borysthenes.

After exhausting all their conjectures, they had relapsed into a gloomy silence, when suddenly they heard the steps of horses, and then the joyful cry, "Marshal Ney is safe! here are some Polish cavalry come to announce his approach!" One of his officers now galloped in, and informed them that the marshal was advancing on the right bank of the Borysthenes, and had sent him to ask for assistance.

When the two corps, Eugene's and Ney's, fairly recognized each other, they could no longer be kept in their ranks. Soldiers, officers, generals, all rushed forward together. The soldiers of Eugene, eagerly grasping the hands of those of Ney, held them with a joyful mixture of astonishment and curiosity, and embraced them with the tenderest sympathy. They lavished upon them the refreshments and brandy which they had just received, and overwhelmed them with questions. Then they proceeded in company towards Orcha, all burning with impatience, Eugene's soldiers to hear, and Ney's to relate, their story.

The officers of Ney stated that on the 17th of November they had quitted Smolensk with twelve cannon, six thousand infantry, and three hundred cavalry, leaving there five thousand sick to the mercy of the enemy; and that, had it not been for the noise of Platoff's artillery and the explosion of the mines, their marshal would never have been able to draw from the ruins of that city seven thousand unarmed stragglers who had taken shelter among them. They dwelt upon the attentions which their leader had shown to the wounded, and to the women and their children, proving upon this occasion that the bravest are also the most humane.

At the gates of the city an unnatural action struck them with a horror that they still felt in all its force. A mother abandoned her little son, only five years old: in spite of his cries and tears, she drove him away from her sledge, which was too heavily laden. She exclaimed, at the same time, with a distracted air, that "*he* had never seen France! *he* would not regret it! but *she* knew France! *she* was resolved to see France once more!" Twice did Ney himself replace the unfortunate child in the arms of his mother, and twice did she cast him from her on the frozen snow.

This solitary crime, amid a thousand instances of the most devoted and sublime tenderness, they did not leave unpunished. The unnatural parent was herself abandoned to the snow from which her infant was snatched, and intrusted to another mother: this little orphan was then in their ranks; he was afterward seen at the Berezina, then at Wilna, again at Kowno, and finally escaped from all the horrors of the retreat.

Frustrated in his plans Ney instead of advancing to join Napoleon was compelled to order his men to return towards Smolensk. At these words they were struck motionless with astonishment. Even his aid-de-camp could not believe his ears: he remained silent, like one who does not comprehend what he hears, and looked at his general in amazement. But the marshal briefly repeating the same order in a still more imperative tone, they were no longer at any loss, but all recognized in it resolution taken, a resource discovered, that self-confidence which inspires others with the same feeling, and a spirit which rises superior to its situation, however perilous it may be. They instantly obeyed, and, without the slightest hesitation, turned their backs on their own army, on the emperor, and on France. Once more they returned into that fatal Russia. Their retrograde march had lasted an hour: again they came to the field of battle marked by the remains of the army of Italy; there they halted, and the marshal, who had remained with the rear guard, then joined them.

Their eyes followed all his movements. What did he intend doing? and, whatever might be his plan, where would he direct his steps, without a guide, in an unknown country? But, while they were thus perplexing themselves, he, with his warlike instinct, had halted on the edge of a ravine of such depth as to make it evident that there was a stream at the bottom of it. By clearing away the snow and breaking the ice, this fact was soon established: and then, consulting his map, he exclaimed, "This is one of the streams which flow into the Dnieper: this must be our guide, and we must follow it; it will lead us to that river, which we must cross, and on the other side we shall be safe." Accordingly, he immediately proceeded in that direction.

A lame peasant was the only inhabitant they could discover; but even this was an unlooked-for piece of good fortune. He told them that they were within the distance of a league from the Dnieper, but that it was not fordable there, and could not yet be frozen over. "It must be so," the marshal remarked; but when he was reminded that a thaw had just commenced, he added, "it does not signify; we must pass, as there is no other resource."

At last at about eight o'clock, after passing through a village, they soon came to the termination of the ravine, and the Russian, who walked before, halted and pointed out to them the river.

Finally, about midnight, the passage began; but the first persons who ventured on the ice called out that it was bending under them, that it was sinking, that they were up to their knees in water; and immediately after that frail support was heard cracking and splitting, as in the breaking up of a frost. All halted in consternation.

Ney ordered them to pass only one at a time: they proceeded with caution, not knowing sometimes in the dark whether they were placing their feet on the ice or into a chasm; for there were places where they were obliged to clear large fissures, and jump from one piece to another, at the risk of falling between them and disappearing forever. The first hesitated, but those who were behind kept calling to them to make more haste.

When at last, after several of these dreadful panics, they reached the opposite bank and fancied themselves safe, a perpendicular steep, slippery as glass, opposed their landing, and many were again thrown back upon the ice, either bruised by it, or breaking it in their fall. It would seem, indeed, as though this Russian river and its banks had contributed with regret, by surprise, and by compulsion, as it were, to their escape.

But what they spoke of as being the most painful of all, were the trouble and distraction of the females and of the sick, when it became necessary for them to abandon, along with the baggage, the remains of their fortune, their provisions, and, in short, all their resources both for the present and the future. They were seen stripping themselves, selecting, throwing away, taking up again, and falling at length through exhaustion and grief upon the frozen bank of the river. The narrators appeared to shudder again at the recollection of the horrible sight of so many men scattered over that abyss, of the continual noise of persons falling, of the cries of such as sank in, and, above all, of the wailing and despair of the wounded, who, from their carts, which could not be trusted to this weak support, stretched out their hands to their companions, and entreated them not to leave them behind.

Their leader at length determined to attempt the passage of several wagons, loaded with these poor creatures; but in the middle of the stream the ice sank down and separated. Then were heard proceeding from the gulf, first cries of anguish long and piercing, then stifled and feeble groans, quickly succeeded by an awful silence. All had disappeared!

But at length Ney had succeeded in reaching Orcha; from this time forward he was the hero of the retreat.

When Napoleon, who was two leagues farther on, heard that Ney had again made his appearance, he leaped and shouted for joy, exclaiming, "Then I have saved my honor! I would have given three hundred millions from my exchequer sooner than have lost such a man."

### § 20. Capture of Minsk by the Russians.

The army had thus for the third and last time repassed the Dnieper, a river half Russian and half Polish, but having its source in Russia. It runs from east to west as far as Orcha, where it appears as if it would penetrate into Poland; but there the high lands of Lithuania oppose its farther progress, and compel it to turn abruptly towards the south, and to become the frontier of the two countries.

Kutusoff and his eighty thousand Russians halted before this feeble obstacle. Hitherto they had been rather the spectators than the authors of our calamities; but from this time we saw them no more, and were at last delivered from the punishment of their joy.

On the 22d of November the army had a disagreeable march from Orcha to Borizoff, on a wide road skirted by a double row of large birch-trees, the snow having melted, and the mud being very deep. The weakest here found their graves; and those of our wounded who, in expectation of a continuance of the frost, had exchanged their wagons for sleighs, were left behind, and fell into the hands of the Cossacks.

It was during the early part of the march to Borizoff that the news of the fall of Minsk[1] became generally

---

[1] **Minsk**: a town on a tributary of the Berezina River, about 400 miles southwest of Moscow. Here Napoleon had immense stores of provisions, clothing, and ammunition. He was pushing forward to reach this place.

known in the army. The leaders themselves now began to look around them with consternation; and, after witnessing such a succession of frightful spectacles their imagination depicted a still more fatal futurity. In their private conversation they did not hesitate to say that, "like Charles XII. in Russia, Napoleon had carried his army to Moscow only to destroy it."

Deploring, then, the rash obstinacy of the stay at Moscow, and the fatal hesitation at Malo-jaroslavetz, they proceeded to reckon up their losses. Since their departure from Moscow they had lost all their baggage, five hundred cannon, thirty-one standards, twenty-seven generals, forty thousand prisoners, and sixty thousand dead: all that remained were forty thousand unarmed stragglers and eight thousand effective soldiers.

With respect to the loss of Minsk the governor of that place had been negligently chosen. He was, it was said, one of those men who undertake everything, who promise everything, and who do nothing. On the 16th of November he lost that capital, and with it four thousand seven hundred sick, the warlike stores, and two million rations of provisions. It was five days since the news of this loss had reached Dombrowna, and the news of a still greater calamity came on the heels of it.

This same governor had retreated towards Borizoff. There he neglected to inform Oudinot, who was only at the distance of two marches, to come to his assistance; and failed to support Dombrowski, who made a hasty march thither: the result was that the latter was overpowered by the fire of the Russian artillery, which took him in flank, and, attacked by a force more than double his own, he was driven across the river, and out of the town as far as the Moscow road.

This disaster was wholly unexpected by Napoleon. Finally, when the emperor learned at Dombrowna the loss of Minsk, he had no suspicion that Borizoff was in such imminent danger, as when he passed the next day through Orcha he had the whole of his bridge-equipage burned.

It was on the day immediately subsequent to that fatal catastrophe, at the distance of three marches from Borizoff, and upon the high road, that an officer arrived and announced to Napoleon this fresh disaster. The emperor, striking the ground with his stick, and casting a furious look to heaven, pronounced these words: "Is it, then, written above that we shall now commit nothing but faults?"

Meanwhile Marshal Oudinot, who was already marching towards Minsk, totally ignorant of what had happened, halted on the 21st. In the middle of the night General Brownkowski arrived to announce to him his own defeat, as well as that of General Dombrowski;[1] that Borizoff was taken, and that the Russians were following close at his heels.

In fact, every disaster which Napoleon could anticipate had occurred; the melancholy conformity, therefore, of his situation with that of the Swedish conqueror, threw his mind into such a state of agitation that his health became still more seriously affected than it had been at Malojaroslavetz. Among the expressions he made use of, loud enough to be overheard, was this: "See what happens when we heap faults on faults!"

His orders, however, displayed decision. Oudinot had just sent to inform him of his determination to overthrow Lambert: this he approved of, and he also urged him to make himself master of a passage across the Berezina, either

[1] Polish generals in Napoleon's Grand Army.

above or below Borizoff. He was desirous that by the 24th the place for this passage should be fixed on and the preparations begun, and that he should be apprised of it, in order to make his march correspond. Far from thinking of making his escape through the midst of these three hostile armies, his only idea now was to beat Tchitchakoff and retake Minsk.

It is true that, eight hours afterward, in a second letter to the Duke of Reggio, he resigned himself to crossing the Berezina near Veselowo, and by retreating directly upon Wilna, by Vileika, to avoid the Russian admiral.

But on the 24th he learned that the passage could only be attempted near Studzianka; that at that spot the river was only fifty-four fathoms wide, and six feet deep; and that they would land on the opposite side in a marsh, under the fire of a commanding position strongly occupied by the enemy.

### § 21. March through the forest of Minsk; passage of the Berezina.

All hope of passing between the Russian armies was thus lost: driven by the armies of Kutusoff and Wittgenstein upon the Berezina, there was no alternative but to cross that river in the teeth of the army of Tchitchakoff, which lined its banks.

After having made his preparations, Napoleon plunged into the gloomy and immense forest of Minsk, in which there was only here and there an open spot surrounding some wretched hamlet or single habitation. The noise of Wittgenstein's artillery filled it with its echoes. The Russian general came rushing from the north upon the right flank of our expiring column, and he brought back with him the winter which had quitted us at the same time with Kutusoff. The news of his threatening march accelerated our steps, and our motley array of from forty to fifty thousand men, women, and children hurried through the forest as rapidly as their weakness and the slipperiness of the ground, from the frost again setting in, would allow.

These forced marches, commenced before daylight, and not terminating until after its close, dispersed all who had previously been together. They lost themselves in the double darkness of the forest and of the night. They halted in the evening, and resumed their march in the morning, in obscurity, at random, and without hearing the signal: the dissolution of the remains of the corps was now completed; all were mixed and confounded together.

In this last stage of helplessness and confusion, as we were approaching Borizoff, we heard loud cries before us. Some rushed forward, fancying it was an attack. It was Victor's army, which had been feebly driven back by Wittgenstein to the right side of our road, where it remained waiting for us. Still, quite complete and full of animation, it received the emperor, as soon as he made his appearance, with the customary but now long-forgotten acclamations.

Of our disasters it had heard nothing: they had been carefully concealed even from its leaders. When, therefore, instead of that grand column which had conquered Moscow, its soldiers perceived behind Napoleon only a train of spectres covered with tattered vestments of every kind, women's pelisses, pieces of carpet, or dirty cloaks, half burned and riddled by the fires, and with nothing but rags on their feet, their consternation was extreme. They seemed terrified at the sight of those unfortunate soldiers, as they defiled before them, with emaciated frames, faces black with dirt, and hideous bristly beards, unarmed, shameless, marching confusedly, with their heads bent, and their eyes fixed on the ground and silent, like a troop of captives.

But what astonished them more than all was to see the number of generals and officers of every grade, scattered about and insulated, seemingly only occupied about themselves, and thinking of nothing but to save the wrecks of their property or their persons: they were marching pell-mell with the soldiers, who did not notice them, to whom they had no longer any commands to give, and of whom they had nothing to expect, all ties between them being dissolved, and all distinctions of rank obliterated by the common misery.

It was, indeed, merely the shadow of an army, but it was the shadow of the Grand Army. It felt conscious that nature alone had vanquished it. The presence of Napoleon animated it. To him it had long been accustomed to look, not for its means of support, but to lead it to victory. This was its first unfortunate campaign, and it had had so many fortunate ones: it only required to be able to follow him. He alone who had elevated his soldiers so high, and now sunk them so low, was yet able to save them. He was still, therefore, cherished in the heart of his army, like hope in the heart of man.

Thus, amid so many beings who might have reproached him with their misfortunes, he marched on without the least fear, speaking to one and all without affectation, certain of being respected as long as glory could command respect. Knowing perfectly that he belonged to us as much as we to him, his renown being, as it were, common national property, we should have sooner turned our arms against ourselves (which was the case with many), as being a minor suicide, than against him.

Some of the men fell and died at his feet; and, though they were in the most frightful delirium, their sufferings never gave its wanderings the turn of reproach, but of entreaty. And in fact, did not he share the common danger? Who of them all risked so much as he? Who had suffered the greatest loss in this disaster?

If any imprecations were ever uttered, it was not in his presence; for it seemed that, of all misfortunes, that of incurring his displeasure was still the greatest: so rooted was their confidence in, and their submission to, that man who had subjected the world to them; whose genius, hitherto uniformly victorious and invincible, had assumed the place of their free-will; and who, having had so long in his hands the book of pensions, of rank, and of history, had found wherewithal to satisfy not only covetous spirits, but also every generous heart.

At the close of the night of the 25th of November, Napoleon made them sink the first trestle in the muddy bed of the Berezina River. But to crown our misfortunes, the rising of the waters had made the traces of the ford entirely disappear. It required the most incredible efforts on the part of our unfortunate engineers, who were plunged in the water up to their mouths, and had to contend with the floating pieces of ice which were carried along by the stream. Many of them perished from the cold, or were drowned by the cakes of ice being violently driven against them by the current and wind.

On the 27th, Napoleon, with about five thousand guards, and Ney's corps, now reduced to six hundred men, crossed the Berezina about two o'clock in the afternoon : he posted himself in reserve to Oudinot, and secured the outlet from the bridges against the efforts of the Russians.

He had been preceded by a crowd of baggage and stragglers, and numbers of them continued to cross the river after him as long as daylight lasted.

But Partouneaux with his division was not so fortunate. At every point where he attempted to pass, he encountered the enemy's fires, and was obliged to turn back : in this way he wandered about for several hours altogether at random, in plains covered with snow, in the midst of a violent tempest. At every step he saw his soldiers pierced through by the cold, and exhausted with hunger and fatigue, falling half dead into the hands of the Russian cavalry, who pursued him without intermission.

This unfortunate general was still struggling with the heavens, with men, and with his own despair, when he felt even the ground giving way under his feet. In fact, deceived by the snow, he was marching upon a lake, which not being frozen sufficiently hard to bear him, he had fallen in and was on the point of being drowned, and then only did he yield and give up his arms.

While this catastrophe was accomplishing, his other three brigades, being more and more hemmed in upon the road, lost all power of movement. They delayed their surrender, however, till the next morning, first by fighting, and then by parleying : at length they all fell, one after the other, and a common misfortune again united them with their general.

Of the whole division, a single battalion only escaped.

During the whole of that day, the 28th, the situation of the ninth corps under General Victor, was so much the more critical, as a weak and narrow bridge was its only means of retreat; in addition to which its avenues were obstructed by the baggage and the stragglers. By degrees, as the action became warmer, the terror of these poor wretches increased their disorder. First of all they had been alarmed by the rumors of a serious engagement; then their terror was increased by seeing the wounded returning from it; and, last of all, they were thrown into the utmost consternation by the batteries of the Russian left wing, some shot from which began to fall among them.

They had been already crowding one upon the other, and the immense multitude heaped upon the bank pell-mell with the horses and carriages, formed there a most alarming encumbrance. It was about the middle of the day that the first Russian balls fell into the midst of this chaos, and they were the signal of universal despair.

Then it was, as in all cases of extremity, that the real dispositions of men exhibited themselves without disguise, and actions were witnessed, some of them the most base, and others the most noble and even sublime. In accordance with their character, some furious and determined, with sword in hand, cleared for themselves a horrible passage. Others, still more cruel, opened a way for their wagons by driving them without mercy over the crowds of unfortunate persons who stood in their way, and crushed them to death. Their detestable avarice made them sacrifice their companions in misfortune to the preservation of their baggage. Others again, seized with a pusillanimous terror, wept, supplicated, and sank under the influence of a passion which completed the exhaustion of their strength. Some were observed (and these were principally the sick and wounded) who, renouncing life, went aside, and, resigned to their fate, sat themselves down, gazing with a fixed and motionless eye on the snow which was shortly to be their winding-sheet.

Numbers of those who started first among this crowd of desperadoes, missing the bridge, attempted to scale it by the sides, but the greater part were pushed into the river. There were seen women in the midst of the stream and among the masses of floating ice, with their children in their arms, raising them by degrees as they felt themselves sinking, and when completely submerged, their stiffened arms still holding them above the water.

In the midst of this horrible disorder, the artillery bridge gave way and broke down. The column entangled in this narrow passage in vain attempted to retrograde. The crowds which were following behind, ignorant of the calamity, and not hearing the cries of those before them, kept urging them on until they pushed them into the gulf, into which they in their turn were precipitated.

Every one then attempted to pass by the other bridge. A great number of large ammunition wagons, heavy carriages and cannon crowded to it from all parts. Pressed on by their drivers and carried rapidly along over a rough and unequalled declivity, in the midst of masses of men, they ground to pieces the poor wretches who were unfortunate enough to get between them, until at length the greater part, furiously encountering each other, were overturned, killing in their fall those who were around them. Multitudes pressed against these obstacles, and becoming entangled among them, were thrown down, and crushed to pieces by other multitudes as they successively stumbled upon them.

Thus these miserable creatures were rolling one upon

the other, nd nothing was heard but cries of rage and of anguish. In this frightful confusion, those who were trodden and crushed under the feet of their companions, struggling to lay hold of them with their nails and teeth, were, like so many enemies, trampled upon without mercy.

Among them were wives and mothers, calling in tones of distraction upon their husbands and their children, from whom they had been separated but a moment before, never again to be united. Stretching out their arms, they entreated to be allowed to pass in order to rejoin them : but they were hurried backward and forward with the crowd, until at length, overcome by the pressure, they sank without being so much as noticed. Amid the howling of a violent tempest, the discharge of cannon, the whistling of balls, the explosion of shells, vociferations, groans, and frightful oaths, this infuriated crowd heard not the cries of the victims it was swallowing up.

The more fortunate gained the bridge by scrambling over heaps of wounded, of women and children thrown down and half suffocated, whom they again trampled beneath their feet in their attempts to reach it. When at last they reached the narrow defile, they fancied that they were safe; but the fall of a horse, or the breaking or displacing of a plank, again arrested everything.

There was also at the outlet of the bridge, on the other side, a morass, into which many horses and carriages had sunk, a circumstance which greatly embarrassed and retarded the entrance. Then it was that, in that infuriated column, crowded together on a single plank of safety, there arose a terrible struggle, in which the weakest least fortunately situated were plunged into the river by their more powerful or more successful comrades. The latter, without so much as turning their heads, and hurried along by the instinct of self-preservation, pushed on towards the goal with unabated fury, regardless of the imprecations of rage and despair uttered by their companions or officers whom they had thus sacrificed.

But, on the other hand, how many noble instances there were of devotion! and why are time and space denied me to relate them? Soldiers, and even officers, harnessed themselves to sledges, to snatch from that fatal bank their sick or wounded comrades. Farther off, and out of reach of the crowd, were seen soldiers, motionless and watching over their dying commanders, who had confided themselves to their care: in vain did the latter conjure them to think only of their own preservation; they refused; and sooner than abandon their expiring leaders, resolved to take their chance of slavery or death.

Above the first passage, where young Lauriston had thrown himself into the river, in order more promptly to execute the orders of Napoleon, a little boat, carrying a mother and her two children, was upset and sank under the ice: an artilleryman, who, like the others, was struggling on the bridge to open a passage for himself, observed the accident, and all at once, unmindful of his own life, he threw himself into the river, and by great exertion succeeded in saving one of the three victims. It was the youngest of the two children: the poor little thing kept calling for his mother in tones of despair, when the brave artilleryman was heard telling him "not to cry; that he had not rescued him from the water only to desert him on the bank; that he should want for nothing; and that he would be his father and his family."

The night of the 28th added to all these calamities. Its

darkness was insufficient to conceal from the artillery of the Russians its miserable victims. Amid the snow, which covered everything, the course of the river, the black mass of men, horses, and carriages, and the noise proceeding from them, were enough to enable the enemy's artillerymen unerringly to direct their fire.

At about nine o'clock in the evening their desolation became complete, when Victor commencing his retreat, his divisions opened for themselves a passage through these despairing wretches, whom they had till then been protecting. A rear guard, however, having been left, the multitude, benumbed with cold, or still anxious to preserve their baggage, refused to avail themselves of the last night for crossing to the opposite shore. In vain were their wagons set fire to, in order to tear them from them; it was only the appearance of daylight which brought them again, but too late, to the entrance of the bridge, which they once more besieged. At half past eight in the morning, seeing the Russians approaching, General Eblé set fire to it by Napoleon's orders; then those who were left on the eastern side of the river "realized that they had lost their last chance."

A multitude of wagons and of cannon, several thousand men and women, and some children, were thus abandoned on the hostile bank. They were seen wandering in desolate troops on the borders of the river. Some plunged into it in order to swim across; others ventured themselves on the pieces of ice which were floating along; and some there were who threw themselves headlong upon the timbers of the burning bridge, which, sinking under them, exposed them at the same time to the horrors of a twofold death. Shortly after, the bodies of many of these unfortunate creatures, wedged in the ice, were seen collecting against the trestles of the bridge. The rest awaited the Russians. The Russian general did not show himself upon the heights until an hour after Eblé's departure; and without having gained a victory, he reaped all the fruits of one.

Napoleon remained till the last moment on these melancholy banks, near the ruins of Brilowa, unsheltered and at the head of his guard, one-third of which was destroyed by the storm. During the day they stood to their arms, and were drawn up in order of battle; at night they bivouacked in a square round their leader; and there the old grenadiers incessantly kept feeding their fires. They sat on their knapsacks, with their elbows planted upon their knees, and their hands supporting their heads; slumbering in this manner, doubled upon themselves, that one limb might warm the other, and that they might feel less the emptiness of their stomachs.

About these bivouacs were collected men of all classes, of all ranks, of all ages; ministers, generals, administrators. Among them was remarked an elderly nobleman of bygone days, when light and brilliant graces held sovereign sway. This general officer of sixty was seen sitting on the snow-covered trunk of some tree, occupying himself with unruffled gayety every morning in adjusting the details of his toilet: in the midst of a hurricane he had his hair elegantly dressed, and powdered with the nicest care, amusing himself in this manner with all our calamities, and with the fury of the elements which assailed him.

Near him were officers of scientific corps, still finding subjects for discussion. Imbued with the spirit of an age which a few discoveries have encouraged to hope for explanations of everything, these individuals, amid the acute sufferings we were enduring from the north wind, were seeking to divine the cause of its unvarying direction. The theory was advanced that, since his departure for the antarctic pole, the sun, by heating the southern hemisphere, had rarefied all its currents of air, elevated them, and left on the surface of that zone a vacuum, into which the currents of air of ours, which were lower on account of being more dense, were violently rushing. That thus the northern pole, loaded with these denser vapors, which had been collecting and cooling since the preceding summer, was discharging them by an impetuous and icy current, which swept over the Russian territory, and stiffened or destroyed everything it encountered in its course.

Others of these officers were remarking with curious attention the regular six-sided crystallization of each one of the flakes of snow which covered their garments.

The phenomena of the simultaneous appearance of several distinct images of the sun, reflected to the eye by means of the icy particles suspended in the atmosphere, was also a subject for observation, and several times momentarily diverted their thoughts from their sufferings.

### § 22. Napoleon abandons the Grand Army and sets out for Paris.

On the 29th the emperor quitted the banks of the Berezina, pushing on before him the crowd of disbanded soldiers, and marching with the ninth corps, which was already disorganized. The day before, the second and ninth corps and Dombrowski's division presented a total of fourteen thousand men; and now, with the exception of about six thousand, they had no longer any form of division, brigade, or regiment.

Night, hunger, cold, the fall of many of their officers, the loss of the baggage on the other side of the river, the example of such a number of runaways, and the much more revolting sight of the wounded abandoned on both sides of the river, and left weltering in despair on the snow, which was dyed with their blood: everything, in short, contributed to discourage them; and they were now confounded with the mass of disbanded men who had come from Moscow.

The whole still formed sixty thousand men, but without the least order or unity. All marched pell-mell, cavalry, infantry, artillery, French and Germans: there was no longer either wing or centre. The artillery and carriages drove on through this tumultuous crowd with no other instructions than to proceed as rapidly as possible.

On the 3d of December Napoleon arrived in the morning at Malodeczno,[1] which was the last point where the Russian general, Tchitchakoff was likely to get the start of him. Some provisions were found there, the forage was abundant, the day beautiful, the sun bright, and the cold bearable. There also the couriers, who had been so long kept back, arrived all at once. The Poles were immediately directed onward to Warsaw through Olita, and the dismounted cavalry by Merecz to the Niemen; while the rest of the army was to follow the high road, which they had again regained.

Up to that time Napoleon seemed to have entertained no idea of quitting his army. But about the middle of that day he suddenly informed Daru and Duroc of his determination to set off immediately for Paris.

[1] **Malodeczno:** a town about seventy miles west of the Berezina River.

Daru did not see the necessity of it. He objected "that the communication with France was again opened, and the most dangerous crisis passed; and that at every retrograde step he would now be meeting the re-enforcements sent him from Paris and from Germany." The emperor's reply was, "that he no longer felt himself sufficiently strong to leave Prussia between him and France. And besides, what necessity was there for his remaining at the head of a routed army? Murat and Eugene would be sufficient to direct it, and Ney to cover its retreat.

"His return to France had become indispensable, in order to secure her tranquillity and to summon her to arms; to take measures there for keeping the Germans steady in their fidelity to him; and, finally, to return with fresh and adequate forces to the assistance of his Grand Army.

"But, in order to effect these objects, it was necessary that he should travel alone over four hundred leagues of the territories of his allies: and that he might do so without danger, his resolution should be there unforeseen, his passage unknown, and the rumor of his disastrous retreat still uncertain; that he would, in short, precede the news of it, and anticipate the effect it might produce on them, and the defections to which it might give rise. He had, therefore, no time to lose, and the moment for his departure had already arrived."

Such were the motives assigned by Napoleon; and General Caulaincourt immediately received orders secretly to prepare for his departure. The rendezvous was fixed at Smorgoni,[1] and the time the night of the 5th of December.

[1] **Smorgoni:** a village about thirty-five miles northwest of Malodeczno, and four hundred and fifty southwest of Moscow.

When Napoleon reached Smorgoni all the marshals were summoned. As they successively entered, he took each one aside in private, and first of all secured their approbation of his plan, gaining some by his arguments, and others by confidential communications.

His manner was kind and flattering to them all; and afterward, having assembled them at his table, he complimented them for their brilliant actions during the campaign. As to himself, the only confession he made of his temerity was couched in these words: "If I had been born to the throne, if I had been a Bourbon, it would have been easy for me not to have committed any faults."

When their interview was over, he made Prince Eugene read to them his twenty-ninth bulletin; after which, declaring aloud what he had confided to each of them privately, he told them "that he was about to depart that very night with Duroc, Caulaincourt and Lobau, for Paris; that his presence there was indispensable for France as well as for the remains of his unfortunate army. It was there only that he could take measures for keeping the Austrians and Prussians in check. These nations would certainly pause before they declared war against him, when they saw him at the head of the French nation, and a fresh army of twelve hundred thousand men.

He added, that "he had ordered Ney to proceed to Wilna, there to reorganize the army; that Rapp would second him, and afterward go to Dantzic, Lauriston to Warsaw, and Narbonne to Berlin; that his own guard would remain with the army; but that it would be necessary to strike a blow at Wilna, and stop the enemy there. There they would find re-enforcements, provisions, and ammunition of all sorts; that afterward they would go into winter quarters on the other side of the Niemen; and that he hoped the Russians would not pass the Vistula before his return."

He said, in concluding, "I leave the King of Naples to command the army. I hope that you will yield him the same obedience that you would to myself, and that the greatest harmony will prevail among you."

As it was now ten o'clock at night, he rose, affectionately pressed their hands, embraced them all — and departed.

Napoleon passed through the crowd of his officers, who were drawn up in an avenue as he passed, bidding them adieu merely by forced and melancholy smiles: their good wishes, equally silent, and expressed only by respectful gestures, he carried with him. He and Caulaincourt shut themselves up in a carriage.

His escort at first consisted only of Poles, afterwards of the Neapolitans of the Royal Guard. This corps consisted of between six and seven hundred men when it left Wilna to meet the emperor: it perished almost entirely in that short passage, though the winter was its only adversary. That very night the Russians surprised and afterward abandoned a town through which the escort had to pass; and Napoleon was within an hour of falling into that affray.

He met the Duke of Bassano at Miedniki, a village about thirty miles west of Smorgoni. His first words to him were "that he had no longer an army; that for several days past he had been marching in the midst of a troop of disbanded men, wandering to and fro in search of subsistence; that they might still be rallied by giving them bread, shoes, clothing, and arms; but that the duke's military administration had anticipated nothing, and his orders had not been executed." But upon Maret replying, by showing him a statement of the immense stores of provisions and clothing collected at Wilna, he exclaimed "that he gave him fresh life; that he would forthwith give him an order to transmit to Murat and Berthier, to halt for eight days in that capital, there to rally the army, and infuse into it sufficient heart and strength to continue the retreat less deplorably."

The remainder of Napoleon's journey was effected without molestation. He went round Wilna by its suburbs, crossed Wilkoski, where he exchanged his carriage for a sleigh, and stopped during the 10th at Warsaw, to ask the Poles for a levy of ten thousand Cossacks, and to promise them that he would speedily return at the head of three hundred thousand men. From thence he rapidly traversed Silesia,[1] visited Dresden and its monarch, and finally reached Paris, where he suddenly made his appearance on the 19th of December, two days after the arrival of his twenty-ninth bulletin.

From Malo-jaroslavetz to Smorgoni, this master of Europe had been no more than the general of a dying and disbanded army; from Smorgoni to the Rhine he was an unknown fugitive, travelling through a hostile country; beyond the Rhine he again found himself the master and the conqueror of Europe. A brief blast of the gale of prosperity once more and for the last time swelled his sails.

Meanwhile, his generals, whom he left at Smorgoni, approved of his departure, and, far from being discouraged, placed all their hopes in it. The army had now only to

---

[1] **Silesia**: a province of southeastern Prussia.

flee; the road was open, and the Russian frontier at a very short distance. They were getting within reach of a reenforcement of eighteen thousand men, all fresh troops, of a great city, and immense magazines. Murat and Berthier, abandoned to themselves, fancied they were quite competent to direct the flight. But in the midst of such frightful disorder, it required a Napoleon for a rallying-point, and he had just disappeared. In the mighty chasm which he left, Murat was scarcely perceptible.

It was then but too clearly seen that a great man is not to be replaced; either that the pride of his followers can no longer stoop to obey another, or that, having always thought of, foreseen, and ordered everything himself, he had formed good instruments, skilful lieutenants, but no commanders.

The very first night a general refused to obey. The marshal who commanded the rear guard was almost the only one who returned to the royal head-quarters. Three thousand men of the Old and the Young Guard were still there. This was the whole of the Grand Army, and of that gigantic body there remained nothing but the head. But at the news of Napoleon's departure, these veterans, spoiled by the habit of being commanded only by the conqueror of Europe, being no longer supported by the honor of serving him, and scorning to act as guards to another, gave way in their turn, and voluntarily fell into disorder.

Henceforward there was no longer fraternity in arms; there was an end to all society, to all ties; the excess of misery had completely brutified them. Hunger, devouring hunger, had reduced these unfortunate men to that brutal instinct of self-preservation which constitutes the sole understanding of ferocious animals, and which is ready to sacrifice everything to itself; nature, wild and barbarous around them, seemed to have communicated to them all its savageness. The strongest despoiled the weakest; they rushed about the dying, and frequently waited not for their last breath. When a horse fell, you might have fancied you saw a famished pack of hounds: they surrounded him, they tore him to pieces, and quarrelled among themselves for his remains like ravenous dogs.

The greater number, however, preserved sufficient moral strength to provide for their own safety without injuring others; but this was the last effort of their virtue. If either leader or comrade fell by their side or under the wheels of the cannon, in vain did they call for assistance, in vain did they invoke the names of a common country, a common religion, and a common cause; they could not even obtain a passing look. The merciless cold of the climate had passed into their comrades' hearts: its rigor had contracted their feelings no less than their features. With the exception of a few of the commanders, all were absorbed by their sufferings, and terror left no room for compassion.

There were a few, however, who still stood firm, as it were, against both heaven and earth: these protected and assisted the weakest; but their number was deplorably small.

### § 23. Sufferings of the Grand Army after Napoleon's departure. Arrival at Wilna.

On the 6th of December, the very day after Napoleon's departure, the sky exhibited a more dreadful appearance. Icy particles were seen floating in the air, and the birds fell stiff and frozen to the earth. The atmosphere was motionless and silent : it seemed as if everything in nature which possessed life and movement, even the wind itself, had been seized, chained, and, as it were, congealed by a universal death. Not a word or a murmur was then heard: there was nothing but the gloomy silence of despair, and the tears which proclaimed it.

We crept along in the midst of this empire of death like doomed spirits. The dull and monotonous sound of our steps, the cracking of the frost, and the feeble groans of the dying, were the only interruptions to this doleful and universal silence. Anger and imprecations there were none, nor anything which indicated a remnant of warmth; scarcely was strength enough left to utter a prayer; and most of the men fell without even complaining, either from weakness or resignation, or because people complain only when they look for kindness, and fancy they are pitied.

Such of our soldiers as had hitherto been the most persevering here lost heart entirely. Sometimes the snow sank beneath their feet, but more frequently, its glassy surface refusing them support, they slipped at every step, and tottered along from one fall to another. It seemed as though this hostile soil were leagued against them ; that it treacherously escaped from under their efforts ; that it was constantly leading them into snares, as if to embarrass and retard their march, and to deliver them up to the Russians in pursuit of them, or to their terrible climate.

And, in truth, whenever, for a moment, they halted from exhaustion, the winter, laying his icy hand upon them, was ready to seize his victims. In vain did these unhappy creatures, feeling themselves benumbed, raise themselves up, and, already deprived of the power of speech, and plunged into a stupor, proceed a few steps like automatons : their blood froze in their veins, like water in the current of rivulets, congealing the heart, and then flying back to the head; and these dying men staggered as if they had been intoxicated. From their eyes, reddened and inflamed by the constant glare of the snow, by the want of sleep, and the smoke of the bivouacs, there flowed real tears of blood; their bosoms heaved with deep and heavy sighs; they looked towards heaven, at us, and on the earth, with an eye dismayed, fixed, and wild, as expressive of their farewell, and, it might be, of their reproaches against the barbarous nature which was tormenting them. It was not long before they fell upon their knees, and then upon their hands; their heads still slowly moved for a few minutes alternately to the right and left, and from their open mouths some sounds of agony escaped; at last, they fell flat upon the snow, burying their faces in it, and their sufferings were at an end.

Their comrades passed by them without moving a step out of their way, that they might not, by the slightest curve, prolong their journey, and without even turning their heads; for their beards and hair were so stiffened with ice that every movement was painful. Nor did they even pity them; for, in fact, what had they lost by dying? what had they left behind them? They suffered so much, they were still so far from France, so much divested of all feelings of country by the surrounding prospect and by misery, that every dear illusion was broken, and hope almost destroyed. The greater number, therefore, had from necessity, from the habit of seeing death constantly around them, and from the prevailing feeling, become careless of dying, sometimes treating it with contempt; but generally, on seeing these unfortunates stretched on the snow, and instantly stiffened, contenting themselves with the thought that they had no more wants, that they were at rest, that their sufferings were over. And, indeed, death, in a situation quiet, certain, and uniform, may be felt as a strange event, a frightful contrast, a terrible change; but in this tumult, this violent and ceaseless movement of a life of action, danger, and suffering, it appeared nothing more than a transition, a slight alteration, an additional removal, which excited little alarm.

Such were the last days of the Grand Army: its last nights were still more frightful. Those whom they surprised marching together, far from every habitation, halted on the borders of the woods: there they lighted their fires, before which they remained the whole night, erect and motionless like spectres. They seemed as if they could not possibly have enough of the heat: they kept so close to it as to burn their clothes, as well as the frozen parts of their body, which the fire decomposed. The most dreadful pain then compelled them to stretch themselves on the ground, and the next day they attempted in vain to rise.

In the meantime, such as the winter had almost wholly spared, and who still retained some portion of courage, prepared their melancholy meal. It had consisted, ever since they left Smolensk, of some slices of horse-flesh broiled, and a little rye-meal made into a sort of gruel with snow-water, or kneaded into paste, which they seasoned, for want of salt, with the powder of their cartridges.

The sight of these fires was constantly attracting fresh spectres, who were driven back by the first comers. These poor wretches wandered about from one bivouac to another, until, struck by the frost and despair together, and giving themselves up for lost, they laid themselves down upon the snow behind their more fortunate comrades, and there expired. Many of them, destitute of the means and the strength necessary to cut down the lofty fir-trees, made vain attempts to set fire to them as they were standing; but death speedily surprised them, and they might be seen in every sort of attitude, stiff and lifeless about their trunks.

Under the vast sheds erected by the sides of the high road in some parts of the way, scenes of still greater horror were witnessed. Officers and soldiers all rushed precipitately into them, and crowded together in heaps. There, like so many cattle, they pressed upon each other around the fires, and as the living could not remove the dead from the circle, they laid themselves down upon them, there to expire in their turn, and serve as a bed of death to some fresh victims. In a short time additional crowds of stragglers presented themselves, and, being unable to penetrate into these asylums of suffering, they completely besieged them.

It frequently happened that they demolished their walls, which were formed of dry wood, in order to feed their fires: at other times, repulsed and disheartened, they were contented to use them as shelters to their bivouacs, the flames of which very soon communicated to the buildings, and the soldiers who were within them, already half dead with the cold, perished in the conflagration. Such of us as survived in these places of shelter found our comrades the next morning lying frozen and in heaps around their extinguished fires; while to escape from these tombs effort was required to enable us to climb over the heaps of those who were still breathing.

Yet this was the same army which had been formed

from the most civilized nation of Europe: that army, formerly so brilliant, which was victorious over men to its last moment, and whose name still reigned in so many conquered capitals. Its strongest and bravest warriors, who had recently been proudly traversing so many scenes of their victories, had lost their noble bearing: covered with rags, their feet naked and torn, and supporting themselves with branches of fir, they dragged themselves painfully along; and the strength and perseverance which they had hitherto put forth in order to conquer, they now made use of only to flee.

The army was in this last state of physical and moral distress when its first fugitives reached Wilna. Wilna! their magazine, their centre of supplies, the first rich and inhabited city which they had met with since their entrance into Russia. Its name alone, and its proximity, still supported the courage of a few.

On the 9th of December, the greatest part of these poor soldiers at last arrived within sight of that capital. Instantly, some dragging themselves along, others rushing forward, they all precipitated themselves headlong into its suburbs, hurrying obstinately on, and crowding together so fast that they formed but one mass of men, horses, and chariots, motionless, and deprived of the power of motion.

The capital of Lithuania was still ignorant of our disasters, when, all at once, forty thousand famished soldiers filled it with groans and lamentations. At this unlooked-for sight, its inhabitants became alarmed and shut their doors. Deplorable then was it to see these troops of wretched wanderers in the streets, some furious and others despairing, threatening or entreating, endeavoring to break open the doors of the houses and the magazines, or dragging themselves to the hospitals. Everywhere they were repulsed: at the magazines, from most unseasonable formalities, as, from the dissolution of the corps and the mingling of the soldiers, all regular distribution had become impossible.

There had been collected there sufficient flour and bread to last for forty days, and butchers' meat for thirty-six days, for one hundred thousand men. Not a single commander ventured to step forward and give orders for giving out these provisions to all who came for them. The commissaries who had them in charge were afraid of being made responsible for them; and the others dreaded the excesses to which the famished soldiers would give themselves up when everything was at their discretion. These commissaries were, besides, ignorant of our desperate situation; and when there was scarcely time for pillage, had they been so inclined, our unfortunate comrades were left for several hours to die of hunger at the very doors of these immense magazines, filled with whatever they stood in need of, all of which fell into the enemy's hands the following day.

At last, the exertions of several of the commanders, as Eugene and Davoust, the compassion of the Lithuanians, and the avarice of the Jews, opened some places of refuge. Nothing could be more remarkable than the astonishment manifested by these unfortunate men at finding themselves once more in inhabited houses. How delicious did a loaf of leavened bread appear to them, and how inexpressible the pleasure of eating it seated! and, afterward, with what admiration were they struck at seeing a scanty battalion still under arms, in regular order, and uniformly dressed! They seemed to have returned from the very extremities of the earth, so much had the violence and persistency of their sufferings wrested and torn them from all their habits, so deep had been the abyss from which they had escaped!

But scarcely had they begun to taste these sweets, when the cannon of the Russians were heard thundering over their heads and upon the city. These menacing sounds, the shouts of the officers, the drums beating to arms, and the wailings and clamor of an additional multitude of fugitives which had just arrived, filled Wilna with fresh confusion.

Every one thought much more of disputing his life with famine and the cold than with the enemy. But when the cry of "Here are the Cossacks" was heard (which for a long time had been the only signal which the greater number obeyed), it was instantly echoed through the whole city, and the rout again began.

This city contained a large proportion of the baggage of the army, and of its treasures, its provisions, a crowd of enormous wagons, loaded with the emperor's equipage, a large quantity of artillery, and a large number of wounded men. Our retreat had come upon them like an unexpected tempest, almost like a thunderbolt. Some were terrified and thrown into confusion, while consternation kept others motionless. Bearers of orders, soldiers, horses, and carriages, were seen hurrying about in all directions, crossing and overturning each other.

In the midst of this tumult, several of the commanders pushed forward out of the city towards Kowno, with all the troops they could contrive to muster; but at the distance of a league from the latter place this heavy and frightened column encountered the height and the ravine of Ponari.

During our conquering advance, this woody hillock had only appeared to our soldiers a fortunate accident of the ground, from which they could discover the whole plain of Wilna, and take a survey of their enemies. Its rough but sharp declivity had then scarcely been remarked. During a regular retreat, it would have presented an excellent position for turning round and stopping the enemy; but in a disorderly flight, where everything which, in other circumstances, might have been of service, became injurious; where, in our precipitation and disorder, everything was turned against us, this hill and its defile became an insurmountable obstacle, a wall of ice, against which all our efforts were powerless. It arrested everything, baggage, treasure, and wounded; and the evil was sufficiently great, in this long series of disasters, to form an epoch.

Here, in fact, it was that money, honor, and all remains of discipline and strength were completely lost. After fifteen hours of fruitless effort, when the drivers and the soldiers of the escort saw the King of Naples and the whole column of fugitives passing them by the sides of the hill; when they heard the noise of the enemy's cannon and musketry coming nearer and nearer every instant, and saw Ney himself retreating with three thousand men; when, at last, turning their eyes upon themselves, they beheld the hill completely covered with cannon and carriages, broken or overturned, and men and horses fallen to the ground, and expiring one upon the other — then it was that they gave up all idea of saving anything, and determined only to anticipate the enemy by becoming plunderers themselves.

One of the covered wagons of treasure, which burst of itself, served as a signal; every one now rushed to the others; they were immediately broken open, and the most valuable effects taken from them. The soldiers of the rear guard, who were passing at the time of this disorder, threw away their arms to join in the plunder; they became so eagerly engaged in it as neither to hear, in fact, the whistling of the enemy's balls, nor to pay the slightest attention to the howlings of the Cossacks, who were at their heels.

It is even said that the Cossacks got mixed among them without being observed; that for some minutes, French and Tartars were confounded in the same greediness; forgetting they were at war, and pillaging together the same treasure-wagons. Two millions of gold and silver then disappeared.

But amid all these horrors there were noble acts of devotion. Those there were who abandoned everything to save some of the unfortunate wounded by carrying them on their shoulders; while others, unable to extricate their half-frozen comrades from the throng, sacrificed their lives in defending them either against their own countrymen, or from the blows of their enemies.

On the most exposed part of the hill, an officer of the emperor, Colonel the Count de Turenne, repulsed the Cossacks, and in defiance of their cries of rage and their fire, he distributed before their eyes the private treasure of Napoleon to the guards whom he found within his reach. These brave men, fighting with one hand, and collecting the spoils of their leader with the other, succeeded in saving them. Long afterward, when they were out of all danger, each man faithfully restored what had been intrusted to him. Not a single piece of money was lost.

This catastrophe at Ponari was the more disgraceful, as

it might easily have been foreseen, and no less easily prevented: for the hill could have been turned by its sides. The property we here abandoned, however, was at least of some use by arresting the pursuit of the Cossacks. While these were busy in collecting their plunder, Ney, at the head of a few hundred French and Bavarians, supported the retreat as far as Évé. As this was his last effort, we must not neglect to describe the close of that retreat which he had continued uninterruptedly, and in the most methodical manner, ever since he left Viazma on the 3d of November.

### § 24. Conclusion.

Finally Ney and his men arrived at Kowno, which was the last town of the Russian empire. On the 13th of December, after marching forty-six days under the most terrible sufferings, they once more came in sight of a friendly country. Instantly, without halting, or looking behind them, the greater part plunged into, and dispersed themselves in, the forests of Prussian Poland. Some there were, however, who, on their arrival on the friendly bank of the Niemen, turned round; and there, when they cast a last look on that land of horrors from which they were escaping, and found themselves on the same spot whence, five months before, their countless eagles [1] had taken their victorious flight, tears gushed from their eyes and they broke out into exclamations of the most poignant sorrow.

"This, then, was the bank which they had studded with their bayonets! this the allied country which had disappeared, only five months before, under the steps of their immense army, and which then seemed to them to be

---

[1] **Eagles**: Napoleon's colors were surmounted by the figure of an eagle.

metamorphosed into moving hills and plains of men and horses! These were the same valleys from which, under the rays of a brilliant sun, had poured forth the three long columns of dragoons and cuirassiers, resembling three rivers of glittering iron and brass. And now, men, arms, eagles, horses, the sun itself, and even this frontier river, which they had crossed replete with ardor and hope, had all disappeared. The Niemen was now only a lengthened line of masses of ice, arrested and chained to each other by the increasing severity of the winter. Instead of the three French bridges, brought from a distance of five hundred leagues, and thrown across it with such audacious promptitude, a Russian bridge alone was standing. Finally, in place of those innumerable warriors, of their four hundred thousand comrades, who had been so often their partners in victory, and who had dashed onward with so much pride and joy into the territory of Russia, they now saw issuing from these pale and frozen deserts only a thousand infantry and horsemen still under arms, nine cannon, and twenty thousand miserable wretches covered with rags, with downcast looks, hollow eyes, cadaverous and livid complexions, and long beards matted with frost; some disputing in silence the narrow passage of the bridge, which, in spite of their small numbers, did not suffice for the eagerness of their flight; others fleeing dispersed over the rough ice of the river, toiling and dragging themselves along from one point to another: this was the whole Grand Army! and even many of these fugitives were recruits who had just joined it!"

Two kings, one prince, eight marshals, followed by a few officers, generals on foot, dispersed, and without attendants: finally, a few hundred men of the Old Guard, still armed — these were the remains of the Grand Army — these alone represented it!

Or rather, I should say, it still breathed only in Marshal Ney! Comrades! allies! enemies! here I invoke your testimony; let us pay the homage which is due to the memory of an unfortunate hero: the facts alone will suffice.

All were flying, and Murat himself, traversing Kowno as he had done Wilna, first gave, and then withdrew, an order, to rally at Tilsit, and subsequently fixed upon Gumbinnen. Ney then entered Kowno, accompanied only by his aids-de-camp, for all besides had given way or fallen around him. From the time of his leaving Viazma, this was the fourth rear guard which had been worn out and disappeared in his hands. But winter and famine, far more than the Russians, had destroyed them. For the fourth time he remained alone before the enemy, and, still undismayed, he sought for a fifth rear guard.

Several thousand soldiers covered the market-place and the neighboring streets; but they were laid out stiff before the liquor-shops which they had broken open, and where they drank the cup of death, from which they had vainly hoped they were to inhale fresh life.

Such were the only succors which Murat had left him; and Ney found himself alone in Russia, with seven hundred foreign recruits. At Kowno, as it had been after the disasters of Viazma, of Smolensk, of the Berezina, and of Wilna, it was to him that the honor of our arms and all the peril of the last steps of our retreat were again confided.

On the 14th, at daybreak, the Russians commenced their attack. One of their columns made a hasty advance from the Wilna road, while another crossed the Niemen on the ice above the town, landed on the Prussian territory, and, proud of being the first to cross its frontier, marched to the bridge of Kowno, to close that outlet upon Ney, and completely cut off his retreat.

Ney, though abandoned by all, neither gave himself up nor his post. After vain efforts to detain these fugitives, he collected their muskets, which were still loaded, became once more a common soldier, and, with only four others, kept facing thousands of the enemy. His audacity stopped them ; it made some of his artillerymen, too, ashamed, and they imitated their marshal : besides it gave time to his aid-de-camp and to General Gérard, to collect thirty soldiers, and to Generals Ledru and Marchand to collect the only battalion which remained.

But at that moment a second attack of the Russians commenced on the other side of the Niemen, and near the bridge of Kowno : it was then half past two o'clock. Ney sent Ledru, Marchand, and their four hundred men forward to retake and secure that passage. As for himself, without giving way, or disquieting himself farther as to what was passing in his rear, he kept on fighting at the head of his thirty men, and maintained himself until night at the Wilna gate. He then traversed the town and crossed the Niemen, constantly fighting, retreating, but never flying, marching after all the others, supporting to the last moment the honor of our arms, and for the hundredth time during the last forty days and forty nights, putting his life and liberty in jeopardy to save a few more Frenchmen. Finally, he was the last of the Grand Army that quitted that fatal Russia, showing to the world how courage battles with ill fortune, and proving that with heroes even the greatest disasters turn to glory.[1]

[1] Marshal Ney, whom Napoleon called "the bravest of the brave," fought

General Dumas was seated in the French headquarters on the Prussian side of the Niemen when a man entered wrapped in a long cloak. His face was blackened with gunpowder, his hair singed with fire. "At last," said he, "I am here." "But who are you?" asked General Dumas in astonishment. "I am the rear guard of the Grand Army — I am Marshal Ney. I have fired the last shot on the bridge of Kowno, I have thrown my musket into the river, and I have walked here across the forest."

Napoleon had entered Russia with an army of over six hundred thousand men. Not more than eighty thousand recrossed the Niemen, and many of them did not live to reach their homes.[1]

under the emperor in several subsequent battles. When Napoleon abdicated and was exiled to Elba, Ney supported the government of his successor and enemy, Louis XVIII. On the escape of Napoleon from Elba, in the spring of 1815, Ney was sent with an army against him, but instead of fighting for Louis XVIII. he took service under his old commander. At Waterloo he led the Old Guard, those men who could die but never surrender. After the final fall of Napoleon, Marshal Ney was tried and sentenced to be shot for treason to the government of Louis XVIII., whose cause he had deserted. Wellington tried to save his life, but in vain. If courage can expiate faults, then his are buried in his grave.

[1] On Napoleon's arrival in Paris he began at once to raise a fresh army. It has been said that it was "an army of boys," for France had lost most of her fighting men on the battle-field, or in Russia. In 1813 he was defeated at Leipsic, and obliged to retreat across the Rhine. The next year he abdicated and retired to Elba.

In the spring of 1815 he escaped from Elba, and raising an army fought and lost the battle of Waterloo.

After his second abdication he was sent an exile to St. Helena, where he died about six years later (1821). His remains were brought to Paris in 1840, and interred under the dome of the Hotel des Invalides, or Soldiers' Hospital. Above his tomb one reads these words: "I desire that my ashes shall repose on the banks of the Seine, among the French people, whom I have so greatly loved."

Thus ended the Russian campaign. Thus did the star of the North triumph over that of Napoleon.

Comrades, my task is done; it is now for you to bear your testimony to the truth of the picture. Its colors will no doubt appear pale to your eyes and to your hearts, which are still full of these great recollections. But who does not know that an action is always more eloquent than its description; and that, if great historians are produced by great men, the former are still more rare than the latter?

# INDEX TO NOTES.

## WITH PRONUNCIATION OF PROPER NAMES.[1]

A-chæ'ans, 37.
A-chā'i-a.
Ad-ra-mȳt'ti-um.
Æ-nē'as.
Æ-ni-ā'nēs.
Ā-gā'si-as.
Ā-gĕs-i-lā'us.
Ā'gi-ăs.
Aid-de-camp, 217.
Ajaccio (A-yat'chō).
Alexander the Great, 149.
Ăl-ki-bī'a-dēs.
Altar, 75.
Amnesty, 13.
Am-phĭp'o-lis.
A-năb'a-sis, 150.
Ăn-ax-ĭb'i-ŭs.
An-tal'ki-dăs.
An-tăn'drŭs.
An-tĭl'e-ŏn.
Ăp-ol-lŏn'i-dēs.
Arcadian, 27.
Ā-ri-æ'us.
Ăr-is-tar'chus.
A-rĭs'te-ās.
A-ris'ton.
Ăr-is-tŏn'y-mŭs.

Ar'me-nē.
Ar'mis-tĭce, 211.
Array, 7.
Ar'te-mĭs.
Ar-te-mĭs-i'ŏn, 146.
Ar-tax-erx'ēs.
A-si'da-tēs.
A-tar'neūs.
Athenian catastrophe, 38.
Augerau (Ōzh-rō').
Augury, 57.

Banished, 145.
Barbarians, 14.
Barras (Bar-rah')
Băs'i-as.
Beauharnais (Bō-ar-nā').
Béranger (Bā-ron-zhā').
Berthier (Ber-te-ā').
Bessières (Bĕs-sē-air').
Billeted, 132.
Bi-san'the.
Bi-thȳn'i-a.
Bi'ton.
Bitumen (Be-tu'men), 15.
Bivouac (Bĭv'wak), 60, 187.

Bœ-o'ti-a.
Bœotian dialect, 31.
Bo-is'kus.
Bō're-ās, 62.
Borizoff, 271.
Borodino, 242.
Bo-rȳs'the-nēs.
Bos'pho-rŭs.
Boulogne (Boo-lōn').
Boyars, 179.
Brăs'i-das.
Bras-i-di'as.
Brienne (Bri-ĕn').
Burial, 56.
By-zan'ti-um, 80, 116.

Carbines, 43.
Car-pæ'an dance, 103.
Cashier, 31.
Caulaincourt (Kō-lan-koor').
Chal-kē'don.
Chal'y-bēs.
Char-mi'nus.
Charpontier (Shar-pon-tē-ā').
Cheir-is'o-phŭs.

[1] In the classical names *ch* has the sound of *k*, e.g. Achaia (A-kā'i-a); the diphthong *æ* has the sound of long *ē*, e.g. Æneas (Ē-nē'as), Kænæ (Kē'nē); *es* at the end of a word has the sound of *eez*, e.g. Apollonidēs (Ăp-ol-lŏn'i-deez); *ti* in Bœotia has the sound of *she*, e.g. (Bē-ō'she-ah). The Russian names may be pronounced as English.

# 316  INDEX TO NOTES.

Cher-so-nē'sus, 119.
Chry-sŏp'o-lis.
Cities, 113.
Claparède (Clap-ar-aid').
Compans (Con-pan').
Convention, 12.
Corn, 9.
Corselet, 52.
Cossacks, 171.
Covenant, 11.
Cubit, 52.
Cuirass, 48.
Cy-re'ian Greeks, 10.
Cy-re'ian Persians, 13.
Czar, 160.

Dance, Carpæan, 103.
Dance, Pyrrhic, 104.
Dar'da-nŭs.
Dăr'ic, 71.
Da-ri'us.
Daru', 179.
Davoust (Da-voo').
De-in'ar-chus.
Dĕk-e-lī'a.
Delta, 125.
Delzons (Del-zon').
Demagogues, 66.
Dĕm-a-rā'tus.
Democrat and Philosopher, 29.
De-mok'ra-tēs.
Deployed, 265.
Der-kȳl'li-das.
Dex-ip'pus.
Dī-ā'si-a, 139.
Di-o-dō'rus.
Dnieper (Nee'per).
Dombrowna, 268.
Dorogobouje, 254.

Dorogomilow, 178.
Dra-kon'ti-ŭs.
Dri'læ.
Dumas (Du-mah').
Duroc (Du-rok').

Eagles, 308.
Ears bored, 32.
Eblé (Eb-lā').
Eckmühl (Ek'mĭl).
Ek-băt'a-na.
E-le'i-ans.
Ephesus, Temple of, 143.
E-pis'the-nēs.
E-rē'tri-a.
E-rē'tri-an, 141.
Erfurt, 204.
Es-thō'ni-a.
Ē-te-o-nī'kus.
Eū-klei'dēs.
Eū-rȳl'o-chus.
Évé (Ā-vā').
Expresses, 205.

Festivals, Olympic, 145.
Fishery, Thunny, 76.
Friedland (Freed'land).

Gérard (Zhā-rar').
Glûs (Gloos).
Gods, The, 89.
Gon'gy-lŭs.
Gor'gi-ŏn.
Gracious, Zeus The, 139.
Great King, The, 124.
Greaves, 69.
Grenadiers, 269.
Guard, The Old, 199.
Guilleminot (Gweel-me-nō').

Gȳ-lĭp'pus.
Gym'ni-as.

Ha'lys.
Har'pa-sŭs.
Hek-a-ton'y-mus.
Hellas, 89.
Hellen'ic, 3.
Hĕr-a-klei'dēs.
Hĕr-ak-lē'ot-ic.
Hĕr'a-klēs, 74.
Herald, 7.
Heralds, 2.
He-rod'o-tus.

Inflated skins, 19.
Invalides (An-val-eed'), 214.
I-ō'ni-a, 21.
Irrigation, 9.

Javelin, 43.
Jomini (Zho-me-ne').
Judges, 67.

Kæ'næ.
Ka-ī'kus.
Kal'pē.
Kal-lim'a-chus.
Kar-du'ki-a.
Ken-trī'tēs.
Ker'a-sŭs, 83.
Ki-lik'i-a, 32.
King, The Great, 124.
Kle-an'der.
Kle-ā'nor.
Kle-ar'chus.
Kle-ar'e-tus.
Kle-on'y-mŭs.
Knidus (Nī'dus).

## INDEX TO NOTES. 317

Knight, 148.
Kœ-ra'ti-das.
Kolomna gate, 173.
Kor-o-nē'a.
Kor'y-las.
Ko-rys-the'ni-a.
Kō-ty-ŏ'ra.
Krasnoe (Kras-no'e).
Kretan, 56.
Kremlin, 238.
Ktesias (Tē'si-ăs).
Ku-nax'a, 1.
Kutusoff, 163.
Ky-nis'kus.
Kўz'i-kŭs.

Laç-e-dæ'mon.
Laç-e-dæ-mo'ni-ans.
Lamp'sa-kŭs.
La-ris'sa.
Latour-maubourg (La-toor'-mō-boor').
Lebure'.
Ledru'.
Lefebvre (Lĕ-fĕv'vr).
Libations, 58.
Lithuania, 194.
Lobau (Lō-bō').
Lon-ti'ni.
Lotos-eaters, 35.
Lyd'i-a.
Ly'kon.

Machiavel (Mak'i-a-vel).
Mæ-sa'dēs.
Mag-nē'tēs.
Mā-krō'-nēs.
Malodeczno, 292.
Malo-jaro-slavetz, 233.
Man-ti-nē'a.

Man-ti-nei'a.
Marchand (Mar-shon').
Ma-ri-an-dȳ'ni.
Mar-o-nei'a.
Marshal Ney (Nay), 311.
Mazeppa, 178.
Media, Wall of, 15.
Me-dos'ar-des.
Měg-a-bȳ'zus.
Meg'a-ra.
Meg-a'rian, 76.
Mercenaries, 75.
Merchant ships, 80.
Mi-le'sians, 76.
Mi-lē'tus, 24.
Miloradovitch, 177.
Mil-ti'a-dēs.
Mil-to-ky'thēs.
Mi'næ, 99.
Minsk, 277.
Mith-ri-dā'tēs.
Mojaisk, 241.
Mortier (Mor-tē-ā').
Moscow, 157.
Moskwa, 171.
Mŏs-y-noe'ki.
Munich (Mu'nik).
Murat (Mu-rah').
Muscovite, 163.
Mȳ'si-a.
Mysian, 104.
Mysians, 35.

Ne'on.
Neufchatel (Nūf-shah-tĕl').
Ney, Marshal (Nay), 311.
Niemen (Nee'men).
Ni-kar'chus.

Ni'ki-as.
Ni-kom'a-chŭs.
Nineveh, 44.

Ŏd'ry-sæ.
Ŏd-rys'ian, 135.
O-dys'seus, 80.
Old Guard, 199.
Olympic Festivals, 145.
O-lȳm'pi-a, Temple of, 147.
O-neir'us, 29.
Oph-ry-nē'um.
O'pis.
O-ron'tas.
Oudinot (Oo-de-nō').

Pæ'an, 34.
Paphlagonian horse, 87
Pā'ri-um.
Partisans, 211.
Partouneaux (Par-too-nō').
Pa-rys'a-tis.
Pĕl-o-pon-nē'si-ans, 37.
Pĕl-o-pon-nē'sus.
Per'ga-mŭs, 140.
Peraldi (Per-al'dĭ).
Pe-rin'thus.
Per'i-klēs, 39.
Phalanx, 8.
Pha-li'nus.
Phar-na-bā'zus.
Pha-si-ā'ni.
Pha'sis, 93.
Phē'rae.
Phi-lē'si-us.
Phil-hellen'ic, 22.
Philo-Laco'ni-an, 113.
Phli-a'si-an, 139.

318    INDEX TO NOTES.

Phŏl'o-ē.
Phry-nis'kŭs.
Phys'kus.
Pino (Pēno').
Pipe, 103.
Pi-sid'i-a.
Pisid'ians, 35.
Pol-y-æ'nŭs.
Po-lўk'ra-tēs.
Pŏl-y-nī'kus.
Poniatowski (Pō-ni-a-tow'ski).
Pontoons, 18.
Postern-gate, 190.
Prō'klēs.
Pro-pon'tis, 125.
Prŏx'e-nŭs.
Pyrrhic Dance, 104.

Reggio (Red'jō).
Regnier (Rā-ne-ā).
Reins, 52.
Rhodian, 43.
Rostopchin, 163, 164.
Ru'ble, 162.

Sacrifice, 2, 91.
Sacrificed, 50.
St. Cyr (San Seer').
Sam'o-las.
Sar'dis.
Sa'trap, 10.
Scu-ta'ri.
Scythians, 188.
Ségur (Sāgur').
Se-li'nus.

Se-lўm'bri-a.
Serfs, 160.
Ses'a-me, 61.
Seū'thēs.
Sikon'yan.
Si-lā'nus.
Si-lē'si-a, 296.
Si-nō'pe.
Sĭt'ta-kē.
Skil'lus.
Skins, Inflated, 19.
Sky-thi'ni.
Smorgoni, 293.
Sneeze, 34.
Sok'ra-tēs, 143.
So-phæn'e-tŭs.
Sophists, 40.
So-tĕr'i-das.
Stāt'ers, 107.
Strelitzes, 190.
Strike our tents, 14.
Sy-ko'ni-ans.

Talent, 7.
Tā'o-chi.
Targeteers, 83.
Tchitchakoff (Chich'a-kŏf).
Te-lĕb'o-ăs.
Temple of Ephesus, 143.
Temple of Olympia, 147.
Thē'bē.
Thē'chēs.
Ther-mō'don.
Tho'rax.
Thra'ki-on, 123.

Thunny fishery, 76.
Thu-ri'an, 79.
Ti-ā'ra, 21.
Tīb-a-rē'nī.
Til'sit, 204.
Ti-mā'si-ŏn.
Ti-me-sil-a'ŭs.
Tīm-e-sīth'e-ŭs.
Tīr-i-bā'zus.
Tis-sa-pher'nēs.
Tra-pē'zus.
Traverse, 90.
Tribute, 13.
Tri-phўl'i-a.
Tri'rēme, 105.
Trō'ad, 140.
Tuileries (Tweel're).
Turrets, 84.
Twer (Wer).

Ve-re'i-a, 238.
Viazma, 243.
Viceroy, 229.

Wall of Media, 15.
War, The, 39.
Witepsk, 194.
Wittgenstein, 237.

Xan'thi-klēs.
Xĕn'o-phŏn.

Zăb'a-tŭs.
Za-kyn'thus.
Zeūs, 29.
Zeūs, The Gracious, 139.

www.ingramcontent.com/pod-product-compliance
Lightning Source LLC
Chambersburg PA
CBHW031854220426
43663CB00006B/615